EXHIBITING FOR MULTIPLE SENSES

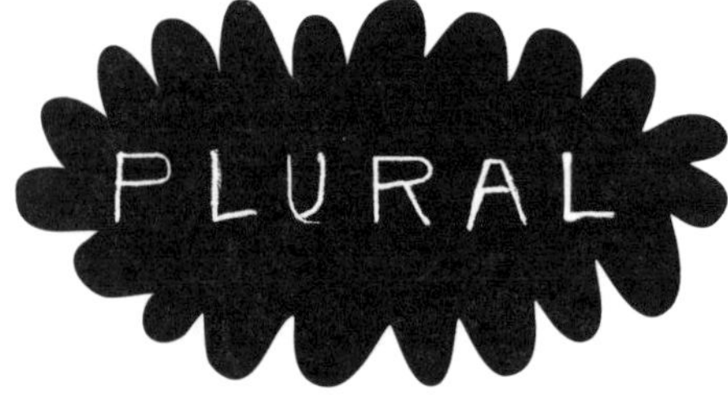

Valiz, Amsterdam

EXHIBITING FOR MULTIPLE SENSES
Art and Curating for Sensory-Diverse Bodies

Eva Fotiadi (ed.)

CONTRIBUTORS

David Bobier
Luca M Damiani
Stephanie Farmer & Hettie James
Eva Fotiadi
David Gissen & Georgina Kleege
Adi Hollander
Lilian Korner
Elke Krasny
Renata Pękowska
Lotte Lara Schrőder
Caro Verbeek

CONTENTS

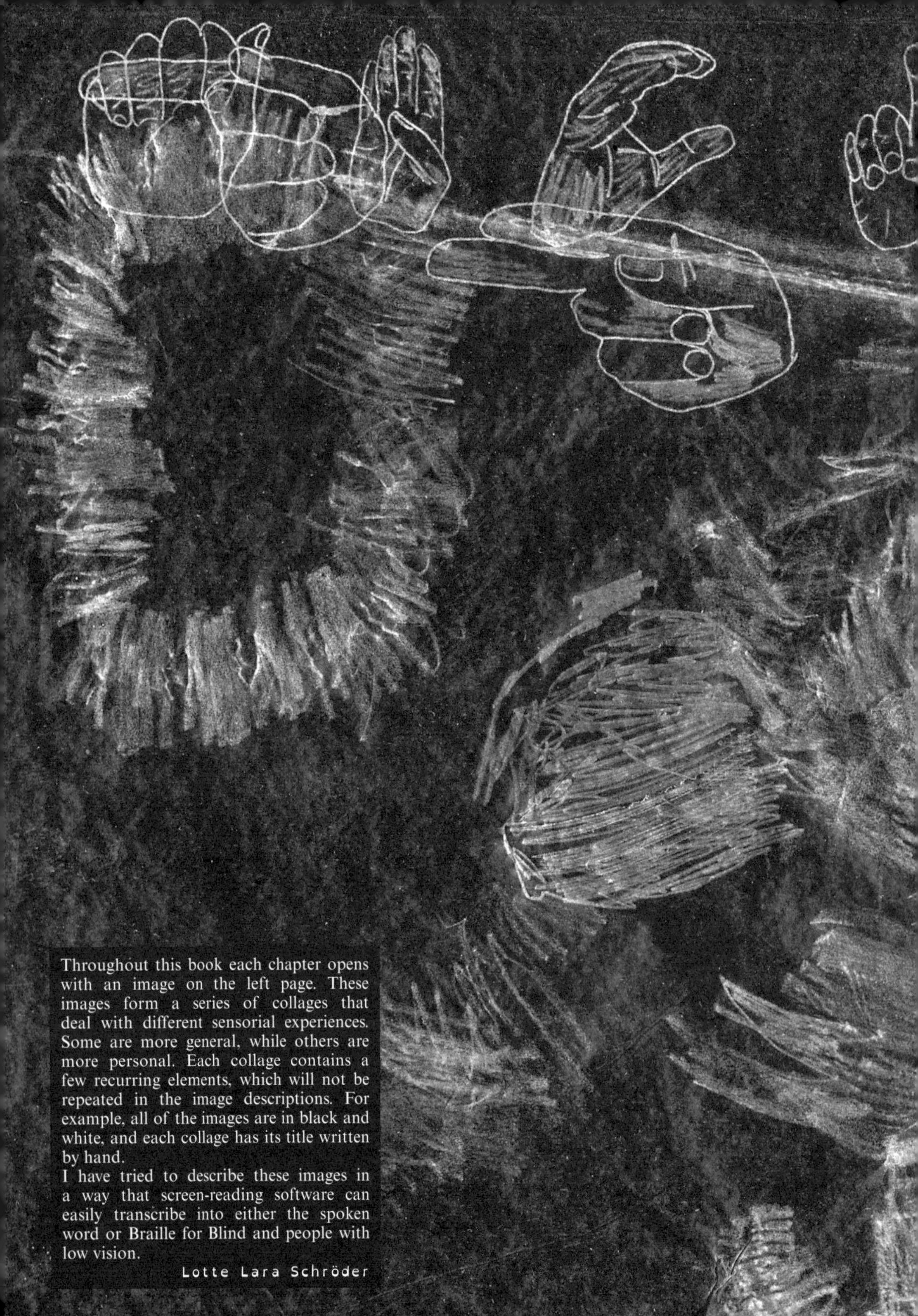

Throughout this book each chapter opens with an image on the left page. These images form a series of collages that deal with different sensorial experiences. Some are more general, while others are more personal. Each collage contains a few recurring elements, which will not be repeated in the image descriptions. For example, all of the images are in black and white, and each collage has its title written by hand.
I have tried to describe these images in a way that screen-reading software can easily transcribe into either the spoken word or Braille for Blind and people with low vision.
Lotte Lara Schröder

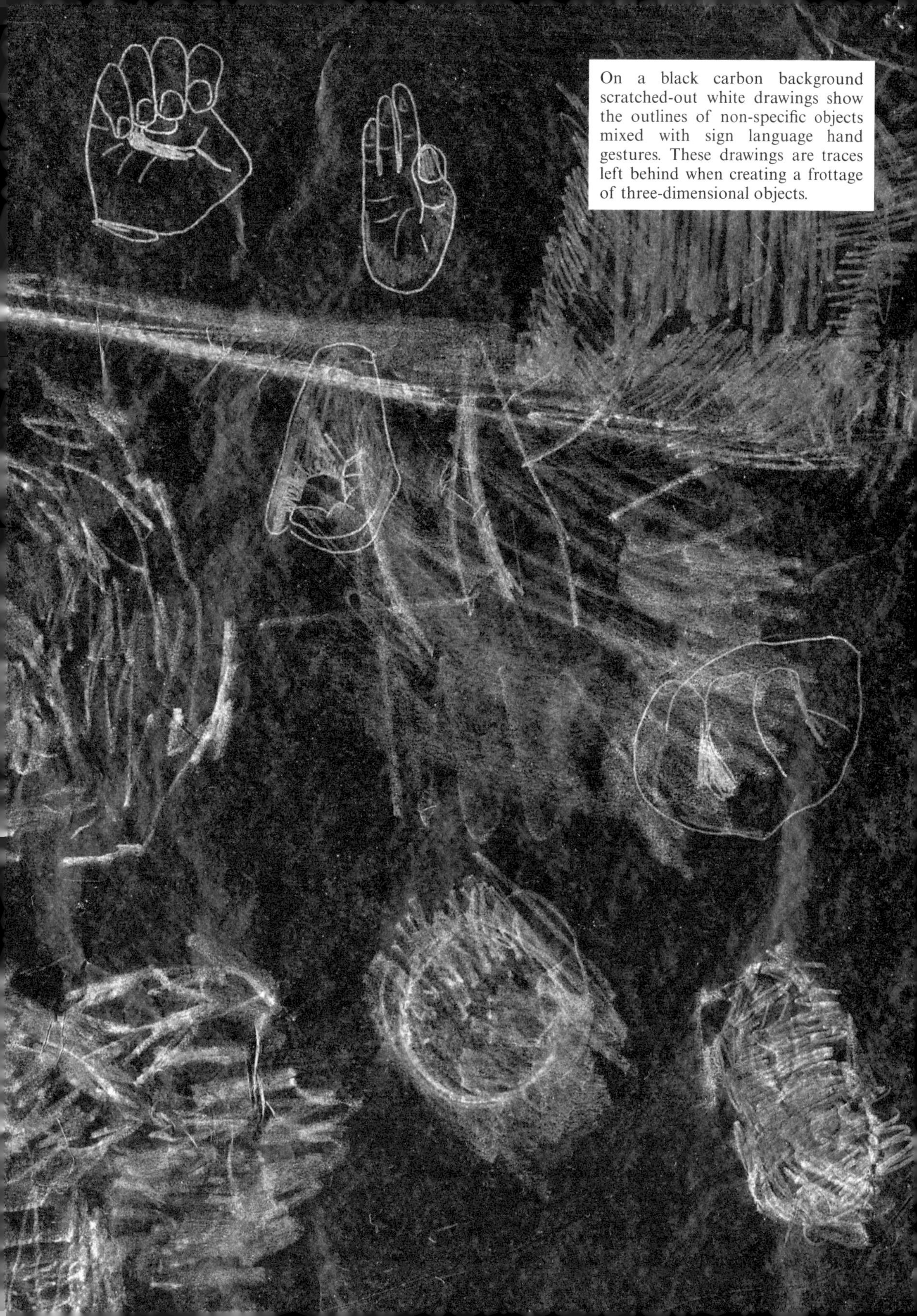

On a black carbon background scratched-out white drawings show the outlines of non-specific objects mixed with sign language hand gestures. These drawings are traces left behind when creating a frottage of three-dimensional objects.

→ TANGIBLE TIME

Tangible Time
This page shows a group of eight 'fidgets', small objects to touch, fiddle, and play with. The fidgets shown (from top left to bottom right): a tomato-shaped clock; a plastic diamond; a small cube-shaped ball game that tests your motor skills and your patience; a slightly fuzzy ball with 14 knobs; an orange-shaped wooden ball with a little stick coming out of it, a chestnut; a small ceramic disc or plate with a black-and-white glaze showing round and oval shapes merging into each other; and a rectangular plastic object, with twenty small, diamond-cut balls on each side that looks like a belt buckle.
Perhaps they are not the usual fidgets, but what constitutes a fidget? Do you have one? Do you ever fidget with your hair? Or perhaps you move around in your chair when you're feeling tense?

INTRODUCTION
Exhibiting for Multiple Senses

Eva Fotiadi

1. Fiona Candlin,
'Rehabilitating
unauthorised touch or
why museum visitors
touch the exhibits',
The Senses and Society,
12:3, 2017, 251–266.

When I was studying art history in Greece, the professor of a twentieth-century art elective course took us to visit a local art museum. At some point during the visit, while we were standing around a group of abstract sculptures and discussing them, the professor asked provocatively: why were we merely looking at the sculptures? Why wasn't any of us touching them? He went on to encourage us to experience the sculptures with our hands as well. I remember thinking that he was being clever with us: of course he knew that touching artworks in exhibitions is forbidden. Often there would also be signs reminding you not to touch. And of course the museum attendants would not stop us from touching the exhibits, because they recognized the art history professor. The museum had close ties with the university. My assumption was that the attendants wouldn't dare correct the professor's behaviour.

That inconspicuous moment at the museum is one of the few things I still remember from that elective course, which for the most part was about individual artists and the classification of art in movements. While I remained convinced that our professor was playing us, from that incident on I unilaterally authorized myself, time and again, to exercise what Fiona Candlin later called 'unauthorised touch' by exhibition visitors.[1]

Touching, smelling, tasting: deliberately engaging multiple senses of the body to experience art and other artefacts on display seems to have been common behaviour for visitors of early museum exhibitions of ethnography, natural history, art et cetera from the seventeenth to the early nineteenth century.[2] Those early museum publics were limited to the social and economic classes that had the time and credentials to visit exhibitions. This changed during the nineteenth century, when museums expanded their opening hours and started accepting working-class visitors. Curators did not trust the uneducated masses to come in physical contact with valuable museum displays.[3] They feared that the exhibits would be damaged and some of them even were so prejudiced that they thought the mere presence of the working class was offending the precious displays. It has furthermore been suggested that this behavioural change should also be considered as part of broader epistemological shifts in the history of Western culture: perceptions of human knowledge and ways of acquiring it, started shifting from a rather multisensory approach up until the Renaissance, towards the gradual prevalence of ocularcentrism linked to ideas of the Enlightenment. These ideas foregrounded objectivity of scientific truth with the eyes as the most reliable witness among the senses. The way to learn from, as well as to aesthetically appreciate objects displayed in exhibitions was no longer by touching them with one's hands, exploring the smells of their materials et cetera, but by studying and enjoying them visually.[4]

Specifically in the context of art displays, it has indeed been shown that alongside the practical and social considerations concerning the safety of exhibited art that limited the acceptable behaviour of visitors, there was an epistemological side as well. The ideas of quality appreciation promoted since the late nineteenth century by founding figures of art history such as Alois Riegl, Heinrich Wölfflin and Erwin Panofsky, favoured sensory models in which sight prevailed.[5]

By the mid-twentieth century, this approach specifically for modern art had found its spatial expression in the pristine gallery space that Brian O'Doherty called the 'white cube', and Drobnick later also the 'anosmic cube'.[6] A space so vacant from anything that could compromise the eye's attention from the art works except, perhaps, for wall labels and texts. The white cube model assumed that modern

2. See, e.g., Constance Classen & David Howes, 'The Sensescape of the Museum: Western Sensibilities and Indigenous Artifacts', in Elizabeth Edwards et al. (eds.), *Sensible Objects: Colonialism, Museums and Material Culture*, Oxford, 2006; Fiona Candlin, *Art, Museums and Touch: Rethinking Art's Histories*. Manchester, UK, 2010; Constance Classen, *The Museum of the Senses: Experiencing Art and Collections*, London & New York, 2017;

3. See, e.g., Fiona Candlin, *Art, Museums and Touch*; Constance Classen, *The Museum of the Senses*.

4. Candlin, *Art, Museums and Touch*.

5. Candlin, *Art, Museums and Touch*.

6. Brian O'Doherty, *Inside the White Cube: The Ideology of the Gallery Space*, expanded edition, Berkeley, 1999 (first publ. 1976); Jim Drobnick, 'Volatile Effects: Olfactory Dimensions in Art and Architecture', David Howes (ed.), *Empire of the Senses: The Sensual Culture Reader*, London and New York, 2005, 265–280.

Exhibiting for
Multiple Senses

7. Nina Levent &
Alvaro Pascual-Leone (eds.),
*The Multisensory Museum:
Cross-Disciplinary
Perspectives on Touch,
Sound, Smell, Memory,
and Space*, Lanham,
Maryland, 2014.

8. Levent, *The
Multisensory Museum*.

art was universally experienced by everyone the same way. Characteristics such as gender, sex, different body proportions or sensory abilities, cultural or economic background were not taken into account.

Yet even if 'normal' art gallery visitors—which is what my fellow art history students and I considered ourselves to be in the early twenty-first century—had fully and unconsciously adopted as self-evident the merely visual engagement with works of art, this embodied behaviour was often at odds with lived experience: from surrealist objects to fluxus multiples, and from happenings and performances to immersive environments, twentieth- and twenty-first-century art is full of works that invite different body parts and senses to engage with them actively. Nonetheless, once these same works become part of art collections and exhibitions, they often end up getting *the eyes* trained to feel the texture of their surface, guess the softness, hardness, temperature or smell of their materials, speculate on how they would move if you would activate their mobile parts et cetera. It so happens that neuroscientists say that the senses function in a multimodal way.[7] For example, people tend to 'eat' their food first with their eyes and nose before it reaches the palate. It has therefore been argued that it is actually redundant to make 'multisensory' exhibitions, because our human bodies respond to sensory stimuli in a multimodal way anyways.[8] Nonetheless, it remains fair to say that in the West, and certainly over the last couple of centuries, we have *trained* primarily our visual skills and corresponding verbal skills at the expense of the rest of our senses.

It has largely been in order to facilitate access and inclusion for the minority of sensory disabled people that public art institutions were forced by state policies to renegotiate their norms of sensory engagement with art. The activism of this minority had an instrumental role in diversifying practices of experiencing art in exhibitions, for example, by means of touch tours and touch models, audio descriptions, accessible fonts, to name a few examples that are in fact also available to non-disabled art patrons. Within many public art institutions, disability access is still often perceived as a set of practices complementary to the institutions' core business of collecting and exhibiting art. It is placed mostly

HAPTIC PERCEPTION

on the task list of education staff rather than of art curators, since it is understood as the facilitation of a small percentage of the population whose bodies differ from the norm.[9]

Nonetheless, disability activists and scholars have pushed since decades in order to 'move disability from the realm of medicine into that of a political minority, to recast it from a pathology to a form of ethnicity', and to assert 'that disability is a reading of bodily particularities in the context of social power relations.' as scholar Rosemarie Garland-Thomson stated about the goals of her seminal work back in the 1990s.[10] This comprises a complex approach to disability as a collective embodied experience, social and political activist claim, and as an analytical category, equivalent to feminism, queerness, race, ethnicity, or coloniality. In the contemporary art field, it seems to be rather recently, and through the work of figures such as Joseph Grigely, Georgina Kleege and Amanda Cachia,[11] that the empirical expertise, critical thinking and practices of experimentation of people who identify either as disabled or as sensory- or neurologically diverse,[12] are becoming acknowledged as producing situated knowledges and critical epistemologies that are relevant beyond their own communities.

Coming from a standpoint of contemporary art history rather than disability art activism, this volume aims to explore contemporary and experimental approaches to the senses in art exhibitions. It does this by functioning within a space between theory of art curating and disability art activism, considering that the encounter of the two areas can be mutually beneficial. The senses are central to aesthetics and the experience of artworks. Therefore, sensorydiverse perspectives—whether derived from hearing or visual impairments, neurodiversity, the sensorial perception of bodies that in other physiological ways differ from a statistical average—may place curatorial preconceptions and embodied behaviours concerning practices of experiencing art into perspective as historically and culturally determined. At the same time, the motivation behind editing this volume lies also in wanting to propose the reverse: contemporary art curating practices and theory can also be valuable resources for disability (art) activism and scholarship. Exhibitions and curatorial projects comprise extremely flexible and malleable

9. For a genealogy of the concept of the 'normal' see the fascinating study by Peter Cryle and Elizabeth Stephens, *Normality: A Critical Genealogy*, Chicago, IL, 2017. The authors show that the idea and practice of taking a statistically average human body as reference for a population as a whole emerged during the nineteenth century and it served scientists in narrowing down the group they studied. Subsequently, the 'normal' body in medicine was established during the twentieth century.

10. Rosemarie Garland-Thomson, *Figuring Physical Disability in American Culture and Literature*, Twentieth Anniversary Edition, New York, 2017 (first publ. 1997), 6.

11. The individuals mentioned reflect a limitation of this research, namely that it draws primarily from the English-speaking academic discourse of disability and crip art activism, even if the case studies originate also from other geographical contexts, for instance the Netherlands. In this edited volume, only the contribution by Lilian Korner expands beyond the English-speaking academic paradigm, by briefly introducing the German-speaking academic discourse on blindness and art.

12. It should be noted here that some people who identify as *d/Deaf* do not identify also as *disabled*. As long as they can use sign language to communicate, their deafness is not restricting them in a way that they experience as disabling.

Exhibiting for
Multiple Senses

13. It should be noted nonetheless that practices of displaying appear across different cultures, periods, but also species, as there are animals whose behaviour includes acts of display. Ivar Gaskell, 'Display displayed', in Johannes Grave, Christiane Holm, Valérie Kobi & Caroline van Eck (eds.), *The Agency of Display: Objects, Framings and Parerga*, Dresden, 2018, 22–44.

terrains where research, experimentation and communication take place, oriented towards a public. And while they may not have traceable effects in 'real life', as it were, they offer us possibilities to process through them, as individuals and as collectives, in real time and retrospectively, the lived experiences of our bodies, cultures and societies.

A sentence from an exhibition wall text that I came across recently on an Instagram story summarizes a great deal of what I advocate for here. The sentence read: 'the possibility of an audience produces the archive of an experience'. While the sentence referred to the content of the exhibition (art and the current war in Gaza), it can be extended to the conditions of the exhibition medium as well. Contemporary art exhibitions are ephemeral, often transferable, public and performative communication vehicles that can take various forms and they are historically so rooted in Western culture that their study tells us a lot about ourselves.[13] The historical context at the moment of writing this introduction, in spring 2025, when acknowledgement and support—financial or other—of the importance of both art and diversity appear to be shrinking in the West, it is indeed a time when archives of experience need to be kept and made public.

In this introductory text, I have chosen to weave together reflections mobilized by engaging with the work of various curators, scholars and artists, emphasizing especially (but not exclusively) this volume's authors and highlighting aspects that I found relevant and inspiring in their work. Except for the essays by Elke Krasny and Renata Pękowska, all other contributions to this book comprise analyses of projects and practices from the perspective of their initiators or makers who focus especially on the research underlying their practices. In what follows in this introduction, I have not attempted to specifically summarize the core of their contribution to this book, as every essay and interview possesses its own texture, rhythm, density, narrative style, and conceptual structures—qualities that I could never fully convey through my interpretation of their content alone.

Sensing from Different Standpoints

In her recently published monograph *The Agency of Access* US-based crip curator and academic art historian Amanda Cachia claimed that when she encounters exhibits with audio components from her point of view at four feet three inches, she is likely to miss the sound.[14] The sound is oriented towards human ears estimated at a higher point in the room. She therefore expands the condition of becoming sensory disabled by one's environment to a broader range of different embodiments than those of people with sensory impairments such as having low hearing or vision.[15] In her practice as curator, Cachia sometimes changes the spatial relations of exhibits to make them inclusive for a variety of bodies. She also works with artists whose art approaches and activates the human body and the exhibition space in ways that alter or challenge habitual behaviour in galleries.

There are, actually, more and more other artists around the world who experiment in related ways. For example, Adi Hollander in collaboration with a team of interdisciplinary artists based in the Netherlands and the US and in partnership with David Bobier and the Canada-based VibraFusionLab (both Hollander and Bobier are contributors in this volume), created a series of prototypes of tactile 'bricks'—as Hollander calls them—that were designed to be combined into modular haptic surfaces such as floors, walls, seats, and banisters.[16] This artistic research project was titled *What Do I Hear? (WDIH?)* and in their design, the project team had the entire human body in mind, aiming to accommodate various embodiments and postures. Designed for spaces where art, film or music are presented, these haptic architectural surfaces enable a body that comes into contact with them to experience sound as vibration 'translating' sound's various parameters, such as density, harmony or direction. The prototypes have led to a series of art installations titled *Haptic Room Studies*, designed for a particular space and/or for a specific music or sound composition. When I talked to visitors in a couple of their exhibitions, some mentioned that the experience made them conscious of how differently the various body parts experienced the vibrations. Somebody noticed that her hips seemed to 'listen'

14. Amanda Cachia, *The Agency of Access: Contemporary Disability Art and Institutional Critique*, Philadelphia, 2025. The term 'crip' has been reclaimed and reinvented from the derogatory English word 'cripple'. Robert McRuer, in his book *Crip Theory: Cultural Signs of Queerness and Disability*, New York, 2006, introduced the term in a theory that drew from queer theory in order to move towards pluralizing disabled identities and criticizing able-bodiedness beyond the mainstream disability studies paradigm at the time.

15. Here I differentiate between becoming disabled by the physical or social environment that is designed for normative (statistically average) bodies, and having a physiological or anatomical impairment.

16. *What Do I Hear?* was initiated in 2021 by the OtherAbilities collective (Adi Hollander, Eva Fotiadi) in collaboration with the media arts center VibraFusionLab (David Bobier, Jim Ruxton, Jenelle Rouse). The participants were: Andreas Tegnander, Mark IJzerman, Alina Ozerova, Ildikó Horváth, Claudio F Baroni, Maria Kandyla, Michele Abolaffio, Rebecca Kleinberger, Akito van Troyer, Mor Efrati, and Yonatan Cohen. For more details, see Hollander and Fotiadi in this volume.

17. Joseph Grigely, *Exhibition Prosthetics: Conversation with Hans Ulrich Obrist and Zak Kyes*, London and Berlin, 2009.

18. Grigely, *Exhibition Prosthetics*.

19. See also Joseph Grigely, *Otherhow: Essays and Documents on Art and Disability 1985-2024*, Ryan Haley, New York, forthcoming in 2025.

20. Cachia, *The Agency of Access*.

21. Beatrice von Bismarck, *The Curatorial Condition*, Berlin, 2022.

better than her shoulders. During the research and development phase of *WDIH?*, the prototypes were tested by both hearing and hearing-impaired people, the latter including some of their creators.

One could also think here of the work of artist Joseph Grigely and his concept of 'exhibition prosthetics' that includes all sorts of conventional elements and practices developed around art, both within and beyond the context of art exhibitions.[17] Posters, invitations, labels, but also written communication in text and image that in Grigely's case includes, most famously, endless Post-its from his written conversations with hearing people. Grigely asks to what extent the various exhibition conventions are actually part of the art, rather than extensions of it.[18] An inherent part of Grigely's work over decades of creating and exhibiting as an artist is also his correspondence with institutions about access, lectures, statements of equality and access, exhibition proposals et cetera, all of which are interwoven with his artistic production.[19]

The art of Adi Hollander as well as Joseph Grigely, both of whom intervene in and activate exhibition infrastructures materially and conceptually, can be considered broadly as examples for what Amanda Cachia called, 'creative access'. The term refers to a methodology in art and curating that 'makes a point of embedding access components—such as audio description, captioning, and the height of work hung on the wall—into the very content of the art itself and, certainly, centering it as an integral and important component of an exhibition for the benefit of disabled and nondisabled visitors'.[20]

Thinking about the relationality of different components in the curated situation of the examples mentioned above brings to mind Beatrice von Bismarck's theory of the curatorial as a professional field in which cultural activities take place and knowledge is produced.[21] Bismarck uses certain concepts as tools, with which she analyses the curatorial and its relational dynamic. In her analysis, she explains how the curatorial both creates relations and is constituted by relations. These relations encompass human actors, institutional actors, as well as non-human agents such as the artworks and exhibition infrastructures (e.g., architecture, display props, wall texts, printed matter). One of the concepts Bismarck introduces as an analytical tool is that of 'constellations', with which she refers to arrangements of spatio-temporal relations in a three-dimensional space, relations of mutual impact between human and non-human agents in the fabric of the curatorial. With origins in astrology and astronomy, the term 'constellations' refers to dynamic relations primarily between non-human agents (celestial bodies), but it also includes the perceiving, looking human subject, a combination that makes the term particularly apt for thinking about exhibitions and curating.

Bismarck's project of theorizing the curatorial is taking into account diversity discourses. Yet unlike, for example, Cachia's standpoint of crip activism, Bismarck does not identify any critical discourse as her main point of view.[22] Rather, she seems to try to think about curating from within the practice and conditions of curating itself. I find that Hollander and Grigely's art, as well as Cachia's curating as infrastructural activism, align quite well with Bismarck's thinking. Be it in a material, experiential or conceptual way: all of them encourage the rearrangement of conventions about sensory and aesthetic perception that have been long at work within the relationalities of exhibition constellations. These conventions include spatial and architectural arrangements that take a statistically average human body as a point of reference, but they also expand on conceptual and hierarchical arrangements between what is defined as the exhibited art, the exhibition's infrastructure and prosthetics.

Since considerable attention has been paid to language in the above discussion, it is also worth mentioning another term used, for example, by the art historian Johannes Grave to describe exhibition props, namely 'parerga'.[23] In its Greek etymology, 'parergon' means that which is besides (παρά) the work (έργο), and which is of less importance than the work. Such hierarchies of importance in the exhibition constellation, whether referring to non-human agents (work vs. parergon), or human actors creating them (artists vs craftsmen; art curators vs exhibition designers, educators), are put into perspective in the work of artists and curators such as Hollander, Grigely and Cachia. By activating the transformative potentials of the exhibition constellation,

22. Bismarck's engagement with diverse approaches is context-specific. For example, in her analysis of the pioneer collective A 37 90 89 and their short-lived project space in Antwerp (1969–1970), she places emphasis on the gender dynamics at work in the distribution of roles between men (in prominent roles) and women (in supporting ones). Moreover, the term 'constellation' in Bismarck's theory evokes curator Okwui Enwezor's term 'post-colonial constellation', a reference that Bismarck acknowledges but she develops her own use of the term. See Bismarck, *The Curatorial Condition*, 72–79, 32. With 'postcolonial constellation' Enwezor referred to the complex geopolitical formations and systems of cultural production shaped by globalization and the enduring impacts of coloniality and imperialism, through which contemporary art is critically refracted and contextualized. Okwui Enwezor, 'The postcolonial constellation: Contemporary art in a state of permanent transition', *Research in African Literatures*, 34: 4, Winter 2003, 57–82.

23. Johannes Grave et al. (eds.), *The Agency of Display: Objects, Framings and Parerga*, Dresden, 2018.

24. Simon Knell (ed.), *Care of Collections*, London & New York, 1994. Bruce, W. Ferguson, Reesa Greenberg, Sandy Nairne (eds.), *Thinking about Exhibitions*, London & New York, 1994.

25. See also Beatrice von Bismarck & Benjamin Meyer-Krahmer (eds.), *Hospitality: Hosting Relations in Exhibitions*, Berlin, 2015.

26. Elke Krasny, Sophie Lingg, & Lena Fritsch, 'Radicalizing Care: Feminist and Queer Activism in Curating— an Introduction', in Elke Krasny, Sophie Lingg, Lena Fritsch, Birgit Bosold & Vera Hofmann (eds.), *Radicalizing Care: Feminist and Queer Activism in Curating*, Vienna & Berlin, 2021, 10–27 (14).

27. Elke Krasny, Sophie Lingg, & Lena Fritsch, 'Radicalizing Care: Feminist and Queer Activism in Curating— an Introduction', in Krasny et al. (eds.), *Radicalizing Care*.

they relativize what is the work and what are its prosthetics, crippling established hierarchies.

Curating as Care

The evocation of the etymological origins of the verb 'curating' in the Latin 'curare', which means 'to care', is occasionally cultivating assumptions about the 'caring' nature of curating. This caring, which initially referred to collections of artefacts and specimens,[24] in contemporary art and museology pays significant attention also to humans who are invited—invited artists, invited guests for events, the public and so on.[25] For all the possibilities and good intentions of infrastructural and conceptual rearrangements that exhibition curating allows for (as discussed above), it is by no means self-evident that it also affects—let alone transforms— the involvement of contemporary art institutions in social and political constellations of power, pushing them towards more inclusive and equitable models.

Elke Krasny, Sophie Lingg, and Lena Fritsch write:

> Claiming curating for any emancipatory and transformative politics and moving curating, care and activism closer together is no easy task. The historical legacies of curating and its entanglements in colonial capitalism and patriarchal statecraft loom large.[26]

They remind us that:

> Caring labor, understood as reproductive labor in Marxist-feminist terminology is the unpaid and underpaid fuel of the capitalist engine, with those performing this work historically understood as dependent and excluded from the idea of modern citizenship.[27]

The subjects that come to mind when reading the above are mainly female and colonized subjects tasked with the *care of others*.

Yet just as the discriminatory politics of labour in colonial and patriarchal societies are interwoven with capitalism, so is also the disenfranchisement of disabled bodies in modern societies, as well as their stigmatization as subjects *in need of care*. The historian of bureaucracies and quantification Dan Bouk and interdisciplinary disability and media scholar Mara Mills, have demonstrated that the term 'impairment', as used today to refer to bodily or health conditions, was coined and spread in the early twentieth century by US actuarial and life insurance companies that were interested in calculating risk of mortality among potential clients. Private data of individuals' lives was made available and shared between life insurance companies so that they could surveil, potentially charge higher fees, or deny clients with high risk of financial loss and death.[28]

As the attention for contemporary feminist, queer, decolonial and other critical and intersectional perspectives increased in the artworld in recent decades, critical explorations of 'care' entered curatorial considerations. In her contribution to this volume, Krasny presents numerous examples of curatorial projects from the past decade that carry the term 'care' in their title. She observes that none of them interpreted the ideas and practices of care in the same way. In several cases the curators appear to have one or more particular contexts in mind: ecological systems, non-Western cultural heritage, indigenous knowledges and traditions, reproductive rights activism, migration, parenthood, health and so on. While most have no explicit reference to the senses beyond vision, the emphasis they lay on care brings senses other than vision to the foreground. Practices of care are linked to senses that involve physical contact, such as touch, but also smell or taste, all of which relate to the caring for humans, as well as to how humans relate to and care for their physical and natural environment. Consequently, when the category of 'care' gains ground in the domains of art and aesthetics, various senses infiltrate exhibitions and other curatorial projects.

So, what critical insights would sensory disability and diversity then bring to art curating from the perspective of care? Crip time is a relevant concept here. The term 'crip time' describes how disabled people experience time

28. Mara Mills & Dan Bouk, 'The History of Impairment', *Osiris*, 39, 2024, 27–56.

29. Alison Kafer, *Feminist, Queer, Crip*, Bloomington, Indiana, 2013; see also Margaret Price, *Crip Spacetime*, Durham, USA, 2024.

Exhibiting for
Multiple Senses

30. This slowing down is fundamentally incompatible with the exhausting acceleration and precarity of neoliberal labour in the art field. See here, for example, the work of the Iranian-American curator Taraneh Fazeli and especially the peripatetic series of exhibitions, public programmes and community projects that she curated under the title 'Sick Time – Crip Time – Sleepy Time: Against Capitalism's Temporal Bullying'. www.alliedmedia.org/leader/taraneh-fazeli.

31. Georgina Kleege, *More than Meets the Eye: What Blindness Brings to Art*, Oxford, 2018.

differently due to factors such as fluctuating energy levels, medical schedules, and societal expectations of efficiency.[29] With such experiences as a starting point, the term has evolved to a broader critique of time and temporality in late-capitalist societies and the accelerated rhythm of life and labour they impose on humans.[30] Often it is invisible disabilities that force subjects to slow down. For example, the sensitivity of neurodiverse people to sensorial over-stimulation has led some museums to establish sensory-friendly opening hours, activities, and spaces for rest.

The well-known slogan of the disability activism movement, 'nothing for us without us', indicates among other things that when people with normative bodies try to care for those with non-normative ones, they often fall into assumptions and even create standardized accessibility solutions that don't always work well for their recipients. In her key book, *More Than Meets the Eye. What Blindness Brings to Art*, blind author Georgina Kleege describes and critically reflects on several examples of touch tours, audio guides or braille signs from the perspective of somebody exposed very early in life to art, and a regular visitor of art institutions. In an interview with architect David Gissen that is republished in this volume, Kleege proposes creative ways of sensorially enriching the experience of art exhibitions, such as recording haptic and sound impressions of artworks and adding them to the artworks' descriptions, or devising collective ways of writing texts about artworks for audio guides.[31]

While Kleege focuses on how cultural institutions could transform their existing practices to improve accessibility, the media arts centre VibraFusionLab (mentioned earlier in this introduction), is exemplary for how interwoven practices of experimental art and curating, inclusion, care, and collaborative work comprise the Lab's foundation from day one. Central to the work of VibraFusionLab is the partnering with practitioners and institutions across the visual and performing arts that want to work with vibrotactile technologies that translate sound to vibration for reasons of access. The initial motivation behind establishing the Lab was to bring these technologies from scientists' labs to the d/Deaf and hard-of-hearing communities. VibraFusionLab has developed expertise adjusting existing as well as

developing new vibrotactile systems, in order to respond
not only to practical access needs and creative access ideas,
but more broadly to the artistic desires and visions of those
who approach the Lab. In his contribution to this book,
David Bobier who is an artist, curator, and the founder of
VibraFusionLab, tells the story of how they started in 2012
and evolved until today. While Bobier does not use the word
'care' even once, care appears embedded in the DNA of
the Lab from its initial conception to its daily practice until
today.

Sensorial Translations and Narrations

In his landmark book *Techniques of the Observer: On Vision
and Modernity in the Nineteenth Century*, Jonathan Crary
analysed optical devices of the past and their phantasmago-
rical effects, showing the kinds of impact that technological
transformations of the visual have entailed.[32] In the early
twenty-first century, we find digital multisensory technologies
occupying the space of the public's fascination with extended
and augmented realities.

One use of digital technologies has been to sensorially 'translate', interpret, or expand existing works of
art. The 2017 exhibition 'Tate Sensorium' at Tate Britain,
London, has become a textbook example of this approach.
Conceived by the creative agency Flying Object, the display
featured four paintings from Tate's collection exhibited each
in a separate room. Using state-of-the-art technologies such
as mid-air haptics, as well as specially designed scents and
flavours, the concept of the show was to add one leading
sensory modality to the visual experience of each painting,
along with other 'secondary' sensory stimuli.

Upon entering the show, visitors received a biometric
wristband that measured their responses to the displays.
Upon exiting, they were given a questionnaire and a chart
combining all of their responses. A limited number of
visitors were allowed per room, for only two to three minutes,
accompanied by a gallery assistant. The repertoire of experiential actions seems to have been quite precisely scripted,
giving a distinctly rigid character to the exhibition visit,

32. Jonathan Crary,
*Techniques of the
Observer: On Vision and
Modernity in the
Nineteenth Century*,
Cambridge, Mass, 1992.

33. For a detailed
description of the
exhibition see Tom
Pursey & David Lomas,
'Tate Sensorium: An
Experiment in Multi-
sensory Immersive
Design', *The Senses and
Society*, 13:3, 2018,
354–366, as well as
Renata Pękowska in this
volume.

34. Michael Fried, 'Art
and Objecthood', *Art
and Objecthood: Essays
and Reviews*, Chicago,
1998, first publ. 1967.

35. Renata Pękowska in
this volume quotes
especially the renowned
anthropologist of the
senses, David Howes, in
*Sensorium: Contex-
tualizing the Senses
and Cognition in History
and Across Cultures*,
Cambridge, 2024.

Exhibiting for
Multiple Senses

36. Proprioception refers to the sense of body position—our awareness of where our limbs are in space—while kinaesthesia relates to the sense of movement. Though often used interchangeably, proprioception is more tied to cognitive awareness, and kinaesthesia to behavioural control. Both are essential to perceiving and coordinating movement, especially in tactile interactions. Catherine L. Reed & Mounia Ziat, 'Haptic Perception: From the Skin to the Brain', *Reference Module in Neuroscience and Biobehavioral Psychology*, New York, NY, 2018, 1-12. doi.org/10.1016/B978-0-12-809324-5.03182-5.

37. Interoception is the perception of the body's internal state. While some define it narrowly—as sensations from the internal organs—others adopt a broader view, seeing it as the overall felt experience of bodily states, shaped by the central nervous system regardless of the specific sensory inputs involved. Erik Ceunen, Johan Vlaeyen & Ilse van Diest, 'On the Origins of Interoception', *Frontiers of Psychology*, 7:743, doi.org/10.3389/fpsyg.2016.00743.

38. Equilibrioception refers to the sensory perception of orientation with regard to gravity and it enables individuals to maintain their balance. Thermoception refers to temperature sensation.

39. David Howes (ed.), *The Sixth Sense Reader*, Oxford and New York, 2009.

something between a ritual and a scientific lab experiment.[33] Unfortunately, little has been published from the analysis of the charts, which could have offered an unusual kind of data from exhibitions—potentially even allowing comparisons across diverse groups of visitors.

In this volume, Renata Pękowska examines aspects of the show, published discussions surrounding it, and visitor recollections. She also connects these insights to her own research into today's digital attention economy and digital dependence. This latter part is key: it reminds us that, beyond any scientific attempts to understand the physiology of sensorial responses, these are always also shaped by the changing technological assemblages that dominate people's daily lives, and by the variations in technologies preferred by—or designed for—bodies with diverse sensory abilities.

One of Pękowska's central questions is: how many senses? Her reflections take the reader from Michael Fried's legendary 1968 essay 'Art and Objecthood'[34]—which practically condemned artists exploring phenomenological perceptions of art as embodied encounters in space and time (such as minimal art, performance, et cetera)—to anthropologists who suggest that different cultures count the body's senses differently.[35] Actually, a consensus on how many human senses there are does not exist in the Western science either: proprioception, kinaesthesia,[36] interoception,[37] equilibrioception, thermoception[38] . . . various counts reach up to nine, twenty-one, or even over the fifty senses.[39] It seems impossible to offer an objective total. Accordingly, even when attempting to translate one sense into another, multiple sensory modalities become woven into the process.

In the research of Adi Hollander and the *Haptic Room Studies* artists' team (whose aim was to translate sound into vibration), attention was given to body positions in contact with architectural surfaces—leaning against, sitting on, standing on, or touching them with one's hand—and to how vibrations travel over and through the body like sound moves through space. The temperature, texture, flexibility, and softness of each material were also considered for their capacity to create comfort for the 'listening' body.

Likewise, when the olfactory art historian and curator Caro Verbeek writes in this volume about the use of scents in art museums, the reader of her text and accompanying images is likely to notice the body's various modes of engagement with smells in exhibitions. Scents can be ambient in space, but in exhibitions they are usually deliberately restricted in location: one must lean toward a scent station, squeeze a pump, smell a straw, scratch and sniff a piece of cardboard, and so on. In short, smelling in exhibitions involves a repertoire of postures, movements, and gestures in space, with varying degrees of proximity to and intimacy with objects—and often some form of touch. In other words, proprioception, kinaesthesia, and balance are integral parts of olfactory curating and exhibition design.

Scents are added to exhibitions as a part of storytelling, to enhance access to content and representation. But what exactly gets translated from the visual to the olfactory? When translating or interpreting (semi-)abstract works of art, scents may be created in response to colour, light, or composition. How did Mondrian's studios smell in the cities where he lived? Scents created for such art-historical representations are sensory interpretations based on olfactory evidence from written sources, photographs, knowledge of materials, and other data. Verbeek's olfactory museology, as a layer in exhibition storytelling, is not specifically intended to enhance access for disabled visitors, yet the exchange with disabled art patrons remains an essential consideration in how olfactory methods are tested and used. As a fairly nascent field evolving around a very neglected sense in the arts, it is possible to embed sensory diversity already in the development of olfactory museology. Interestingly, one of Verbeek's pieces of advice for curators working with smells is to avoid asking people questions such as 'What do you smell?'—to prevent feelings of inadequacy. It is often difficult to name smells, but relatively easy to describe the memories or associations they evoke.[40]

The challenge of narrating sensorial experiences beyond sight recurs in experimental artistic and curatorial work involving multiple senses. It's not only with smell that language falls short—touch can be equally elusive. Both the American scholar Georgina Kleege and the German art historian Lilian Korner describe reaching the limits of their language when asked to articulate tactile experiences.[41]

40. Caro Verbeek in this volume. See also, Cretien van Campen, *The Proust Effect: The Senses as Doorways to Lost Memories*, Oxford, 2013.

41. See Georgina Kleege, *More than Meets the Eye*; Georgina Kleege, 'The Art of Touch: Lending a Hand to the Sighted Majority', *Journal of Visual Culture*, 20:2, 2021, 433–451, and Gissen and Korner in this volume.

Kleege's work revisits assumptions about blind people's perception of art, tracing them back to eighteenth-century philosopher Denis Diderot and his Enlightenment-era reflections on blindness and art. In their essay for this volume, Lilian Korner turns to another of Diderot's contemporaries, the German Alexander Baumgarten—founder of philosophical aesthetics. Rather than criticizing Baumgarten's visual bias, Korner is more interested in adapting his methodology to develop a new framework for haptic aesthetics, along with a language to match. In their practices, both Kleege and Korner collaborate with museums to experiment with vocabularies for touch-based engagement with artworks. Their projects have been realized in institutions such as the Contemporary Jewish Museum and SFMOMA in San Francisco, and the Museum für Angewandte Kunst in Frankfurt.

The idea of integrating disabled experiences into curatorial practice—not just for accessibility, but as a creative and conceptual resource—is gaining ground. A most notable recent example that is also discussed in this book is 'Ensemble', a 2024 exhibition at London's ATP Gallery, by the curatorial duo Hettie James and Stephanie Farmer. The show featured audio descriptions conceived as artworks in themselves. Six artists were invited to contribute a personally significant work—one that had never been, and would never be, publicly exhibited. Inspired by Kleege's critique of exhibition audio guides and their limited engagement with diverse voices, 'Ensemble' proposed an alternative. James and Farmer designed a collaborative, game-like process reminiscent of the Surrealists' exquisite corpse. Participants worked in groups to create audio descriptions without ever seeing the artworks, working only from verbal accounts. The process was designed not only to produce meaningful audio pieces for many different audiences, but also to offer the contributing artists an innovative kind of engagement with their unrevealed works. Moreover, the essay of James and Farmer reflects a quite self-aware curatorial inquiry— questioning both the limits of exhibition formats (which need revision when the works exist only in sound) and their own assumptions. Their noticeable use of phrases such as 'we hoped', 'we believed', or 'we wanted' underscores the consciously exploratory character of their curatorial endeavour.

The book closes on a different note, with a visually-driven piece by artist Luca M Damiani. The piece comprises part of his long-term, auto-ethnographic research into neuro-diversity and sensory processing. Damiani's work explores how a neurodiverse brain—especially in the aftermath of a severe brain injury—navigates and interprets the surrounding environment. Using graphic techniques, the artist's digital compositions fuse imagery, text, medical data, and sensory inputs into an intricate, hybrid language. Here, art, therapy, research, and code merge into a sensory logic uniquely his own.

SCENTSCAPE

Exhibiting for
Multiple Senses

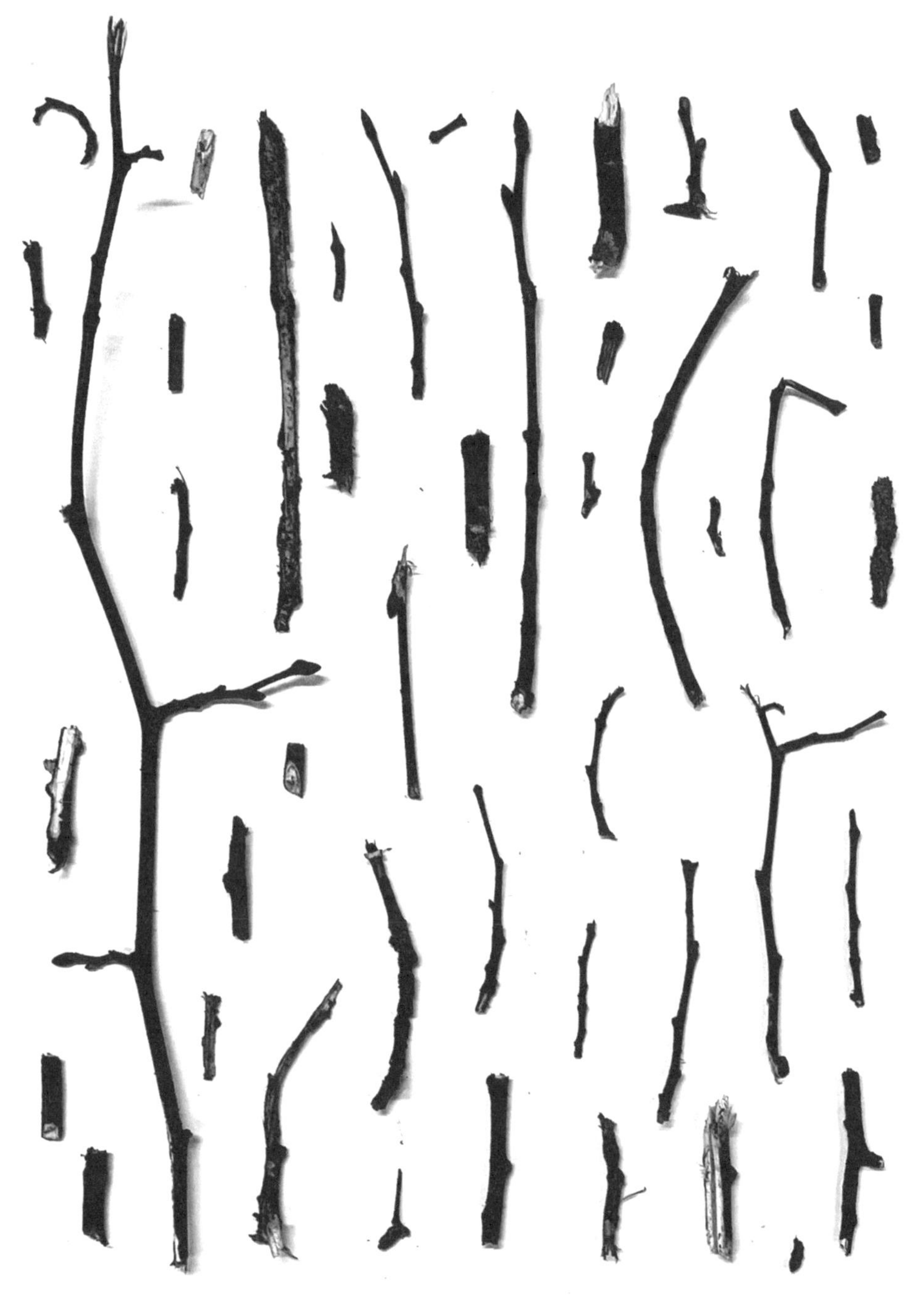

Hot Texture

This page features a group of sticks, placed on a flat surface in an orderly fashion, yet without a clear system. One stick is very large and four are half that size. Then there are around 35 sticks that are about half the size of the medium-sized ones.

Now, can you imagine you lie with your bare back on this group of sticks? How might you feel? Can you feel all the different sizes? How do the sticks connect to your own bones? Can you feel all the fragments of your own body?

THE MUS~~T~~KY MUSEUM
Working with Scent in a Heritage and Art Context to Enhance Accessibility for People of ~~Other~~ All Abilities

Caro Verbeek

Dedicated to the visionary sensory literature and disability scholar Dr Piet Devos (1983–2024)

1. Beata Labuhn, 'Breathing a Moldy Air: Olfactory Experience, Aesthetics, and Ethics in the Writing of Ruskin and Riegl', *Future Anterior,* 13:2, 2017, 103–117, 103.

2. Lewis Kachur, *Displaying the Marvelous: Marcel Duchamp, Salvador Dali and Surrealist Exhibition Installations,* Cambridge, 2001, 68.

Nietzsche famously complained about the musty smell emanating from collections of antiquities in museums.[1] Since the emergence of the white cube, efforts were made to get rid of the mouldy smells of the past in an attempt to create a 'neutral' space. From an olfactory point of view this led to a 'tabula rasa' or an inodorous space that enabled the (intentional) addition of smells by artists such as Marcel Duchamp, who—in 1938—filled an entire gallery with the smell of coffee, functioning as a wordless and surreal poem, or Edward Kienholz who reproduced the smell of a bar for his installation *The Beanery* in the 1960s, to name just a few examples.[2]

Whereas these instances were still quite rare at the time, over the past few decades a true renaissance seems to be unfolding in the realm of 'olfactory museology', or the intentional use of smell in heritage institutions, rendering these spaces 'musky' (or at least fragrant and odorous) rather than 'musty' (although the latter can evoke nostalgic sentiments as we will see later). Surprisingly, and perhaps paradoxically at first sight, the most recent and elaborate developments in this field are taking place in institutes that exhibit *visual* art; the very museums that have promoted and sustained the 'scopic regime' that dominates Western culture.[3] Smell is finally (or rather again) embraced as a serious part of (high) culture and heritage.[4] But how can scents be used in storytelling and make art museums more accessible? And how can scents be implemented safely, practically, and meaningfully?

In this article I would like to share some of the experiences and insights I gained over the past twenty-five years of working with smell (including failures), briefly discuss the different types of olfactory museology that can be distinguished, and finally highlight three case studies that were part of my own practice, with an emphasis on my most recent olfactory project related to Piet Mondrian which addresses the question 'Can we smell abstraction?'.

3. A few examples of olfactory projects in museums of visual art are: 'Sleeping Beauties: Reawakening Fashion', at the Metropolitan Museum of Art, New York (2024); 'The Essence of a Painting: An Olfactory Exhibition', at Museo del Prado Madrid (2022); 'Fleeting: Scents in Colour', at Mauritshuis, The Hague (2020); 'There's Something in the Air: Scent in Art', at Villa Rot Burgrieden (2015); 'The Art of Scent: 1889–2012', at Museum of Arts and Design, New York (2012).

4. See for example: Cecilia Bembibre & Matija Strlic, 'Smell of Heritage: a Framework for the Identification, Analysis and Archival of Historic Odours', *Heritage Science*, 5, 2017. Published online: doi.org/10.1186/s40494 -016-0114-1 and Caro Verbeek, 'Presenting Volatile Heritage: Two Case Studies on Olfactory Reconstructions in the Museum', *Future Anterior*, 13:2, 2017, 34–42.

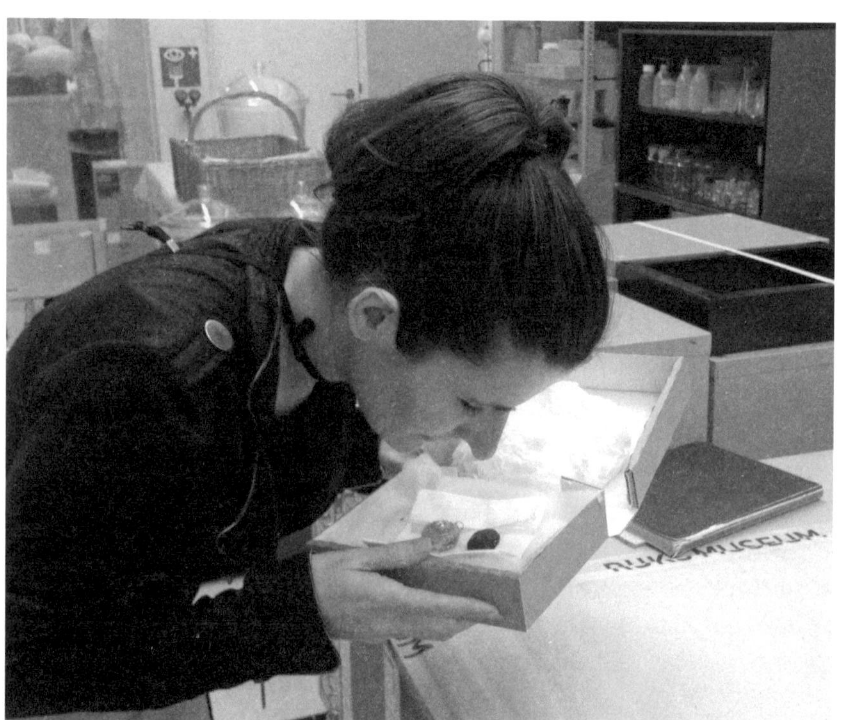

The author, Caro Verbeek sniffing a pomander (jewel filled with fragrances) at the Rijksmuseum Amsterdam. Photo: Suzanne van Leeuwen, 2013.

5. Rachel Herz & Gerald Cupchik, 'An Experimental Characterization of Odor-evoked Memories in Humans', *Chemical Senses*, 17, 1992, 519–528.

An 'Olfactory Odyssey' and General Do's and Don'ts

When I started working with smell in museums, I soon noticed the considerable and lasting impact it had on audiences. Some of them told me their art experience had deepened and had become more memorable even months afterwards. I observed participants of olfactory tours, including children, scrutinizing paintings with more attention, patience, and curiosity than I had ever witnessed. Surprisingly, many of them seemed to become very talkative, eager to share what they just went through while smelling scents related to paintings, stories, and artefacts. This is probably the result of olfaction's unique capacity to trigger early, vivid memories.[5]

Interestingly, soon after these first endeavours, I learned that people of diverse abilities were intrigued by olfactory interventions as well, including those with anosmia ('smell blindness') because they felt their situation was acknowledged by the emphasis on the importance of smell in history and culture, making them feel recognized. Blind people and people with low vision generally felt like they were given access to heritage and art that is usually not available to them.

Needless to say, it was also challenging to work with scent in these 'bastions of vision', and not in the last place because there is a high level of 'odorphobia' (fear of smells) and unfamiliarity with this fleeting material, especially among conservators who worry about the collection. For those interested in working with smells who need to reassure worried colleagues, these are some important rules of thumb:

• Never work with liquid scents (I once accidentally dropped a bottle with the smell of the Battle of Waterloo near the information desk at the Rijksmuseum, the scent lingered there for weeks), but work with 'dry diffusion' (scented air) or scented pieces of cardboard instead (more on distribution methods will follow during the case studies).

• Avoid any sulphureous compounds, for those will affect silver (instantly blackening the material). This makes creating 'stench' rather challenging as most disagreeable smells contain sulphur.

• When working with stench, always make sure this isn't the final smell offered to your audience or people will leave sad, annoyed or angry (such is the emotional impact of smell).

• Always make sure that the scents you use are connected to artefacts, depicted stories or depicted odorants and such. This enables multisensory and/or meaningful storytelling in your institution connected to your theme/vision/collection.

• Try to avoid questions like 'what do you smell?' Also try not to inform visitors about associations and memories, this to prevent people from feeling inadequate, because it's very hard to name smells, but relatively easy to describe our recollections and connotations.

• Try to connect to perfumers, smell marketeers, chemists, educators, scent historians, and art historians. But if this is truly challenging don't hesitate to just start, possibly with simple materials.[6]

OLFACTORY MUSEOLOGY
A Categorization

When charting 'olfactory museology', although it is an emerging and changing field, it is already possible to discern between four types of practices, (more or less) coinciding with four different roles:

1. Artists: From the 1890s onwards, artists and performers started to integrate smell into their total works of art, including dance, cinema, theatre, and sculpture. Especially the Futurists and the Surrealists (Duchamp was already mentioned) addressed the sense of smell regularly and meaningfully.[7] This type of art practice is now referred to as 'olfactory art'. In 2013 Peter de Cupere introduced a helpful definition in his 'Olfactory Art Manifesto': '[when] smell [is used] as a medium that gives context and/or can be the concept of the work'.

6. Museum professionals (and others) interested in implementing smell in their practice can consult several online open-source publications such as: Lizzie Ostrom, *How to Use Scent in Events: Odette Toilette's Guide for Museums*, London, 2016 and Caro Verbeek, *In Search of Lost Scents at the Rijksmuseum: Scent as a Medium in a Museum of Visual Art (Vision document)*, Amsterdam, 2020 and Odeuropa, *Olfactory Storytelling Toolkit*, Sofia Ehrich et al. (eds.), Amsterdam, 2023.

7. Caro Verbeek, 'In Search of Lost Scents: the Olfactory Dimension of Futurism', in *Yearbook of Futurism Studies*, Berlin, 2021, 247–275 and Caro Verbeek, 'Surreal Aromas: (Re)constructing the Volatile Heritage of Marcel Duchamp', in *Belle Haleine: The Scent of Art*, Heidelberg, 115–124.

8. Bembibre, Strlic, 'Smell of Heritage'.

9. Odeuropa was a smell heritage and olfactory mining project led by Inger Leemans. The author was manager of the olfactory events and olfactory museology sub-project, which was continued by Sofia Ehrich.

10. Odotheka is an international archive of smells of heritage objects. For more information see: www.heritageresearch-hub.eu/project/odotheka/

11. Jorge Otero-Pailos & Adam Jasper (eds.), 'Smell and Preservation', Future Interior, 13:2. 2017.

12. One such example of the diagnostic use of the nose in a heritage context would be the sniffing session with IFF perfumers and the author, led by head of furniture conservation Paul van Duin and GC-specialist Henk van Keulen at the Rijksmuseum (2012) which was dedicated to determining the contents of an apothecary cabinet from the eighteenth century. For more information see: www.futuristscents.com/2020/03/28/redolent-remedies-sniffing-out-a-historical-apothecary-cabinet/.

2. Curators: Over the past two decades or so museum professionals (other than artists) have started to curate 'olfactory art exhibitions', focusing mainly on works with an olfactory dimension as a theme or strategy or on (the history of) perfume. A true pioneer in this field is Jim Drobnick, who also authored *The Smell Culture Reader* in 2006. 2012 marked the year perfume critic Chandler Burr curated 'The Art of Scent' at the Museum of Art and Design in New York. In 2015 Tinguely Museum in Basel presented 'Belle Haleine: The Scent of Art' while in the same year I co-curated 'There's Something in the Air: Scent in Art' at Villa Rot in Burgrieden, including both historical and contemporary olfactory art practices. An exhibition that addressed the presentation of scents on a meta-level was 'Smell as a Criterion: Towards an Olfactory Politics in Curating' took place in Porto Alegre (Brazil) during the 10th Mercosul Biennial in 2016. Many have followed since.

3. Heritage professionals and conservators: Scent heritage professionals began to analyse and preserve the olfactory dimension of artifacts and spaces professionally around 2015. A pioneer in this field is Cecilia Bembibre, who has reconstructed the smell of the library of Saint Paul's Cathedral in 2017.[8] She was also responsible for creating a 'book odour wheel' (which categorizes different book scents) and promoting scent as heritage under the umbrella project 'Odeuropa' (2021–2023).[9] Also worth mentioning is the scent preservation project 'Odotheka', a Polish initiative lead by Matija Strlic (2022–ongoing).[10] Architectural historians such as Jorge Otero-Pailos are trying to reconstruct ambient scents of architectural heritage.[11] Last but not least, heritage professionals also use their nose diagnostically, for example to assess the state of objects and the presence of mould or to know which materials were used.[12]

4. Educators (and curators): Olfactory interventions to mediate between visual art and different audiences are often supported and initiated by the education department, mostly because scents can make exhibitions more accessible and inclusive. 'Fleeting: Scents in Colour'

(2021), curated by Ariane van Suchtelen and Lizzie Marx
for the Mauritshuis in The Hague, was initiated by the
curators, but with the help of educators (and myself). In this
exhibition, the public was able to smell seventeenth-century
objects, land- and cityscapes and (olfactory) events by means
of 'corona-proof scent stations' that were equipped with
footpumps and scent compositions made by International
Flavors & Fragrances (IFF), Hilversum. The case studies
below fall under this final category.

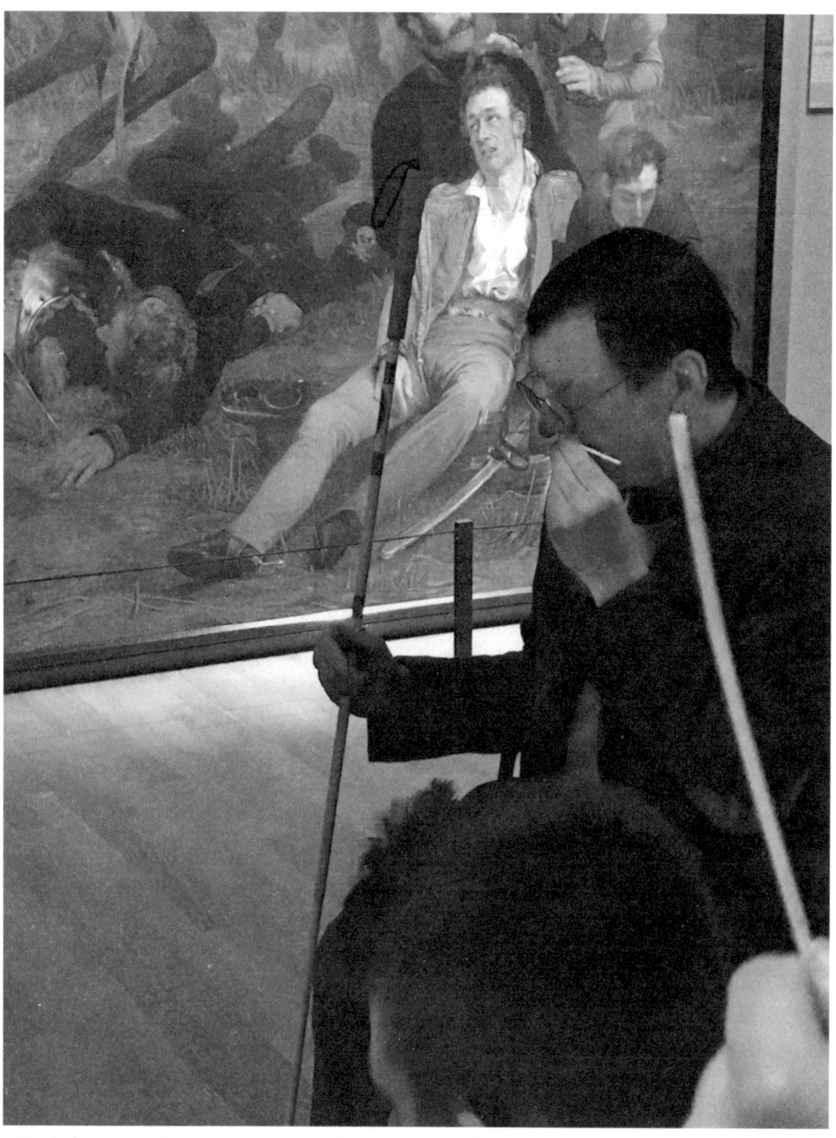

Blind photographer Hannes Wallrafen smelling the scent of *The Battle of Waterloo*
(Jan Willem Pieneman, oil on canvas, 1824) at the Rijksmuseum, 2020.
Photo: Cathelijne Denekamp.

13. For those interested in the project 'In Search of Lost Scents' ARIAS and the author created a podcast that can be found here: www.arias.amsterdam/in-search-of-lost-scents/.

14. Caro Verbeek, 'Seeing by Smelling: How to Enhance the Experience of Blind and Low Sighted People in a Museum of 'Visual' Art', *Futuristscents*, 2020.

CASE STUDY 1:
IN SEARCH OF LOST SCENTS AT THE RIJKSMUSEUM AMSTERDAM (2015–2020)

'In Search of Lost Scents' was part of my creative industries PhD-project (2015–2020) on the role of smell in art history and museology.[13] Together with IFF Hilversum (under the guidance of Bernardo Fleming) and the Rijksmuseum (supervised by Pauline Kintz) we developed a dozen of scents based on the collection of the Rijksmuseum, spanning the period between the Middle Ages and the twentieth century, and ranging from paintings to artefacts and even an airplane. In addition, we researched the effect of smells on different target groups (children, adults, families, people of diverse abilities).

The most popular scent was unquestionably the (re)construction of the scent of the Battle of Waterloo, composed by senior perfumer Birgit Sijbrands. This scent combined the emanations of the battlefield, including gunpowder, horses, moist earth, anxiety sweat, and last but not least, Napoleon's perfume called 'aqua mirabilis' which he used amply, and which is very similar to eau de cologne 4711. Yielding a historical sensation, personal memories, and an immersive experience all at once, this scent triggered people's imagination. Many reported having a sensation of being 'in' the depicted scene instead of just watching it from a distance.

In 2019 inclusion manager Cathelijne Denekamp (Rijksmuseum), Hannes Wallrafen (Geluid in Zicht) and I organized a tour for a group of blind individuals and people with low vision. It struck me how these particular individuals seemed to possess a vast(er) vocabulary to describe smells and seemed eager to share personal stories connected to memories that the various smells evoked, even involving visual memories that were tied to some of the scents. Wallrafen, a former photographer who had turned blind later in life, was particularly moved by the scent of the Battle of Waterloo which was created for an 1824 painting by Jan Willem Pieneman:

> I already knew I could see by listening, but now I know I can see by smelling too. The scent enables me to envision the complexity of the scene.[14]

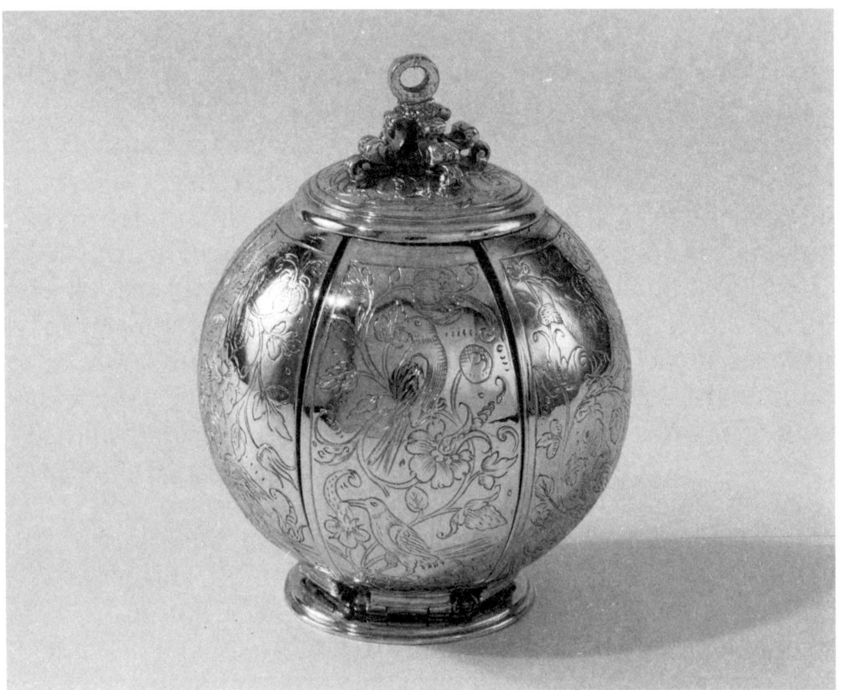

Anonymous, pomander, ca. 1600–1625, 7 cm. (height), silver. Collection Rijksmuseum Amsterdam.

During the tour we also highlighted a 'pomander'. This is a spherically shaped item made from precious metal which was usually filled with fragrances such as spices, animal excretions such as musk and civet, and floral material to protect oneself from diseases (before Pasteur's discovery that germs cause diseases, it was generally believed that malodours were responsible for the spread of diseases). The Rijksmuseum displays their pomanders behind glass, making them inaccessible to our noses and hands, and depriving them of their original function. That is why during tours I carry my own specimen in addition to one of the scents that they might have contained. Another participant who, unlike Wallrafen, had always been blind told me:

> I clearly remember that silver piece of jewellery. Maybe because we both smelled it and were able to hold one in our hands. More in general, the scents really contributed to the stories surrounding the

Exhibiting for
Multiple Senses

15. Idem.

16. Caro Verbeek, Inger Leemans & Bernardo Fleming, 'How can scents enhance the impact of guided museum tours? towards an impact approach for olfactory museology', *Senses & Society*, 2020, published online: doi. org/10.1080/17458927. 2022.2142012.

17. Caro Verbeek, *In Search of Lost Scents at the Rijksmuseum: Scent as a Medium in a Museum of Visual Art (Vision document)*, 2020, 15.

18. In 2010 Jorg Hempenius and the author won a pitch and created the olfactory project 'Inhaling Art' for the Van Abbemuseum, produced by Loes Janssen and Steven ten Thije. In 2019 Jorg Hempenius and the author contributed to 'Multisensory Museum', curated by Marleen Hartjes.

objects, not the artefacts themselves. Being 100% blind, I do not feel any connection to, for example, paintings. The scents really made me empathize with people from different eras though. I have an excellent sense of imagination.[15]

Some of the more general outcomes of a quantitative analysis of the answers to the questionnaire were that people become more talkative when there is a scent involved; they pay attention to different details (for example the sky and the earth of the Battle of Waterloo painting); they (want to) stay longer; and they generally appreciated the tour with a higher grade than those who took the same tour without smells.[16] A final insight I would like to share in this context is how children's attention span was lengthened considerably.[17]

CASE STUDY 2: 'DELINKING AND RELINKING', VAN ABBEMUSEUM (2020–ONGOING)

The ambition to be an inclusive, accessible, and multi-voiced museum has been the goal of the Van Abbemuseum since Charles Esche became its director in 2004. Accessibility expert Marleen Hartjes was partially responsible for their long-term exhibition of the museum's collection titled 'Delinking and Relinking' (18 September 2021–1 June 2026). The show aims to inform and heighten the aesthetic appreciation of art by people of different abilities, for example through tactile replicas and olfactory interpretations of artworks.

Having worked with the Van Abbemuseum on several projects before, in 2020 art historian Sofia Ehrich, scent marketeer and expert Jorg Hempenius (iScent), and I created five smells to accompany five paintings and another three ambiently diffused smells for art installations (the latter won't be discussed in this context).[18] These scents were distributed on scratch&sniff cards with texts printed in both ink and braille containing one sentence that described how the scent was related to the paintings. For example: for Constant Permeke's painting *The Sower* (1935), we opted for the smell of moist earth, which aimed to convey both the countryside the artist lived in and loved, and what is depicted on the canvas. For a painting by Charley Toorop that shows a common lodging house (1928) which is characterized by the contrast of dark and light colours, of poverty and hope, we chose a smell with a similar dark-light contrast. Lily of the valley was supposed to evoke the lighter colours as well as memories of childhood, referring to the baby positioned between adults with grim faces. A more abstract olfactory translation was a painting by Chagall (*Hommage à Apollinaire*, 1913) representing the passing of time. As smells are inherently fleeting, visitors were asked to focus on that aspect. Finally, we created a smell for Cé Röling's *Yearly Fair in Sicily* (1933), focusing on the elements in the painting such as cattle and the change of the seasons.

All the paintings were pre-selected by the curators. This means that they weren't necessarily the most suitable for olfactory interpretations (as a scent historian I usually search for strong connections). The Van Abbemuseum has expressed the wish to involve scent experts before they curate artworks for their next semi-permanent display.

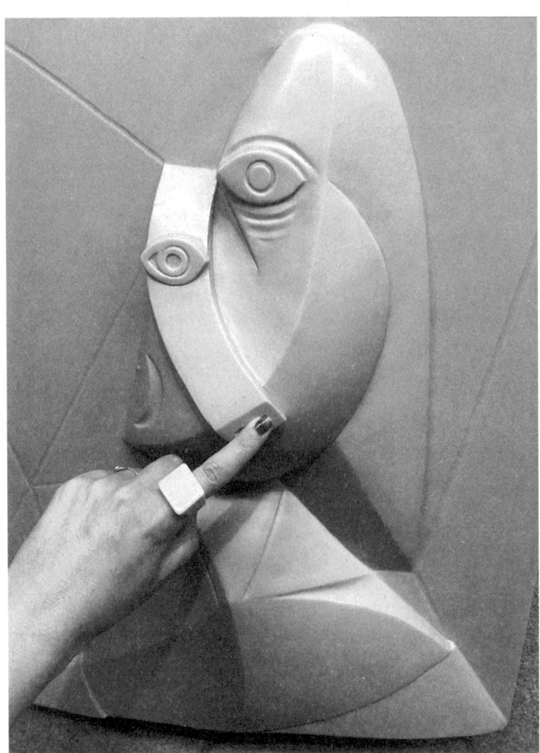

Tactile interpretation of a work by Picasso, Van Abbemuseum Eindhoven. Photo: Caro Verbeek, 2024.

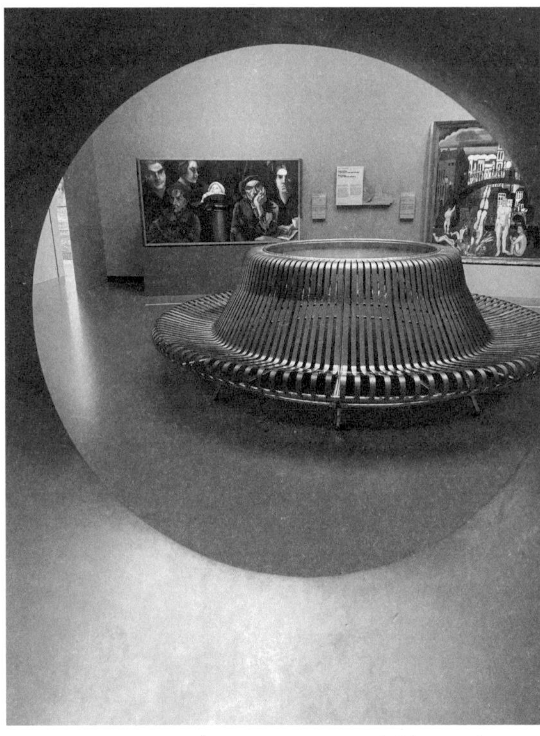

Installation view of scent room, 'Delinking and Relinking', Van Abbemuseum Eindhoven. Photo: Caro Verbeek, 2024.

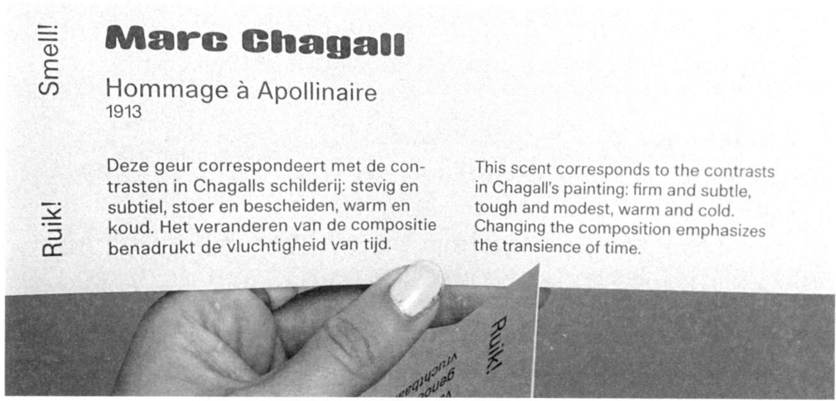

Jorg Hempenius, Caro Verbeek, Sofia Ehrich, scented scratch&sniff card for Marc Chagall's *Hommage à Apollinaire* (1913), with a short description of the relation between the scent and the artwork. Photo: Caro Verbeek. The first batch of cards was printed in braille. The cards will be discontinued and replaced by more sustainable scent stations.

19. Interview between author and Bram Groenteman on 09 September 2024. Personal archive.

Qualitative Assessment

As I did not conduct quantitative research in this case, I asked some of the visitors if they could share their experiences with me for the purpose of this article. One of them was curator Bram Groenteman who visited the presentation in 2021 with his (then) fellow students of the track Curating Art and Cultures. Head of Collections Steven ten Thije asked the students to focus on their experience and to leave out theoretical frameworks. Groenteman noticed how his peers who study modern and contemporary art seemed to be more receptive to the smells than those studying more traditional art. Additionally, the first group appeared to be more open to the abstract scents (Chagall), whereas the students who engage with 'older' art were more compelled by recognizable scents (Permeke). One of the main discussions afterwards was on the role of interpretation (by the scent's maker) when it comes to translating a work of art into a smell (as opposed to creating a tactile replica, which naturally also requires quite some interpretation that seeing people might not be aware of).[19] This question was echoed by editor of this volume Eva Fotiadi:

> The smells made me spend more time looking at the paintings than I would otherwise. As the scented paper

came with a short text about what the smell was trying to convey, I tried to figure out whether I agreed.[20]

The individual texts were considered 'too instructive' and taking away 'some of the associative freedom' according to Fotiadi.

Designer and experience expert Simon Dogger also reflected on the scents, the medium (cards) and the texts:

> The fact that the scents and descriptions are accessible and lead to associations and an image in your mind is of absolute additional value. I don't know if other blind and partially sighted people have a high level of associative thinking, but it works well for me. In addition, the fact that you can take the card with you and smell it again at a later time is a very interesting aspect of these tactile cards.[21]

Unfortunately for Dogger (and presumably others), in the near future the scented cards will be replaced by scent stations (created by perfumer Jorg Hempenius) for environmental and practical reasons as the amount of paper and odorants proved to be both expensive and unsustainable. Furthermore, scratch&sniff doesn't allow for all the nuances in a scent to come out. Hempenius:

> When a composition is printed in scratch&sniff, some of the top and base notes seem to become somewhat obscured. Scents in flasks with pumps or boxes with tiny sniffing holes will help maintain their full scope.[22]

The animalic notes in the work by Röling described earlier, which shows numerous cows, for example, turned out to be more subtle than envisioned. Distribution methods are often highly challenging as all the aspects described above have to be taken into account.

20. Interview between author and Eva Fotiadi on 08 October 2024. Personal archive.

21. Interview between author and Simon Dogger on 17 October 2024. Personal archive.

22. Interview between author and Jorg Hempenius on 10 September 2024. Personal archive.

Exhibiting for
Multiple Senses

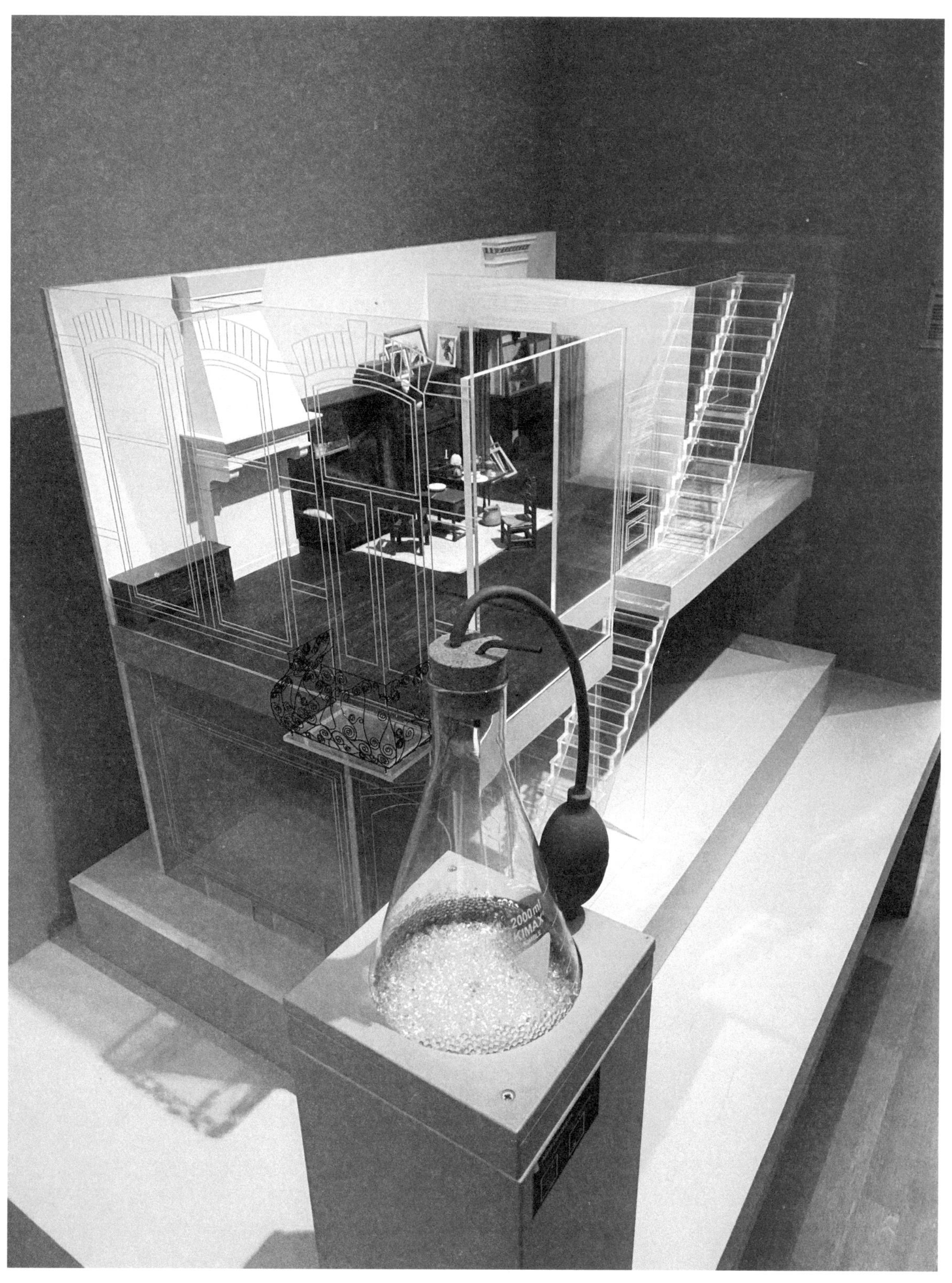

Installation view scent station with model of Amsterdam Studio, 'Mondrian & De Stijl', Kunstmuseum The Hague.
Photo: Caro Verbeek, 2024.

CASE STUDY 3:
CAN YOU SMELL ABSTRACTION?
The Scentscapes of Mondrian's Studios at Kunstmuseum The Hague (2022–ongoing)

23. The research project and tour 'Clapping to the Beat of Piet' at Kunstmuseum The Hague was financially supported by CLUE+, Vrije Universiteit Amsterdam.

What Does Abstraction Smell Like?

When I started working as a curator at the department of Mondrian and De Stijl at Kunstmuseum The Hague in 2021, one of my first endeavours was to try to make Mondrian's art more accessible through sensory interventions and embodiment exercises. For this purpose, I started the (research) project and sensory tour 'Clapping to the Beat of Piet', later aided by education specialist Richtje Reinsma (Fontys Hogeschool) and her students who assessed the tour and provided me with feedback.[23] We then refined the (historically informed) sensory interventions including dance and movement, (jazz) music, sound (described by Mondrian), clapping

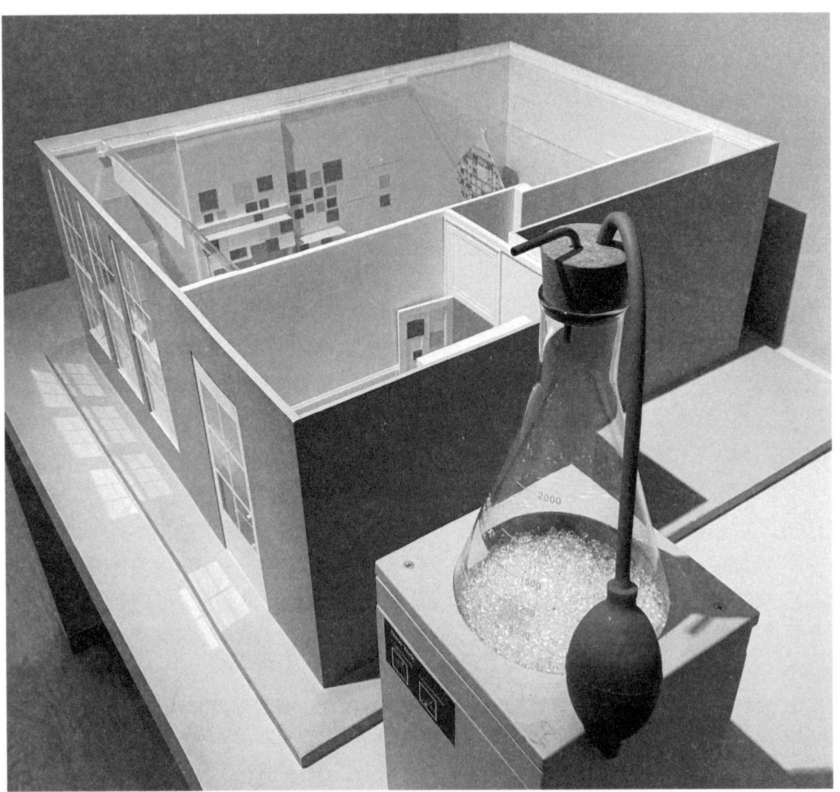

Installation view scent station with model of New York Studio, 'Mondrian & De Stijl', Kunstmuseum The Hague. Photo: Caro Verbeek, 2024.

(to Mondrian's visual rhythms), and smell, the focus of this case study.

It can be difficult to connect scent to abstract art, since no smell sources are depicted. But I formulated the following question (which can be extrapolated to other abstract artists' studios as well): 'If we (re)construct the scents of Mondrian's consecutive studios in Amsterdam, Paris, and New York, would this allow the audience to smell his development towards abstraction?' In the celebratory year 2022 (his 150th day of birth), we presented Kunstmuseum The Hague's very first scentscape, based on the study of materials, activities, nose witness reports, and photographs of Mondrian's studios.

Olfactory Facts in Mondrian's Life and Work

At the beginning of his career Mondrian—whose grandfather was a perfumer—studied, lived and worked in Amsterdam (1892–1911), painting in a traditional naturalistic style that echoes the Hague School. In this phase he mainly focused on the external, visually observable world. That is why he collected all kinds of objects such as copperware, Japanese prints and also Persian carpets and cashmere shawls that appear on his paintings and on photographs. The latter two types of textiles are known to have emanated heavy odours of camphor and patchouli. These substances were used as natural 'mothballs' and can be categorized as 'colonial' scents, which were omnipresent in Amsterdam around 1900. In addition, Mondrian and visiting artists smoked plenty of tobacco (another colonial product), such as cigars, pipes and cigarettes. Of course, the fresh smell of turpentine (a substance from fir trees) must have permeated every corner of the room as a constant base note (restorer Ruth Hoppe established this through chemical analysis). Finally, the perfumers decided to add a 'musty' touch, since many buildings in Amsterdam at the time were subject to mildew.

It is important to note that his environment did not always smell exactly the same of course, as a letter from Mondrian to his friend Aletta de Iongh demonstrates:

Since I blackened a wall of the studio with coal tar, it smells so much of tar that you might get a headache, and I will just leave too. I thought the smell would go away sooner. So should we postpone until next week?[24]

In Paris (1911–1914 and 1919–1938) the artist started to work in a more abstract style, which was reflected in his interior; he attached mirrors and cardboard rectangles in the primary colours to the white studio walls and he got rid of anything 'unnecessary', since he no longer painted the external world. This rendered the scent of his studio less dense and layered, yet some aromas remained: Mondrian and his visitors smoked their beloved cigarettes, and the smell of turpentine perpetuated as a common thread. One scent—or rather bouquet of scents—which reflected how the industrialization of the metropole occasionally slipped in; when he opened his windows, the smell of burning coals and heated metal from the nearby station Gare Montparnasse must have disturbed the paradisiacal and clear atmosphere in his studio.

Yet the most annoying according to the artist was that his paintings got so dirty from the polluted air that he had to cover them with a cloth.

In a rare literary text, Mondrian commented on Parisian scents himself, but reflecting on those he found outside, as a mixture of modern and natural scents:

The boulevard is more thought-concentrated. I see the colours and shapes. I hear the sounds. I feel the spring warmth, I smell the spring air, the gasoline, the perfumes, I taste the coffee.[25]

Fleeing from the Nazis (he was deemed a 'degenerate artist',) Mondrian arrived in New York in 1940, where he stayed until his death in 1944. His style changed quite substantially one last time, culminating in his final painting *Victory Boogie Woogie* (1944). Far away from the war, Mondrian enjoyed the bustling city life and, of course, the exciting rhythms of the boogie-woogie to which he danced if his health allowed him to. He discovered tape as a new medium here, so that he could make his compositions as playful and dynamic as the music he loved and improvise more easily. This also meant

24. Letter from Piet Mondrian to Aletta de Iongh, May 1909, collection Kröller-Müller Museum Otterlo.

25. Piet Mondriaan, 'De groote boulevards', *De Nieuwe Amsterdammer. Onafhankelijk Nederlandsch weekblad*, 1920; reprinted in: Piet Mondriaan, *Twee verhalen*, (introduced by August Hans den Boef en een studie van Carel Blotkamp, Amsterdam, 1987, 13–20.

Exhibiting for Multiple Senses

26. The historical background of the scents of Mondrian's studios is described elaborately in: Caro Verbeek, 'Kun je abstractie ruiken? Hoe de geurtransities van Mondriaans ateliers zijn artistieke ontwikkelingen markeren (én bewerkstelligen)' (Can you smell abstraction? How the olfactory transitions of Mondrian's studios marked (and enhanced) his artistic development), *KM Magazine*, 2022, 20–24.

that the smell of glue made its first (abundant) appearance in his work environment. Moreover, his coal stove had now been replaced by (odourless) central heating. The scent in his studio was now as clear, fresh and 'flat' as the picture plane of his canvases. This was the smell of modernism and optimism echoing the ideal pristine atmosphere once envisioned by his colleague Theo van Doesburg:

> An absolute cleanliness, a constant light, a clear atmosphere. […] Men can certainly learn more from doctors' laboratories than from artist's studios. The latter are cages that smell of sick monkeys.[26]

Execution

After a brief based on the information provided above, perfumers Anh Ngo, Birgit Sijbrands and project leader Bernardo Fleming (IFF Hilversum) then composed three scents. To safely distribute the smell, a small amount of each liquid was poured over Styrofoam beads in a 2000-ml flask. These were used to enlarge the surface that can give off scent to the air in the container. Hempenius—who also creates devices to distribute smell—created stoppers with pumps and a straw so that visitors could circulate the scented

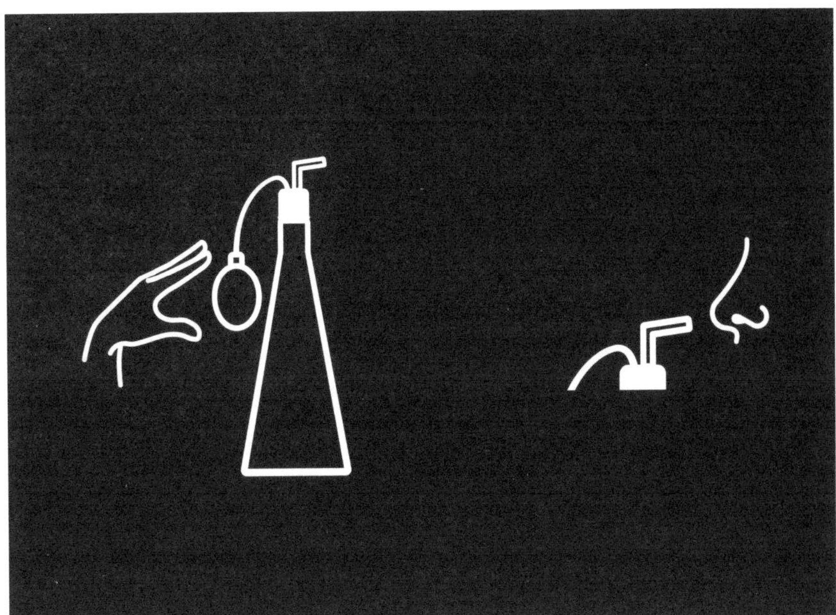

Label with textual instructions and icons: 1. Squeeze (the pump). 2. Smell (the straw), for Mondrian scent stations, 'Mondrian & De Stijl', Kunstmuseum The Hague, design by Dwi Tirtadji and design department Kunstmuseum The Hague.

air and move it towards their noses. This method is called
'dry diffusion' and it's considered a responsible way of
working with scent in museums as liquids are not allowed nor
desirable in a heritage context (as mentioned before). Berend
Visser (Kunstmuseum The Hague) designed pedestals that
prevented the flasks from falling and from being lifted. And
graphic designer Dwi Tirtadji (Kunstmuseum The Hague)
created icons that demonstrate how the stations are supposed
to be handled (as many visitors aren't accustomed to using
their nose in a museum). The three flasks were installed next
to three mock-ups of Mondrian's studios. A general text
about the smells of Mondrian's studios accompanies the
installation.

Quantitative and Qualitative Assessment

Jolanda van Zijl (accessibility manager Kunstmuseum The
Hague) and I designed a questionnaire related to all sensory
interventions, including the scents. Questions ranged from
'Did the sensory interventions increase your knowledge?'
to 'Did this tour alter your perception of Mondrian?' and
'Did this tour alter you perception of art in general?'. We
then organized a dozen tours, with groups ranging from
five to fifteen people equalling eighty-six participants.
Neurologist Jules Claus analysed the results of the survey's
multiple-choice questions. One of the outcomes revealed
that among all sensory interventions, music and smell scored
highest when it comes to 'understanding' Mondrian's work
better, as opposed to people's expectation that smelling
merely leads to emotional or 'fun' experiences and not to
knowledge. Another result was that the smells on display
seem to yield an immersive experience (just like in the case of
the Battle of Waterloo). People often reported that they felt as
though they were physically inside Mondrian's studio, standing
beside him while he works and they experienced an increased
level of empathy for the artist as an actual human being. In
addition, the answers to the open questions ('What did you
find most surprising?' and 'What do you expect to remember?')
showed that smell was mentioned more often than any other
sense (only surpassed by a combination of senses).

Exhibiting for
Multiple Senses

27. An article on the more scientific outcomes of the research of 'Clapping to the Beat of Piet' from an interdisci-plinary perspective (neuro-aesthetics, phenomenology, art and sensory history) by neurologist Jules Claus and myself is in preparation. Psychologist Crétien van Campen took on an advisory role in this endeavour.

Interestingly, six participants (circa five per cent) who were blind or had low vision that were part of a delegation of Kubes (a Dutch organization that aims to make art and culture accessible for people with a visual impairment), seemed particularly enthusiastic about the musical and 'proprioceptic' (the sensation of movement and one's own body) elements of the tour which allowed them to feel Mondrian's rhythmic paintings by imagining movements and hearing rhythms. This is thought-provoking since Mondrian often indicated that his goal was to convey inner movement or a 'dynamic equilibrium'. The essence of his art can be made accessible to people of other abilities if you offer the right tools. Members of this group also mentioned the artificiality of the scents more than other target groups, possibly because smelling in combination with looking at the models contributes to a heightened sense of reality.[27]

The Nose Knows

The same scentscape was also introduced during lectures at universities and art academies between 2021 and 2023. In an attempt to engage in 'comparative smelling' in a playful manner, I made participants guess which scents belong to his Amsterdam and New York studios by handing out blotters (cardboard papers with scent) or by wafting aromatized hand fans. I then explain that just like his art, the scent of his studios became 'lighter' over time and more pristine as he started to work more abstractly and that his Amsterdam studio smelled 'darker' just like his colour palette at the time. Surprisingly, 95 per cent of participants connected the right smell to the studios after this simple cue. Synesthetic (addressing other senses than the one that is triggered) language appears to be quite accessible and understandable when it comes to smell (for example 'a green smell' or a 'loud aroma').

Specifically for visitors who smell the scents without guidance, and who often resort to the dichotomy 'foul-fragrant' or 'nostalgic' (in relation to the Amsterdam studio), we (only recently) introduced a 'scent wheel' in the gallery. Adding descriptors can help people deepen their understanding of what it is they are smelling and discern between different notes, and learn when odorants reoccur.

Final Note

Museums in the late twentieth and early twenty-first century have decontextualized both artworks and human bodies, detaching them from their multisensory surroundings and capacities, reducing art and other historical objects to a merely visual and textual affair. Intentionally (re)introducing smells within curatorial practices and storytelling restores the multisensory context and meaning of artworks (and what they depict) and takes the entire body with its numerous sensory faculties into account. It fosters a more inclusive and accessible art experience both for people who are blind or have low vision and sighted people. For the first group it seems to enhance their imagination; not necessarily to imagine the artworks, but rather the stories behind them. For the latter group the combination of seeing and smelling can additionally lead to an altered gaze; the scents direct their eyes to different details for example. But people of all abilities seem to become more communicative, feel immersed, feel emotionally involved, spend more time in front of an artwork, and are more likely to remember their experience. Using smell in a meaningful way can bring people together instead of setting them apart based on their abilities. Moreover, blind individuals or people with low vision could help sighted people—who are usually highly ocularcentric in their approach to life and art—to recognize that art does not represent mere visual affairs, but rather an amalgam of impressions. Ideally, smells, sounds, tactile impressions, dance/movement, and images could all be combined within art and heritage contexts and people of all abilities brought together rather than divided through separate tours.

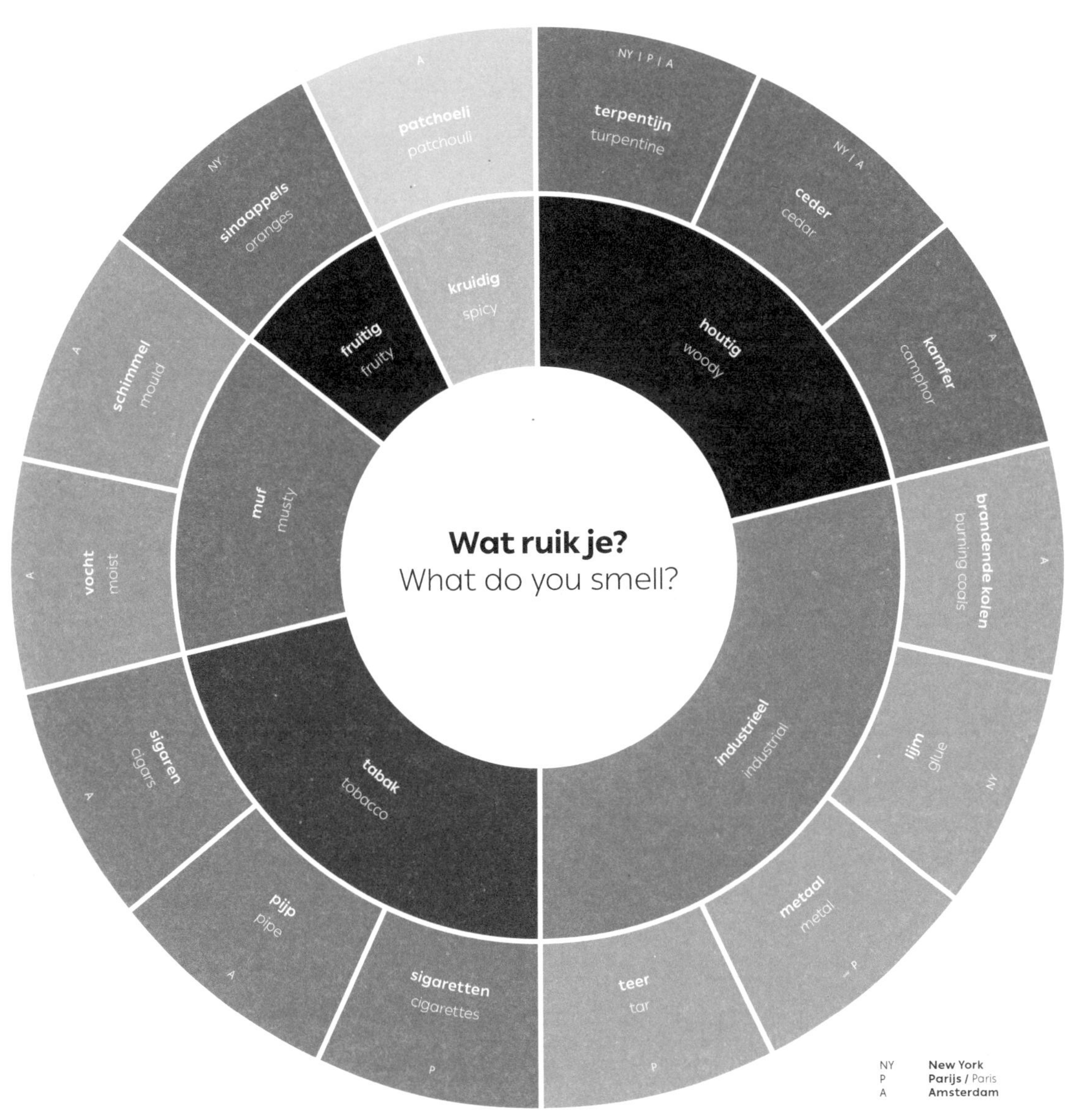

Caro Verbeek (concept and research), Dwi Tirtadji (design), odour wheel with scent components found in Mondrian's studios in Amsterdam, Paris and New York, 2024, 'Mondrian & De Stijl', Kunstmuseum The Hague.

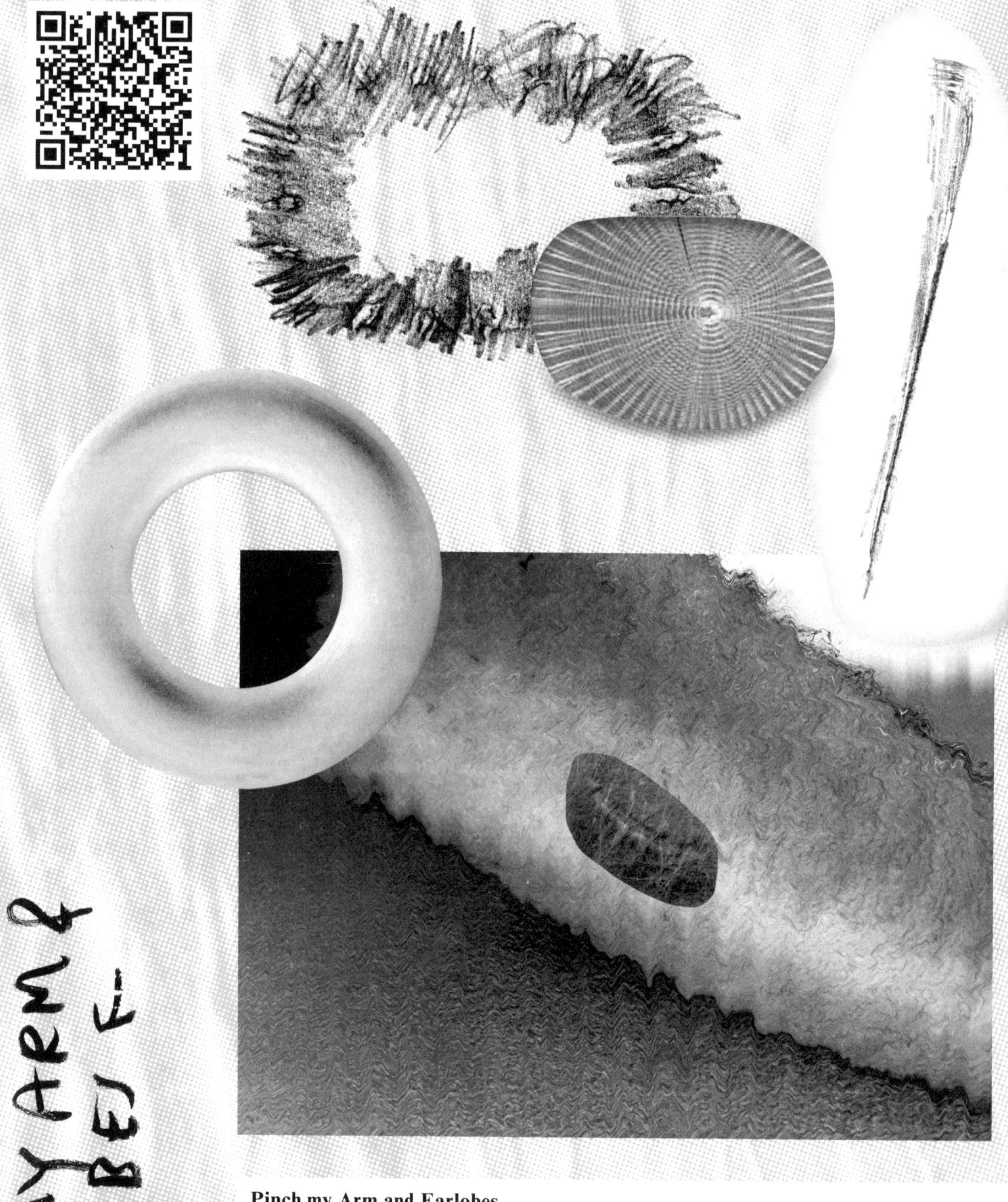

Pinch my Arm and Earlobes

The background of this collage is a dotted raster image of a tree bark. In the top left corner is a QR code. When scanned, it takes the reader to a piece of music (a collection of sounds) that corresponds to this page. To the right are three oval shapes. The one on the left is scratched with a black pencil on the grey background. The middle one contains tree rings. The one on the right shows a pencil drawing that resembles a needle or thorn. The bottom half of the page features an image of an arm distorted by a wavy texture. One spot has been cut out and inverted, highlighting the bitemarks on the arm. Above that photo of the arm is a circular plastic training ring for your hands. This can also be used as a teething or bite ring.

What is the sensation of biting? A mind-calming, stress-releasing activity? Do you ever bite your partner? What happens in your body when you bite really hard into your arm? And what happens when you bite on a piece of wood?

MORE THAN MEETS THE EYE
Interview with Georgina Kleege

David Gissen

Introduction

Georgina Kleege's writings on her and others' experiences and theorizations of blindness, such as *Sight Unseen* (1999), have become central to the field of disability studies. Her 2018 book, *More than Meets the Eye: What Blindness Brings to Art*, combines memoir and analysis of theoretical texts in a larger exploration of the relationship between blindness and the fine arts. In addition to her writing, Kleege consults with museums and other arts institutions, exploring how her and other blind people's experiences might inform future curatorial and programming activity. Such work increases the accessibility of exhibitions while transforming the interpretations of museum collections in often highly provocative ways. The following interview revisits some key ideas from *More than Meets the Eye*, while exploring the book's implications for the conservation and preservation of art and architecture.

DAVID GISSEN (DG): Your book *More than Meets the Eye* shifts the implied relationships when we use terms such as 'disability', 'access' and 'culture'. We often imagine how culture can be made more accessible to those with various disabilities. There are many cultural institutions that try to make their cultural artifacts more accessible to people with visual and mobility impairments. Your book flips such thinking around—you claim that institutions and the non-disabled public might understand culture more deeply through a disability perspective. For example, you use the term 'gaining blindness'. I was wondering if you could explain what this term means and the larger ideas it represents.

GEORGINA KLEEGE (GK): The concept of 'gaining blindness' comes from my observation that we always talk about 'losing sight'. So blindness is always understood as a loss. But I think the lived experience of many blind people is that blindness, vision impairment, is a different way of perceiving the world, and that there are gains in that difference. I'm sensitive to the other extreme, which is the ways in which sometimes blindness and other disabilities are understood as being compensated for by some divine intervention: the idea of the 'blind seer'—that you don't have physical vision, but you can see the future. It's not about that. It's just a question of people who learn to direct their attention to other facets of the environment or other facets of culture. So that's what it really means.

When it comes to access and, in this case, particularly when it comes to cultural access to arts institutions, I think too often there is an understanding that the cultural institution bestows access, and then the people who have received the access then go away. What I'm advocating for is that there is a more two-sided interaction. And that when you give blind people access, they have something to bring to the table in terms of a different perspective. And I think this has implications across the board, and it has to do with why diversity can be challenging to people, because if you open up the culture then the culture is going to change. And you have to be ready to say 'That's OK', and 'I'm happy there is this change, and things aren't going to stay the way they've always been'.

DG: In fact, you proposed that museums employ blind docents to interpret works for nonblind people. I'm curious how you imagine this as an intervention into the space of the museum—both from the larger conceptual level that you've already addressed and from the everyday experience of a museum visitor. What happens? Is this about a person explaining what it is like to touch an artwork?

GK: I've actually had this experience since I wrote the book, at the Contemporary Jewish Museum in San Francisco. I was part of a project on an exhibit that they called 'Jewish Folktales Retold: Artist as Maggid'. It was a show of all commissioned works by contemporary artists, and their task was to make a work that was somehow related to Jewish folktales. They brought me in to work with the 3D works in the exhibit—there were mostly 2D works, but they had some works of sculpture—and they let me get my hands on the work, and they let me in some instances talk with the artists. I was present when at least one of the pieces was installed, so I was handling parts of it as it was being installed. And then they recorded audio and video of this and they put it up on their digital website. My point was, and this is a point I made in the book, is that I love touch tours—whenever anybody gives me the opportunity to put my hands on a work of art I'm happy—but it always feels sort of unfulfilling, because I do it, I touch the work, and then it's like 'OK. Goodbye! You can go home'. And I feel like I have a lot to say about the experience, and I know that people are really, really curious about: what is it like to touch that sculpture, what does that feel like, what did you get out of the experience? So, this was an occasion to model that reciprocal exchange—to say what it feels like, to say how my haptic explorations of those pieces actually enhanced meaning.

So we did that, and then we also did a docent tour for blind and visually impaired people, because they couldn't allow everybody to touch the art—the other blind people. But the artists, since they were all living and available, we got each of them to donate some of their materials, and some of them had scale models, and so on and so forth. So we went around the gallery, and I gave my spiel. But we had a little cart that we pushed around that had these materials. Because the media that were involved were not typical sculptural media, so there was a piece in handmade paper, and a piece in cast silicone, and a piece in carved Styrofoam, so they were not typical stone or bronze. There were a lot of interesting tactile and haptic features that I could draw out. People could hear what I was talking about, but also handle something that gave them some more information.

In addition, I'm co-curating an exhibit of tactile art at a gallery in Massachusetts in the spring. One of the things that is interesting about that is that artists typically submit images—so I made the stipulation that they would have to submit a detailed description of the work, because one of the curators is blind. But also that they would have to give a description of its tactile features—what are the rewards of touching this particular piece?

When you hang around artists and they're hanging around their work, they're always touching, and patting, and fondling, and brushing off the dust, and all that sort of stuff. Even if it's a 2D work that you wouldn't imagine being touched.

DG: I want to take this idea of the institution 'gaining blindness' a bit further. I'm wondering if you've ever imagined what disability might bring to the actual maintenance, and conservation, or reconstruction of culture.

GK: I've been involved in a couple of projects at the San Francisco Museum of Modern Art. There is an initiative funded by the Mellon Foundation called the Artist's Initiative, and basically artists propose a project, and they come in and work with pieces in the collection. And I teamed up with a collaborator who I've written about in the book, Fayen d'Evie, and we did a bunch of projects with pieces—I think the title was something like 'Multisensory Encounters'—so we worked with a sound piece by the artist Bill Fontana that was site specific, it was designed for the atrium of that building, but it was only up for a certain amount of time. And we did a bunch of projects where we took people, who were mostly staff people at the museum, up and down the different levels so you could hear it from different levels. And we would stop at each level and record people's impressions, how it changed, and all this sort of stuff. So it became an extended description of the piece that could serve as a kind of conservation—because it's an ephemeral piece, it's no longer there—but how do you preserve a record of the experience?

So we did that, and then we worked with this Richard Serra piece, *Sequence*, which is now gone from the museum, but it was there for a few years in a sort of custom-built studio, which—if you know it—is this big bronze thing that you walk through. I think he once referred to it as a choreographic object because you walk through it and you have this experience. It sort of defeats the idea of a single vantage point; you can't see the piece from anywhere. So we did a lot of work moving through the piece. We did recordings of us moving through the piece making sounds, because it's very resonant. They gave us permission to use my cane to shoreline in the piece, which is a process that blind people use where you find the edge. So we wanted to activate its sonic qualities. Again, it was recording a range of different experiences in the piece that we could document in sound and in writing to preserve a record of the piece. Now it's gone back to Stanford, I guess.

I'm doing another project just now with Vija Celmins' exhibit that is at SFMOMA now, which is work that is completely inaccessible to me. It's all 2D work, a lot of it is drawing. So we were working to develop detailed audio description of the work, but that would also work as detailed mapping of the different pieces. There is a process that I've learned to do where, rather than asking somebody like the docent, 'Describe this to me', and you have the single authoritative perspective, to take a group of people and say 'What do you see?' then 'What do you see?' then 'What do you see?' In collaboration there is a creative process where more and more information is added on, and there is some opportunity for debate, refinement of 'Oh, I thought it was *this*, but now what you say shows me *this*'. And so, what you get is this very rich verbal account, which then theoretically could also serve as a form of preservation. So rather than saying 'Drawing in Graphite on Paper', you have all this other information that, again, can serve as preservation of direct viewer interaction.

DG: Three hundred years ago, if you sought to reconstruct a lost work of architecture or art from Greek and Roman antiquity you probably relied on ancient written descriptions of those works. In those particular cases, writing was the only surviving representation of lost or ruined architecture and art. So your exploration of writing as a type of preservationist record has some precedents. But in the past 150 years, we've witnessed a real shift away from any use of written description in preservation and conservation to a more pronounced emphasis on optical evidence. We've also witnessed increased emphasis on the optical characteristics of works in the preservation and conservation of culture.

After I read your book, I was thinking about this issue, and one of the things that I kept thinking is that so much of the culture and accessibility discussion is about accessing space. What would it mean to make these latter characteristics of time more accessible? The evidence of time's impacts on architecture and art are often discussed as changes to a surface; and this is presented as an optical effect. I don't know if you've thought about this in great depth? For example, you've written at length about your experiences in a medieval cathedral and at Stonehenge. Your work seems to be a pathway to think about the effects of time in very different ways—that are completely outside of the repertoire of preservation and conservation practice.

GK: I'm thinking about architectural sites and time. That's interesting. Even in a day, how does a room change? That might be about light. It might be about weather. But the changing light, it might be different seasons of the year, and how things are different in different seasons. There is also—and this is part of what I was mentioning when I was writing about my experiences visiting cathedrals—there is the experience of the space as emptied of people, which seems to me to be completely false, because these are spaces that were never intended to be emptied of people. They were spaces that were meant to function with people, but also with ritual. And so every aspect of

it is impacted by what the people are doing, what the priests are doing, that there is sound, that there is music, that there is light coming in through stained glass. I can't remember if I wrote about this or not, but I had a very profound experience at the Durham Cathedral. There is a chapel there where St. Bede is buried. And on his birthday, they have a ritual where the choir processes down, and you go from this large cathedral with that kind of sonority into a more confined space, and it's really profound. And the congregation gets up and you follow the choir, and then there are all these people in there and they're singing and ... wow. And that's time-related in that you celebrate that birthday once a year.

There is also an emotional response to visiting a place that has changed over time, and you know it has changed because of interactions with human bodies and the elements: the steps of the cathedral have a trough because people have stepped there. And that I find interesting because it speaks of the architectural object as a living thing that goes on and changes. Some of that change can be understood as deterioration, but some of it can be understood as what just happens over time.

DG: There is one experience in your book that might represent a firmer shift away from the optical, and it's one that I thought would be a conservator's nightmare! You wrote about the way that animals living inside Stonehenge enabled you to experience the age of the structure and the structure's architectural characteristics. I was wondering if you could talk about that.

GK: That was a wonderful experience. I was there and I had no expectations. The rules are that at Stonehenge you have to make an appointment to gain access, but it was not the tourist season, and I was there with my late husband, and we were just walking around, and the guard came up to me and said, 'Would you like to get inside?' I said, 'You bet'. And she said, 'Well, could you wait until this tour bus goes away, because if one person goes inside everyone wants to go'. It was November, so there were not a lot of people. So we went inside, and the first thing that interested me was that it is warmer inside that circle. And it is November in Britain; there was not a lot of sun, but whatever there was, heated those stones. Then she was telling me rather more than I needed to know about the many, many varieties of lichen that exist on those stone—I mean there is some huge number of lichens that are living on those stones. And then she said, 'Here, touch here', and so I touched there, and there was this little vibration. And I said, 'What the hell is that?' And she said, 'Birds have nested'. And this was way down inside the stone. Obviously, the birds have been doing this for centuries, and that each generation of bird can dig in a little deeper, so they had their little burrows in there. So yeah, from a conservator's point of view…. But by the time anybody thought of preserving those stones, those birds had laid claim to that as their territory. So what are you going to do? Put a net over them? These are things that have been on the landscape for however many centuries, so of course animal life is going to inhabit them.

DG: This will change how I teach Stonehenge to my students. No one thinks of those stones as creating interior warmth or vibrating. We don't think of them as moving. This speaks to your large point about what we gain from your interpretations and experiences of artifacts.

Your description of Stonehenge also reveals a tension in your book: In the introduction you argue that touch is an overemphasized sense in discussions of accessibility and blindness. But you often describe the privilege that you've had to touch works. And if I understand what you're saying correctly, you think touch is a fascinating discussion in issues of accessibility when it transgresses cultural boundaries, but when it's just simply 'touch this thing because you have a disability', it becomes a form of simplistic charity.

GK: In the book when I was talking about the figure of the hypothetical blind man, what I object to is: 'No eyes equals really big hands'. And even in those representations of sighted people who are all eyes, it ignores the fact that you have other senses such as hearing. And also it's not just the hands, it's also proprioception and kinaesthesia—it's the haptic experiences of moving around and near objects that I think often get terms of the blind people. And also I want to get away from the idea that blind people have some super-sensitive touch sensation. I mean, a lot of my experiences in touch tours come from having a lot of experience in touch tours. And pushing past maybe what is initially offered, which is 'Here you can feel the outlines of a horse', as if looking at art is just about identifying the objects depicted. As we were saying earlier, there are all sorts of aspects of texture, temperature, density, and sonority. What happens when you tap it? (taps the microphone) Those are things that I think need to be incorporated into any kind of access provision.

One of my first projects with Fayen d'Evie was at the Kadist Art Foundation in San Francisco. I realized that I have a really big vocabulary to talk about the visible, and I think we all do, but talking about touch sensation, it feels sort of impoverished to me—it's hard, it's soft. So, we thought maybe we should come up with an enhanced vocabulary to talk about these things. What we ended up doing was to recognize that different types of artwork require, and invite, and incite, and provoke different types of touching with different parts of your body. Sometimes you do want to trace it delicately with your fingertips. And then sometimes, there is the desire to manipulate. Sometimes there is a desire to grasp or hold with your fist. Sometimes it's about moving around and through, and feeling different volumes rising and falling around you. And so, having an awareness that the touch experience is not always the same. It really was a sort of experience of the artist telling you what to do: 'Go ahead, grab and pull'.

The other people who I think should be brought into these conversations more are art preparators— people to hang the works. Because they know a lot. They're handling works and they say 'This has to go this way', 'The centre of gravity is like this', and that stuff is really, I think, fascinating. The hierarchies that exist in museums— nobody asks them to talk about it, but they have a lot of knowledge.

DG: It would be great to have you work with an architect who would think about how to hang work differently. Through your writing, the ubiquitous use of pedestals in museums require more thought (or might be an irrelevant form of display). This is one, among other kinds of tropes of display, that could be rethought.

GK: Well, exactly. I've been thinking about this because I'm curating this show in Massachusetts. One thing that is apparent is that if you're having work that people are supposed to touch, hanging it on the wall is not necessarily the best place. And also, if there are multiple people wanting to touch the same thing, it somehow works better if everything is off the walls and in the centre, because then people can reach in from different angles. Exactly, so to think about how you make the space work for different types of engagement with different types of art.

DG: This issue of *Future Anterior* is about disability and preservation, but the category of 'disability' is one I've often resisted. I am an amputee and you are blind. I don't know what it's like to experience the world as you experience it, and you don't know what it's like to experience the world as I experience it. First, I think it's important to mention that your books enabled me to come more out of the 'disability closet', so thank you.

GK: Well, don't thank me yet. (laughter)

DG: But what do you think about disability as a broader category? And what does disability mean when we talk about the future accessibility of cultural artifacts, the future of preservation, or of culture, more generally? What do you and I have to offer collectively in our camaraderie as disabled people?

GK: I do embrace my identity as a disabled person, and I feel a strong connection with a disability community, which includes blind people, but is not limited to blind people.

Back in the 1970s when I was a student and first had experience in activism, it was a moment when, like, the blind people were over here, the deaf people were over there, the wheelchair users were over there. And I can remember vividly being in meetings when someone would say, 'Well, we have shared interests and goals', and everyone in the room would say 'Really? Really? How could that be that I have anything in common with these other people?' But I think that moment was really what led to the Americans with Disabilities Act. Because, prior to that, different groups were competing— not literally. And it's not as if we've completely joined the gaps. But for me, the connection is real.

People sometimes say to me, 'Oh I don't think of you as disabled'. The fact is I am disabled. What are they saying? They are saying, 'I think that you're like me, and that's better than being like you'. So there is a certain amount of education that has to happen in those regards.

There is also the argument that I know, because I write about blind artists, and some of them were kind of hesitant about being in the book—'I don't want to be categorized', 'I don't want to be pigeon-holed', 'I don't want to be ghettoized'. You get shuffled into the special category of 'Here is work by blind artists, and over here is work by the *artists*'—the regular artists. And a lot of people resist that. And then, there are kind of perks to the heroic-overcoming narrative that a lot of people partake in. It's like, 'Oh, you're so amazing. You can paint these paintings, but you can't see!' It feels good to be praised, but you have to think: 'What am I being praised for?'

I think that if I try to say what disabled people, as I understand it, have in common—one thing is that we don't think that the world was created with us in mind. Which is in some ways a statement about exclusion, but in the other it's a statement about resourcefulness and innovation. Because you could say, 'I'm a blind person, I move through a space that was not designed with me in mind.' But are there things that I do in that space that could inform the way that other people use that space? When I can describe a public space that I find more accessible than other public spaces, how is that created by architecture? And how can I disseminate that information so that it gets absorbed into architectural knowledge?

DG: Let me revisit part of my question, how can we—disabled people—imagine ourselves as intervening into the conservation and preservation of the cultural past? This is an issue of accessibility of course, but how might your ideas help inform how we rethink preservation and conservation?

GK: When we think about restoring or preserving the built environment of the past or conserving today's built environment for the future, we need to recognize that all sorts of people with all sorts of embodiment have inhabited and continue to inhabit those spaces, whether or not designers or architects had us in mind when they created those spaces. While it's true that people with disabilities have experienced and continue to experience ostracism, exclusion and segregation, I don't think we want our ideas about the past or

the future continually to reinscribe that exclusion. So it seems vitally important for conservation and preservation to seek out and include the perspectives of people who use, navigate and perceive those spaces in atypical ways.

This text was first published in *Future Anterior: Journal of Historic Preservation, History, Theory, and Criticism*, Vol. 16, No. 1, 2029, 57–67.

CAMARADERIE

David Gissen with
Georgina Kleege

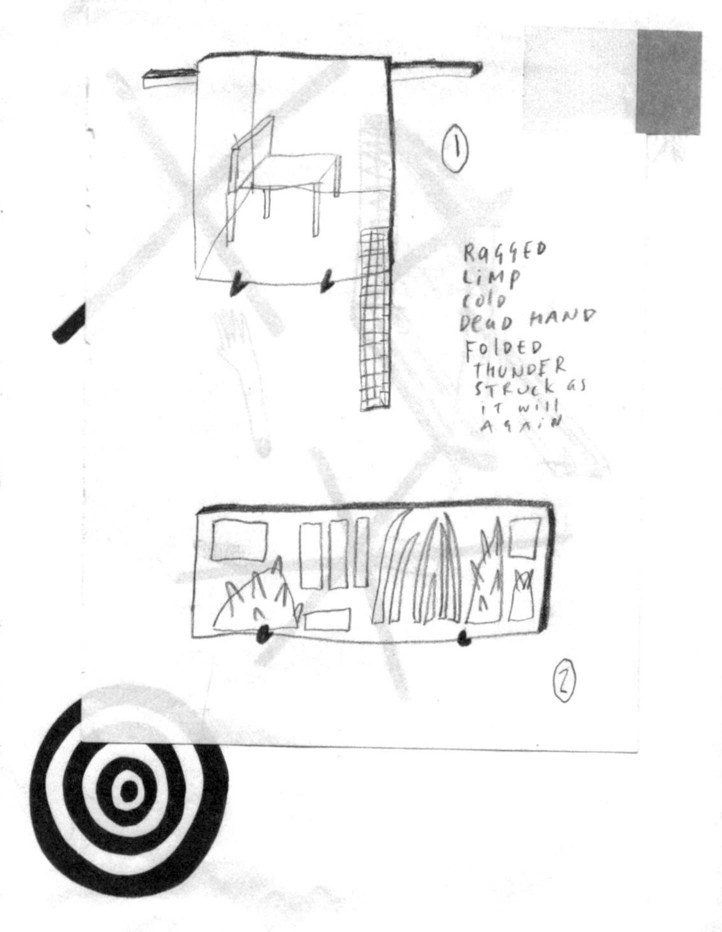

PRESSURE CHEST

Pressure Chest

This background image is a black-and-white photograph with a dotted texture showing a patch of melted snow. However, it could also represent something that fell from the sky and left a big splash on the ground. Half on top of that is a white drawing sheet, glued to another sheet with two x's and concentric circles shining through to the top sheet. The top one contains an overlapping sketch of a bed in a room (1) and a rock garden (2). In this drawing these sketches are hanging from the wall, in a way that people could touch them. The text on the drawings reads: 'ragged, limp, cold, dead hand, folded, thunder struck as it will again'.

When you lie face-down in the grass, can you feel your chest sinking in the soil? How does the pressure of gravity influence your everyday movements? And in the club, where do you feel the subwoofer? Into which organ do the bass notes enter?

'ENSEMBLE' APT Gallery, London, 2 to 26 May 2024

Hettie James & Stephanie Farmer

1. This exhibition was made in partnership with APT Gallery, and funded by Arts Council England.

2. All six artists in 'Ensemble' signed a Letter of Agreement to confirm that the original artwork chosen had not been exhibited before and will not be in the future.

3. Georgina Kleege, *More than Meets the Eye: What Blindness Brings to Art*, New York, 2018, 14.

With audio description (AD) exhibited as an art form in its own right, Hettie James and Stephanie Farmer reflect on curating their audio-based group exhibition 'Ensemble'[1] finding creative possibilities in collaboration and co-creating artworks.

No artwork to look at. None. A slightly shocked expression often swept across people's faces when we explained this. Our exhibition was to be a collection of six artworks, with each artwork made up of two audio descriptions, from two different perspectives, played back-to-back. The first description would be made by the artist of the original artwork; the second by a collaborative creative group. Together, these descriptions would create one new artwork, an audio description artwork.

The new AD artworks would be exhibited in their own right, without their related original artworks to help confirm or deny the audience's interpretations. For this to really work, the original artworks themselves had to be completely inaccessible to the audience, now and in the future.[2] Artworks that had been exhibited before or even ones with similar iterations couldn't be chosen, so no one could look these up on the internet 'to give themselves a clue' about what the artwork 'actually' looks like.

We wanted to challenge the 'long philosophical tradition that conflates seeing and knowing'[3] and increase knowledge about AD. We started to consider ways in which AD can be used and produced collectively, inspired by the W-ICAD (Workshop for Inclusive Co-created Audio Description) model.[4] Audio description was originally developed as an access tool for blind and partially blind audiences to experience artworks, exhibitions, museums, film and theatre productions. We were inspired by the accessibility of AD for all audiences, referred to by Georgina Kleege as 'the wheelchair ramp analogy'.[5] By using this analogy, Kleege points out how everyone can benefit from AD.

We discussed these possibilities of AD as a creative and inclusive art form in our conversations with Art in Perpetuity Trust (APT) in the two years leading up to 'Ensemble'; where we talked about the concepts and ideas for an exhibition that thought about access from the start. As a charity founded by artists in 1995, we were drawn to its inbuilt creative community, where all members contribute to the running of the organization, including its gallery and artists' studios. We considered the possibility of shared knowledge within APT's network and how this could impact 'Ensemble' as well as future exhibitions, art practices and conversations.

We believed the artists exhibiting in 'Ensemble' would probably describe from a place of contextual knowledge, perhaps adding in snippets of information that wouldn't necessarily be known otherwise. They could let us in on reasons for certain decisions made while making the artworks that are not initially apparent. The collaborative team's AD, on the other hand, would be different as they would be encountering the work for the first time, without any prior knowledge of the artwork or even the artist's practice, using conversations with each other to help understand, interpret and describe the artworks. These two different ADs, the artist's and the collaborative group's, would be created in utter isolation, with no insights shared by either party. The artist was to present the artwork to the collaborative team without a word and leave while discussions ensued.

To create these dual ADs, artists—Louise Ashcroft, Cash Aspeek, Terence Birch, Fran Cottell, Colin Lievens, and Dr Aaron McPeake[6]—would all participate together in an audio description training day.[7] While some of the artists had experience in making and using audio description, we wanted the whole group to learn or re-learn skills all together.

4. Alison F. Eardley, Vanessa E. Jones, Lindsay Bywood, Hannah Thompson & Deborah Husbands, 'The W-ICAD Model: Redefining Museum Access through the Workshop for Inclusive Co-created Audio Description', *Curator, The Museum Journal*, July 2023, 1–24. We attended the W-ICAD symposium at Westminster University, March 2023.

5. Georgina Kleege, *More than Meets the Eye: What Blindness Brings to Art: What Blindness Brings to Art*, New York, 2018, 105. Kleege is referring to how her sighted students benefited from having the film *The Sessions* audio described.

6. Cash Aspeek and Fran Cottell currently have studios at APT, and studio holder David Bloor was the audio and installation technician for 'Ensemble'.

7. In partnership with APT and funded by the Association for Art History, we organized a previous AD training day with Mind's Eye, June 2023 (see footnote 8).

Exhibiting for
Multiple Senses

8. Mind's Eye is a UK
audio description
service set up by Anne
Hornsby in 1992.

Learning in this communal way, we hoped, would encourage conversations about how we each perceive artworks differently and how this affects how we communicate them. We all met together at Deptford Library with AD pioneer Anne Hornsby from Mind's Eye,[8] who travelled down from Manchester to lead us through the information and exercises.

In one exercise (which you could try with a friend, foe or colleague!) we had to sit, back-to-back, and describe a room of our choosing to the other person, while they sat in silence, without the chance for question or interruption. When recalling a room, most will jump to a room they have a distinct memory of or know well. But how do you tackle this—do you describe as if you are moving around the room? Or do you describe the things that first hit you when you enter—the warmth of the sun streaming in through the windows, the musty smell of your granny's living room curtains? You are describing the known, the understood, to someone who doesn't have the same information—doesn't know how your granny's house smells—so you must describe this further: is it musty from the moth balls hidden in the drawers or is it the cigarette smoke that clings to the curtain's fibres?

Through this exercise, is the listener stepping into the room with the describer, are they stepping into the room through the mind of the describer, are they co-creating a new room in their mind?

This idea of the listener's role as co-creator was one of the most exciting concepts for us. In 'Ensemble' each person, as listener or beholder,[9] would be realizing the artworks; interpreting and translating the words and descriptions, imagining the artworks in their minds, co-creating their own distinct artworks into existence. The artworks would then be inherently affected by and reflective of each person's lived experience and perception of the world.

By thinking about the audience's role as co-creators, we considered our own roles as curators. We decided to place ourselves in the role of the audience, encountering the work through AD alone. We didn't want the assumed privilege of any additional information or perceived greater understanding, removing a sense of hierarchy in the making and experiencing of the exhibition. This decision to not experience the artists' original physical artworks was particularly important during our online group crit, a collaborative critique session for the artists.

Each artist had to select an artwork to describe, write their first draft, and read this out to the other artists, ourselves, and Anne Hornsby. Neither we nor Anne had experienced the original artworks.[10] This removed the possibility of us steering or influencing these conversations with our own experience of the works. Reading an AD aloud or hearing it out loud, as opposed to hearing it in your internal brain voice, can be an illuminating process. Is the written word laid out differently when it is expected to be spoken or heard? How does it change if it is?[11]

9. See Ken Wilder, *Beholding: Situated Art and the Aesthetics of Reception*, London, 2023.

10. This is not how Anne Hornsby usually works as an audio description trainer; however, she agreed to in this instance.

11. We have been interested in the written word spoken out loud since our 2021 exhibition 'A Garden with Animals' at 7B Agar Grove, London. This was produced in response to the archive of the art critic and poet Ian Hamilton.

Exhibiting for
Multiple Senses

12. Anonymous, 'Group Crit Artists' Feedback', online, 29 February 2024.

13. Fran Cottell in Fran Cottell & Collective Agency, *Construction*, 2024. Exhibited in 'Ensemble'.

14. Cash Aspeek in Cash Aspeek & Collective Agency, *Threadbound*, 2024. Exhibited in 'Ensemble'. In this Cash describes how the work 'could be propped up on its toes, on a shelf at about head height, or it could, more comfortably, lay in your hands'.

15. 'It is quite hard to get feedback [...] I did a performance and it wasn't until ten years later that people told me what they thought about it. I had no idea it worked.' in Fran Cottell, 'Post-show Interview with Fran Cottell', unpublished, conducted by Hettie James and Stephanie Farmer, online, 12 July 2024.

16. Hettie James, 'Post-show Interview with Dr Aaron McPeake', unpublished, conducted by Hettie James and Stephanie Farmer, online, 25 July 2024.

17. Colin Lievens & Collective Agency, *Tissue*, 2024. Exhibited in 'Ensemble'. Within the artist's AD there is an anecdote about Colin's mum's house.

By reading their first drafts aloud in the group crit, the artists had a sounding board. Having group discussions after each of the artists' AD, with questions such as 'I didn't quite understand what you meant there? It would be helpful to expand on [...]', gave artists immediate and direct feedback. Listening to others brought out how we each focus on different aspects when experiencing an artwork—in a way 'to better imagine another's world'[12]; for some placement is important, for others texture, colour, or smell. Should a description include its immediate surroundings, especially when an artist considers their work as site-specific or 'related to a specific situation'?[13] A number of artists resolved this challenge by describing their work without a fixed location.[14]

Artists don't often get this kind of critical response to their work, and even if they do, it is often after the completion of the work.[15] This process of creating AD for 'Ensemble' expressed the importance in creating a group show where the artists are brought together to learn, reflect, and communicate instead of creating in isolation and perhaps only meeting at the private view. Post-show, we talked about having an additional group crit for the artists when developing their audio descriptions to include people and communities not represented by the 'Ensemble' artists and creative team.[16]

Having listened to other ADs, the artists could consider parts they had not included, such as bringing in more emotive personal anecdotes in addition to the context of their artist practice.[17] We had not expected this to happen,

perhaps naively, given that another of one of our rules was
that artists should choose 'an artwork that is significant to
your past, present or future practice.'[18] Of course, including
these anecdotes made sense, especially as many of the
artworks were old—some nearly twenty years. Through
this process of creating their audio descriptions, the artist's
thoughts would naturally travel back to the time of the
artwork's creation, making possible new revelations about
the work, through revisiting it in the context of their practice
now. We imagined artists picking an artwork housed in their
studios, unexhibited, either because it didn't quite fit in a
show, or because a body of work in which it could sit had
not yet materialized. Despite this, these works are kept. They
are moved from studio to studio, home to home, because
there is something inherent in their nature that is inextricably
important to the artist.

Now to the collaborative team…

This was taken up and developed by Collective Agency's
Joe Rizzo Naudi, a partially blind writer, and curator Sasha
Galitzine, who had been discussing aspects of 'Ensemble'
with us, at a time when they were working on 'Behold'[19],
a group show about touch. To create the descriptions, Joe
decided to work with a team of writers: Jen Calleja, Timna
Fibert, Ella Frears, Annie Hayter, Autumn Sharkey, and
artist Nicole Clif. This process introduced the possibility
of writers being involved in the making of an artwork, as

18. Hettie James &
Stephanie Farmer,
'Artists' Info Document',
unpublished, emailed to
artists, December 2023–
May 2024.

19. 'Behold',
Hypha Studios,
www.hyphastudios.com/
behold-a-group-show-
about-touch-curated-by-
sasha-galitzine-with-
graham-little/. Accessed
13 October 2024.

Exhibiting for
Multiple Senses

20. Terence Birch &
Collective Agency,
Parker, 2024. Exhibited
in 'Ensemble'. Terence
provides the title,
dimensions and date of
his original artwork
close to the beginning
of his audio description.

21. Yusuf Osman,
'Feedback', unpublished,
emailed by Joe Rizzo
Naudi to Hettie James
and Stephanie Farmer,
19 June 2024.

22. Anonymous,
'Ensemble Visitors'
Feedback', online and
at APT, May 2024. This
was a response to the
question: what are your
thoughts about audio
description?

opposed to the more traditional role of writing a response to it.

Each of the artist's original artworks were encountered by Joe and two people from the collaborative team. They chatted about the artwork with Joe, who sat with his back to it; he could ask questions but not experience the artworks directly himself. Having recorded and transcribed these conversations, Joe edited them down to a set of notes. He dictated a five-minute audio recording for each artwork based on his memory of these notes. Joe then used this recording to draft a description text, returning to the original notes for details and inspiration. Next, in a process similar to the artist's online group crit, Joe sent the draft description texts to Sasha. She gave feedback on them having not experienced any of the original artworks or been present at the description conversations. Following her feedback, Joe finalized Collective Agency's collaborative descriptions and voiced the text as audio recordings.

We reflected on the two processes for creating the audio description artworks in 'Ensemble'. How would each artwork evolve, shift, and develop as the two audio descriptions unfold?

Having not prescribed a 'right way' to describe the artworks, most artists didn't follow the more traditional format of audio description, with 'tombstone' information prefacing the main body of text.[20] People visiting the show had different preferences. Some liked the ADs where title, form and date were explained near the beginning. Others preferred a sense of ambiguity and questioning which created more room for their imagined artworks to evolve. One person said that the lack of consistency in the artists' descriptions made them 'difficult to follow' and that 'it is really important to try and be consistent and logical when describing something'.[21] While for another person, audio description as 'poetry and experiential, rather than about practicality and accuracy [...] was a positive'. Some enjoyed the artist's 'view / language being entangled with the writer's distanced and writerly AD'[22], emphasizing the exchange between the two ADs in each artwork. These preferences ultimately embody how different minds and bodies benefit from multiple voices and ways of communicating and describing.

We considered how the artworks would be experienced at
APT Gallery.

Our intent was to create a shared, communal environment—
the audience experiencing the works together at the same
time—creating an ensemble of multiple imagined artworks
co-existing simultaneously in the space. While headphones
create loud and crisp sound, they can create a sense of
entering an insular or separated space, blocking out noises
and others from the outside, which is why we decided to have
the audio works played aloud. Projected sound has a different
feeling in terms of life or span; unlike those never-ending
podcasts or Spotify playlists we are so used to listening to via
headphones, sound played aloud has a sense of temporality,
expanse and space.

    Creating this sense of space, we hoped, would help
people to respond to the works, influencing our decisions
about the curation of the six artworks and the design of the
exhibition space. We thought about timings. We had already
decided that each artwork would last from ten to twelve
minutes, long enough to give the two perspectives but not
so long that they would be overwhelming or too much to
process in one go. Having said this, we realized that even our
ten to twelve minutes may prove, for many people, pretty
challenging, especially as most may never have heard or used

Exhibiting for
Multiple Senses

23. Alison F. Eardley,
'Ensemble Foreword',
Ensemble Audio /
Digital Guide, May 2024,
www.aptstudios.org/
ensembleaudiodigital
guide. Accessed
13 October 2024.

24. 'Beyond the Visual:
Blindness and Expanded
Sculpture', July 2023–
July 2026, is a collabo-
ration between Chelsea
College of Arts, the
Henry Moore Institute
and Shape Arts, with Dr
Ken Wilder as Principal
Investigator, Dr Aaron
McPeake as Co-Investigator
and Dr Clare O'Dowd as
Research Curator.

audio description before. Dr Alison Eardley describes how people tend to 'look briefly at an artwork and then move on to the next piece'[23] when the focus is on the visual as the primary sense. As the works were audio, we could give each artwork space through time. We decided to play the artworks on the hour, at quarter past, half past, and quarter to. This created a brief gap for people to chat to their friend about what they had imagined, move to a different seat in the space, pop to the loo, ask the invigilator a question or sit and contemplate.

AD lends itself to being accessed in many ways; it can be listened to at home, online, in text and audio formats and translated into multiple different languages. Although we had imagined the works listened to within a communal gallery space, we were aware that for some people, visiting a gallery isn't always possible whether that's for geographical, financial or health reasons. Inspired by Dr Ken Wilder and Dr Aaron McPeake's research project 'Beyond the Visual'[24], we were intrigued by how different senses and places might influence the interpretations of the works. Did surrounding objects, noises, smells that weren't present at APT Gallery morph or add to the creation of the artworks in people's minds, giving them a new context that the minimal white cube space didn't provide?

APT's gallery, an old rag and metal warehouse, is made up of two main spaces, with a middle segue space sandwiched in between. These two areas we named 'front space' and 'back space'—yes—nothing fancy but very fitting. Although not always known for its comfort or welcoming nature, the minimal white space does provide a unique sensory experience, with little to affect or de-focus people's minds and imaginations. Arguably, the main stimuli in APT's spaces were going to be the other people experiencing the show.

In the back space, where the audio artworks would be playing, we planned to have a variety of different seating options, from benches to bean bags, placed along the walls of the gallery, to suit different bodies and needs. This meant people would be, more often than not, facing across the room, to where another person might be sitting. While we imagined some people may close their eyes or stare into space, some may want something to focus on. For this we decided to create a large central white canvas box. This could act as a screen, so no one had a direct opposite line through the space to another, to diffuse any potential self-conscious-ness created from the feeling of watching or being watched by others in the space. It could also act as a literal as well as metaphorical 'blank canvas' for people to project their imaginings and thoughts onto or even into. More than one audience member at 'Ensemble' joked that the original physical artworks were being kept, or even hidden in this box, taunting them with the possibility of some kind of reveal, reminding us of Ryan Gander's 'Locked Room Scenario'.[25]

Of course, while benches and chairs were unlikely to be moved, the large black bean bags we suspected (and hoped) would migrate and end up dotted around the space. We wanted to make sure that while used, in all their glory, they didn't turn into some sort of unexpected obstacle course, especially for wheelchair users and those who were blind and partially blind. We had already been considering a raised path to lead people around the space, inspired by Jack Warne's 2023 exhibition, 'Blind at The Age of Four'.[26] Here a bumpy patterned aluminium anti-slip path (think fire escape stairs),[27] a sculpture in its own right, enabled blind and partially blind people to navigate the space more freely, and also mapped a possible route around the exhibition for everyone.

In came our carpet path.

We had been encouraged to visit 'World Unseen'[28] at Somerset House in April 2024. With only one day left open to the public, we scurried over. They had created, like in

25. Ryan Gander, 'Locked Room Scenario', Dairy distribution depot, www.artangel.org.uk/ project/locked-room-scenario/. Accessed 18 October 2024.

26. Jack Warne, 'Blind at the Age of Four', 9 Gransden Ave, www.3-o-n.com/album. Accessed 14 November 2024.

27. This path was designed by Joe Rizzo Naudi and Jack Warne in collaboration with the rest of the curatorial team. The pattern on the footpath is called 'propeller plate'.

28. 'World Unseen', Somerset House, www. somersethouse.org.uk/ whats-on/canon-world-unseen. Accessed 18 October 2024. An exhibition by Canon in partnership with RNIB.

Exhibiting for
Multiple Senses

29. NaviLens is a navigation and labelling app for blind and partially blind people that uses QR codes to translate signage into audio messages.

30. This carpet is now owned by APT for use in future exhibitions.

31. We discussed these options in conversations with Joe Rizzo Naudi and Dr Alison Eardley.

32. See Tom Humphries, 'Talking Culture and Culture Talking' in Dirksen Bauman (ed.), *Open Your Eyes*, Minneapolis, 2008, 35–41.

Jack Warne's exhibition, a path to guide visitors around the East Wing Gallery, in coordination with NaviLens.[29] Canon incredibly agreed to give us this specially designed, weighted, thick, black, cushiony carpet path, so that it would have a second life and to help people access another exhibition. We were able to lay this through APT Gallery, leading people from the entrance through the front and middle space, then running around the back space, in between the white canvas box and seating. The carpet acted as a guide in 'Ensemble', but also as a noisy-step dampener, a way to soften APT's echoey industrial space.[30]

The acoustics of the gallery was one area that we failed to fully compensate for; even with our carpet path and bean bags, the 4.5-metres-high ceilings meant the audio works bounced around the space, creating acoustic shadows. This made the artworks more difficult to hear or process for some listeners. Other listening options such as a dedicated quiet space, a choice of listening devices and a British Sign Language (BSL) video were things we considered post-show for future exhibitions.[31]

There were other elements we would also improve if putting on 'Ensemble' again. Although we provided BSL interpretation on specific dates of the exhibition and for one of our events, we should have connected with the d/Deaf community more. Had we done this, we could have considered how the audio descriptions would translate into BSL and been aware of d/Deaf 'talking culture'[32] and storytelling; we could have opened up other avenues of creative possibilities for audio descriptions. In hindsight, we should have also worked more closely with local community groups from the very beginning of the project to involve them in the process and development of the show.

One aspect we hadn't fully considered was the power of workshops to create a sense of a temporal community. Dr Aaron McPeake ran a workshop that encouraged participants to sit in the back space with the Ensemble artworks and creatively respond whilst listening. With a jumble of pencils and pens to draw, doodle or write, and air-dry clay to sculpt and squish, people could sit with each other at a table or on the seats in the gallery and respond to the works. People participating found the 'opportunity to be completely free

and experiential'[33] the most enjoyable part of the workshop.
Responding in this way helped them to engage, relax, and
maintain concentration throughout the total six artworks.[34]
If we did 'Ensemble' again, we could give people this option
to respond in a creative way, as another form of feedback,
alongside the traditional (rather dry and formal) written
Q&A usually collected.

In Collective Agency's workshops[35] Joe and Sasha
used group creative imagination and word play games;
participants peered into an imaginary box, describing what
they found inside and then passing on to the next. These
objects sometimes fed off each other in some sort of loopy
story, flitting between seemingly random objects of curious
combinations. Once more at ease, the group separated
into two to discuss two hidden artworks in the space,
mirroring the interactions that the collaborative team had in
producing Collective Agency's description for 'Ensemble'.
Conversations were retold, expanded upon and questioned,
back to the collaborative circle where they had begun. These
workshops, like the artists' training and online group crit,
confirmed to us how collaborative and collective practical
learning can benefit exhibition making. The more people
there are creating and using audio description in the future,
the further it will develop; evolving and animating it as an art
form.[36]

Could audio descriptions move more into an
imaginative realm—describing artworks that only exist in the
mind—or could they be used as an act of archiving a memory
to describe artworks that no longer exist?

33. Anonymous, 'Dr
Aaron McPeake Workshop
Feedback', online and
at APT, May 2024.

34. The duration of the
six artworks is one and
a half hours in total.

35. These were
supported by The de
Laszlo Foundation.

36. Louise Ashcroft
reflected that she
could use AD in
teaching art students
in Louise Ashcroft,
'Post-show interview
with Louise Ashcroft',
unpublished, conducted
by Hettie James and
Stephanie Farmer,
25 July 2024.

37. Clem Adelman, 'Kurt Lewin and the Origins of Action Research', *Educational Action Research*, Vol. 1, No. 1, 1993, 7–24.

38. Sarah Walsh, 'Feedback', unpublished, emailed to Hettie James, 17 October 2024.

39. Georgina Kleege, *Sight Unseen*, London, 1999, 5.

40. Georgina Kleege, *More than Meets the Eye: What Blindness Brings to Art*, New York, 2018, 12.

41. Anonymous, 'Ensemble Visitors' Feedback', online and at APT, May 2024. This was a response to the question: how would you describe the exhibition to someone in five words?

42. Anonymous, 'Ensemble Visitors' Feedback', online and at APT, May 2024. This was a response to the question: what are your thoughts about audio description?

'Ensemble' was a kind of 'action research'.[37] The process of 'Ensemble' itself—particularly 'the very act of delivering the AD workshops' and training around the exhibition—'enabled us to improve the way we approach access at each stage of the project', as reflected by Sarah Walsh, APT's Administrative Director.[38] We aimed to rethink the roles of curator, artist and audience. By working with artists and a collaborative team, we learned the unique contributions each could bring to audio description making. As the artist, collaborative team and audience worked together as co-creators of 'Ensemble', the artworks brought together multiple perspectives. The two ADs, placed side-by-side or back-to-back, allowed differences in style, focus and voice to be more clearly understood and compared, 'to catch a glimpse of sight unseen'.[39]

By exhibiting audio description as an art form in its own right, without its original physical artwork, 'Ensemble' has responded to Georgina Kleege's call for 'innovations that could elevate audio description to the status of a new literary and interpretative genre'.[40] The exhibition was described in five words as something that 'reimagines the experience of art',[41] with audio description considered a 'generative writing orientation, emergent art form'.[42]

Throughout the development, exhibition and reflection process, we found AD has the potential to bring together multiple voices, minds and bodies to help everyone engage with artworks and exhibitions, especially when co-created in a collaborative manner. Our hope is that more and more people will use and create AD, further developing the ways we can challenge how artworks and exhibition making are perceived.

ACOUSTIC SHADOWS

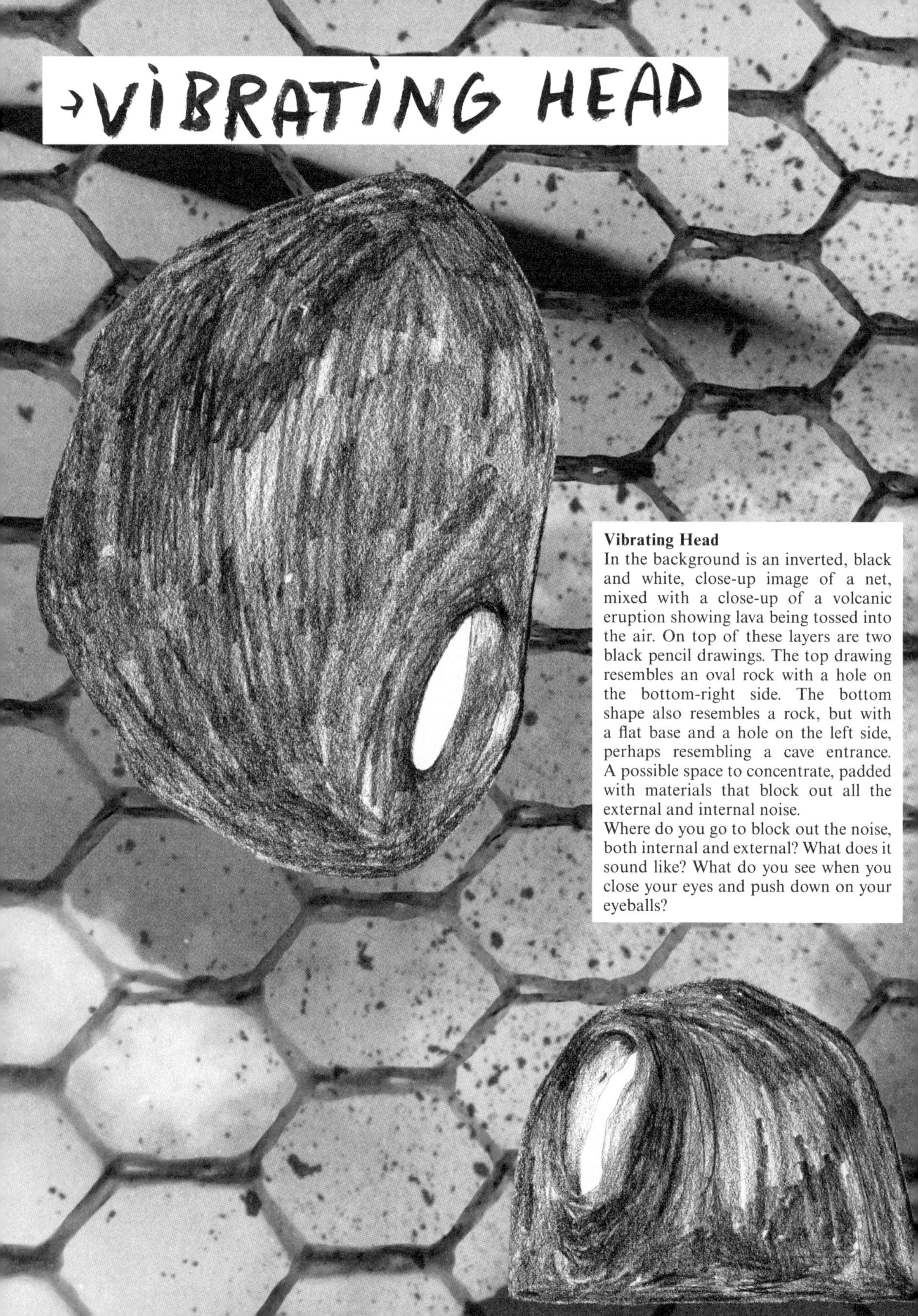

Vibrating Head
In the background is an inverted, black and white, close-up image of a net, mixed with a close-up of a volcanic eruption showing lava being tossed into the air. On top of these layers are two black pencil drawings. The top drawing resembles an oval rock with a hole on the bottom-right side. The bottom shape also resembles a rock, but with a flat base and a hole on the left side, perhaps resembling a cave entrance. A possible space to concentrate, padded with materials that block out all the external and internal noise.
Where do you go to block out the noise, both internal and external? What does it sound like? What do you see when you close your eyes and push down on your eyeballs?

AESTHETICS OF BLIND TACTILE SENSATIONS
Attempts at Describing the Tangible

Lilian Korner

1. Aristotle, *De Anima*, Book II, Chapter 11.

2. Museumbund, *Das inklusive Museum: Ein Leitfaden zu Barrierefreiheit und Inklusion*, 2013, 38.

3. This text was first published in the *Journal of Disability Studies* in the German-speaking region. It has been revised and translated for the present publication, and therefore primarily German sources are taken into account.

4. S. Saerberg, 'Sensorische Räume und museale Regimes. Von visueller Dominanz zu sensorischer Diversität', in *Wege zur Kultur. Barrieren und Barrierefreiheit in Kultur- und Bildungs-einrichtungen*, A. Tervooren & J. Weber (eds.), Böhlau. 2012, 172.

Introduction

Between the tangible and the act of touching, the same relation-ship exists: for if touch is not a single perception, but several, then the tangible must necessarily be experienced in multiple ways. Yet it remains a question whether touch is a single percep-tion or multiple [perceptions], and what the organ of the faculty of touch is.[1]

The cultural participation of Blind and visually impaired people in fine arts institutions generally takes the form of an audio-description or of tactile models of the works in question.[2,3] But there is a distance between the original objects and both descriptions and tangible models; after all, 'do not touch' applies.[4] Yet if, by way of exception, touching is permitted, one experiences a phenomenon which the Blind writer and disability studies scholar Georgina Kleege describes as follows:

> Initially, our goal was to develop some sort of vocabulary and taxonomy of tactile aesthetics. Whenever I have been called upon to describe what it is like to touch a work of art, I find myself at the limits of my language. It seems that I must always fall back on binary oppositions: hard versus soft,

rough versus smooth, warm versus cool. Our conversations as we handled the work were frequently guiding each other to touch in particular ways: 'Tap it here', we would say, or 'Pinch this while you tug on that', or, 'Careful! That edge is pretty sharp'.[5]

Kleege's observation corresponds with literature relating to the sense of touch around which a vast field of metaphors and references has accumulated. However, there is no similar analytical language for touch, as there is for sight.[6,7] So, we arrive at the intersection of a dilemma that is both epistemic and ethical: firstly, there is no 'School of touch', no categories and practices with which to refine this particular sense. Moreover, it is usually forbidden to touch art works, meaning that Blind and visually impaired people basically are prevented from forming an independent 'reception' of the work.[8] Because the perception of touch is systematically ignored by academic institutions, we also lack proper methods and language to describe this perception effectively.[9] Alexander Gottlieb Baumgarten came up with an impressive formulation about this, within the framework of philosophical thinking, in his lecture 'Aesthetica' 1750/58. According to Baumgarten it is the task of aesthetics 'to advance knowledge even beyond the confines of the things clearly recognised by us'.[10]

Cultural historian Anselm Haverkamp suggests that aesthetics functions as a philosophical concept capable of structuring experiences that have not yet been articulated in language, and thus are not part of academic discourses yet.[11] Building on Haverkamp's work, Christoph Menke argues that in Baumgarten's view, both representation and its form should connect with the principle of established, habitual practice in order to be normalized.[12] Baumgarten traces such practices back to Latin poetry, seeing aesthetics as both an instrument and a discipline that makes sensory experiences communicable, even when they haven't yet been conceptualized or objectified.[13] Applying this three-step approach of form, content, and practice to the sense of touch leads to a dual hypothesis. Our sensory awareness of touch maintains its formal expression through corresponding linguistic idioms. By examining these touch-related idioms,

Exhibiting for
Multiple Senses

5. G. Kleege, 'The Art of Touch: Lending a Hand to the Sighted Majority', *Journal of Visual Culture*, 20(2), 2021, 437.

6. U. Brandes, 'Körperlose Berührung: In Kunst- und Ausstellungshalle der Bundesrepublik Deutschland', *Tasten*, Steidl Verlag ,1996, 9–18; F. Korner, 'Wahrnehmungspolitiken: Ein Plädoyer gegen den Okularzentrismus', *Form, Magazin für Haltung und Design*, 295, 2022b, 135.

7. C. Classen, *The Deepest Sense: A Cultural History of Touch*, 2012, among others, is of relevance for the discussion in English, though not prioritized for monetary reasons.

8. For the connection between the museum and ocularcentrism, see historical work by T. Bennett, *The Birth of the Museum: History, Theory, Politics*, 1995, among others.

9. The aesthetic side of the problem can, in the words of Miranda Frickers, be described as epistemic injustice. Shelley Tremain, 'Epistemic Injustice and Disability', in *The Routledge Handbook of Epistemic Injustice*, I.J. Kidd, J. Medina, & G. Pohlhaus Jr. (eds.), 2017, sketches how disability systematically impedes the development of epistemic resources. A necessary development is the expansion of the Blind Perception Style.

10. A.G. Baumgarten, *Ästhetik*, D. Mirbach (ed. and trans.), 2007, 13.

11. A. Haverkamp, '"Wie die Morgenröthe"': Baumgartens Innovation', in *Baumgarten-Studien: zur Genealogie der Ästhetik*, R. Campe, A. Haverkamp & C. Menke (eds.), 2014, 34.

12. C. Menke, 'Die Disziplin der Ästhetik und die Ästhetik der

Disziplin', in *Baumgarten-Studien: zur Genealogie der Ästhetik*, R. Campe, A. Haverkamp & C. Menke (eds.), 2014, 247.

13. E. Ostermann, *Die Authentizität des Ästhetischen. Studien zur ästhetischen Transformation der Rhetorik*, 2002, 79.

14. As Geese and Schulz rightly observe, women and non-cis-gender people are under-represented among blind scientists, both within the represen-tation of blindness, as well as within German research. N. Geese & M. Schulz, 'Die Autoethno-grafie in den Critical Blindness Studies: Überlegungen zum Ver-hältnis von Forschenden zum Erkenntnisgegenstand', in *Disability Studies im deutschsprachigen Raum: Emanzipation und Vereinnahmung*, D. Brehme et al. (eds.), 2020; Geese & Schulz, 2022.

15. In this sense the text contributes to chances and possibilities of the affirmative models of disability. J. Swain & S. French, 'Towards an affirmation model of disability', *Disability & Society*, 15(4), 2000.

16. M. Schillmeier, 'Der Blinde als der Andere: Moderne Praktiken epistemischer Politik', in *Andere Bilder: Zur Produktion von Behinderung in der visuellen Kultur*, B. Ochser & A. Grebe (eds.), 2013, 33.

17. C. Länger, *Im Spiegel von Blindheit: Eine Kultursoziologie des Sehsinnes*, 2002, 5.

18. Länger, *Im Spiegel von Blindheit*.

19. M. Schulz & N. Geese, 'Critical Blindness Studies in den Disability Studies', In *Handbuch Disability Studies*, A. Waldschmidt (ed.), 2022, 413.

we simultaneously develop the content—that is, the systematic study of touch. This is where Blindness comes in again. The situation concerning the knowledge about touch appears to resemble that of its 'most prominent knowledge carriers'.[14] Due to their epistemic marginalization, Blind people are often treated as objects of care and inclusion, and rarely as independent subjects who create knowledge or insight.[15, 16] My first focus here is to move away from this deficit-oriented perspective and instead recognize the specific ways of perceiving and knowing that emerge from Blindness. In the section dealing with the Blind Perception Style, I will develop an independent epistemic position of Blindness, thus determining the form of the representation. I will provide an overview of the connections between touch and Blindness. Lastly, I will present the outcome of touch practices which I carried out in the Blind Perception Style with objects in the Museum für angewandte Kunst in Frankfurt. And so we remain loyal to Baumgarten: he developed his aesthetics by studying the artistic form and artistic materials.

The Blind Perception Style

When the tactile sensations of Blind people are discussed here, 'Blind' refers neither to the medical nor to a purely normative category, but rather a particular epistemic position.[17] While entirely relevant in an everyday-life context, the categorization into various degrees of visual impairment plays a minor role for the following observations.[18] The basic assumption is that Blindness comprises certain forms of knowledge, the content of which has only recently become a subject in academic literature.[19]

In order to categorically define this knowledge, I should like to refer to the Blind Perception Style as first formulated by the Blind sociologist Siegfried Saerberg, in his ground-breaking study *"Geradeaus ist einfach immer geradeaus"* [Just Go Straight Ahead].[20] With 'Blind Perception Style' we can understand 'an ordered whole of subjective reality constitution.'[21] The term 'Subjective reality constitution' recurs in the phenomenological basic tenet which for Saerberg, in keeping with Merleau-Ponty, signifies a physical 'living-in-the-world'.[22, 23] The body is a temporally

and spatially expanded prerequisite of our self-perception.[24]
Everything that is perceived is pre-structured by the body's
structure before we become aware of it. If the body's structure determines the structure of perception, then we must
not imagine an ideal body, but rather consider the body in
its individual reality. Specifically: 'if the body is a 'means to
have the world', a Blind body also has a Blind world.[25] The
advantage of this phenomenological position is that it can
operate beyond the dualism of physiological conditioning
and social construction.[26] So, Blind perception is not simply
constructed socially by a way of a particular composition of
knowledge elements, but is inscribed in experience through
bodily facticity.[27]

The Blind Perception Style describes the embodiment
of sensorial configurations of Blind people's everyday
routines, as unconscious or embodied knowledge, which
must first be brought to speech.[28] Saerberg is interested in
orientation practices in public space; touch therefore only
plays a part insofar as the white cane is deployed as a sensory
prosthesis.[29] Touch by hand only occurs in order to 'better
determine the object character of' an unexpected obstacle.[30]
The Blind Perception Style encompasses a whole ensemble
of non-visually structured perceptions; touch and the
tactile sense form only one subset. However, if we focus on
this subset, we can demonstrate the marginalization of the
Blind Perception Style through it. Particularly in aesthetic
or artistic contexts, blind people appear primarily as those
who perceive through touch. The systematic devaluation
of blindness often occurs precisely because the form of this
perception style is repeatedly defined and judged by visual
standards. By examining this dynamic, we learn more about
the Blind Perception Style in general and about potential
tactile knowledge and its linguistic composition in particular.
With this perspective, we now enter the field of art.

Art and the Sense of Touch

Since the formulation of the cultural model of disability[31]
and the attempt to formulate an independent Disability
Aesthetics,[32] there has been a growing interest in the
connection between cultural phenomena of disability and

20. S. Saerberg,
"Geradeaus ist einfach
immer geradeaus": Eine
lebensweltliche
Ethnographie Blinder
Raumorientierung, 2006,
18.

21. Saerberg,
"Geradeaus ist einfach
immer geradeaus", 55.

22. The basis for this is
formed by Saerberg the
Phenomenology of
Perception by the
French phenomenologist
and Husserl critic,
Merleau-Ponty (1908–
1961). His works are
primarily philosophi-
cally and not very
sociologically
orientated. His ideas
are based time and again
on the phenomenon of
blindness and touch
with the white cane.

23. Saerberg,
"Geradeaus ist einfach
immer geradeaus".

24. M. Merleau-Ponty,
Phänomenologie der
Wahrnehmung, 1966, 125.

25. Merleau-Ponty,
Phänomenologie der
Wahrnehmung, 1966, 176.

26. S. Dickel, '(New)
Disability Memoirs als
wegweisende Texte für
eine kritische
Phänomenologie',
Zeitschrift für
Disability Studies, 1,
2023, 4; B. Hughes & K.
Paterson, 'The Social
Model of Disability and
the Disappearing Body:
Towards a sociology of
impairment', Disability
& Society, 12(3), 1997,
329.

27. Saerberg,
"Geradeaus ist einfach
immer geradeaus", 56.

28. S. Saerberg,
'Inklusives Handeln
zwischen Vergesell-
schaftung, Sinnlichkeit
und Subjektivierung',
Zeitschrift für
Inklusion 3, 2022.

29. Saerberg,
"Geradeaus ist einfach
immer geradeaus", 98.

30. Saerberg, "Geradeaus ist einfach immer geradeaus", 116.

31. D.T. Mitchell & S.L. Snyder, *The Body and Physical Difference: Discourses of Disability*, 1997; A. Waldschmidt, 'Disability Studies: Individuelles, soziales und/oder kulturelles Modell von Behinderung?', *Psychologie & Gesellschaftskritik*. 29(1), 2005, 9-31.

32. T. Siebers, *Disability aesthetics*, 2010.

33. A. Hackel, *Paradox Blindheit: Inszenierungen des Sehverlusts in Literatur, Theater und bildender Kunst*, 2017.

34. G. Mosel, *Blindheit und Kunst*, 2013.

35. O. Käfer, *Blindheit in der Kunst: Darstellung und Metaphorik*, 2016.

36. Schillmeier, 'Der Blinde als der Andere'.

37. D. Diderot, 'Brief über den Blinden, zum Gebrauch für die Sehenden', 1749, *Diderot. Philosophische Schriften*, 1, ed. A. Becker, 2013.

38. Diderot, 'Brief über den Blinden', 13, translation in K.E. Tunstall, *Blindness and Enlightenment: An Essay with a New Translation of Diderot's Letter on the Blind (1749) and a Translation of La Mothe Le Vayer's Of a Man-Born-Blind (1653)*, Continuum, 2011.

39. Diderot, 'Brief über den Blinden', 13.

their respective structures of representation. Astrid Hackel's study[33] is cited as being exemplary in the area of Blindness. It is by no means an unknown phenomenon in the history of art: for instance, in 2001 the influential art historian Moshe Barasch presented a study on the image of the Blind person. Günter Mosel[34] and Otto Käfer[35] are also well informed. Despite that, they share a 'blind spot' when it comes to naming Blind creators of art and their perception. Thus, these works conform with the modern tradition, for which blindness constitutes a puzzle or a metaphor, but not an independent style of perception.[36] To clarify this point, a brief historical overview will show that the linking of art and blindness leads, time and again, to touch, from there back to blindness and then to art.

Denis Diderot's work *Letter on the Blind for the Use of Those Who Can See*[37] is one of the most influential writings on Blindness. It contains the following passage on the relationship between art and blindness: 'By using his hands to study how the parts of a whole must be arranged such that we call it beautiful, a blind man can manage to apply this term correctly, but when he says that's beautiful, he is not judging it to be so'.[38] The French philosopher stresses that this is not an independent judgement, but 'he is simply repeating the judgement of the sighted'[39] when an object has to be termed beautiful. Diderot thus describes a dual devaluation: both of blind people and of the sense of touch. According to him, blind people may well create artefacts; these may be considered beautiful in the way that this judgement is used in the fine arts, but this particular way of assessing beauty is not accessible to them, and because of that, their creations are regarded as mere craft, not fine art. In this way, sight is established as the primary mode of perceiving beauty and becomes the standard for judging art. This follows from the assumption that touch can perceive forms that are useful, but not beautiful. Consequently, the blind person who perceives through touch is deemed incapable of independently forming a judgement about beauty in art—their access to beautiful perceptions is fundamentally denied, due to the devaluation of touch.

Despite this problematic judgement, Diderot already shows a sensitivity to the difference between various styles of perception. For instance, one of the Blind protagonists of his text answers the question if he would have wanted to see. His reply:

> If I wasn't so curious, I'd just as well have long arms, as it seems to me that my hands could teach me more about what's happening on the moon than your eyes or telescopes can, and besides, eyes stop seeing well before hands stop touching. It would be just as good to improve the organ I already have, as to grant me the one I lack.[40]

Diderot is not the only one. Figures and metaphors of Blindness feature in French and German literature of the Enlightenment.[41] The metaphorics of Blindness are all too often the reverse side or an integral part of the so-called 'dark enlightenment'. It should be clear that this does not entail a departure from the dominant metaphor of light, but rather a continuation or refinement of it. Somewhat more subtle are those positions that initially engage with questions of perception without explicitly metaphorizing Blindness or Blind people. The Frenchman Condillac and the German Herder are prominent examples. The former even declared touch to be the first, or primary sense, 'which is taken as a model for all human perception'.[42] Only after the tactile exploration of space, might it be possible—if at all—to evaluate the information provided by vision.[43] Whereas Condillac sought to reverse the sensory hierarchy, Herder—building on Diderot's ideas—developed an aesthetics of reception that is grounded solely in the sense of touch.[44] At the same time, however, he drew on developmental psychology, which presupposes visual experience from early childhood.[45] This raises the question of how tactile experience can be conceptualized independently of sight—starting with the challenge of even naming and distinguishing the two senses. Since Herder (who was sighted) relied on models of perception that are already shaped by visuality, his haptic aesthetics remains dependent on the visual: it is 'parasitic in the sense that it draws on the operations of "seeing", even as it seeks to define the qualities of touch'.[46]

40. Diderot, 'Brief über den Blinden', 18.

41. K. Nonnenmacher, *Das schwarze Licht der Moderne. Zur Ästhetikgeschichte der Blindheit*, 2006; N. Binczek, *Kontakt: Der Tastsinn in Texten der Aufklärung*, 2007.

42. E.B. Condillac, *Abhandlung über die Empfindungen*, trans. E. Johnson, newly edited and published by L. Kremendahl 1983.

43. F. Korner, 'Wahrnehmungspolitiken. Ein Plädoyer gegen den Okularzentrismus', *Form, Magazin für Haltung und Design*, 295, 128–136, 2022b.

44. J.G. Herder, 'Plastik: Einige Wahrnehmungen über Form und Gestalt aus Pygmalions bildendem Traume', in *Werke in zehn Bänden. Band 4: Schriften zu Philosophie, Literatur und Altertum 1774–1787*, J. Brummack & M. Bollacher (eds.), 1994, 18.

45. Herder, 'Plastik', 24.

46. N. Binczek, *Kontakt: Der Tastsinn in Texten der Aufklärung*, 2007, 381.

47. K. Harrasser, 'Die Fabel der Arachne: Im Untergewebe taktiler Medialität', in *Auf Tuchfühlung: Eine Wissensgeschichte des Tastsinns*, K. Harrasser (ed.), 2017, 176.

48. R. Prange, *Die Geburt der Kunstgeschichte*, 2004, 99.

49. R. Arnheim, 'Über Victor Löwenfeld', *Der geteilte Mensch: Kunst, Wahrnehmung, Gesellschaft – Ausgewählte Essays*, 1998.

50. H. Körner, *Ein Blinder Bildhauer. Der Mainzer Jakob Schmitt*, Krach, 1984.

51. G. Révesz, *Die Formenwelt des Tastsinnes*, Bd. 2: Formästhetik und Plastik der Blinden, 1938b.

52. Révész, *Die Formenwelt des Tastsinnes*, 1938b, 266.

53. It is remarkable that Volkmar Mühleis also largely bases his study on Merleau-Ponty's phenomenology (Mühleis, *Kunst im Sehverlust*). Therefore, it might be appropriate to examine the philosophy of the French phenomenologist to assess the role blindness and sight play in the conception of the body.

54. Mühleis, *Kunst im Sehverlust*, 20.

55. Mühleis deals mainly with male artists. In comment 359, fourteen artists were listed: eleven male and three female. It continues to be essential to approach the art history of Blind people in accordance with criteria of the gender-critical history of art as well.

56. Mühleis, *Kunst im Sehverlust*, 23.

57. Mühleis, *Kunst im Sehverlust*, 188.

In the following century, practical interest in touch shifted more towards experimental psychology,[47] after beauty in art was unequivocally localized in visual reception at the end of the eighteenth century.[48] The connection between the sense of touch, Blind Perception Style and art was only reopened by the Viennese art historian and psychologist Victor Löwenfeld. He set up an art class in the Hohe Warte Institute for the Blind in Vienna—at the time, the largest of its kind for Jewish life in Europe. The pupils were taught to produce sculptures based on their own perception. The experiment ended with the *Anschluss* (annexation of Austria by Germany) in 1938. Löwenfeld emigrated and the institute was forced to cease its previous operation.[49] It remained the only attempt in the German-speaking region to establish art education that included the Blind Perception Style and not only focused on the creation of handicraft products.[50] With the concept of art focused on the visual aspect and a depreciation of the aesthetic potential of touch, as formulated by Diderot, Blind artists' creations were under threat of constant discredit. This is most clearly reflected in the study of tactile perception by the psychologist Géza Révesz.[51] He studied the sculptural products of Blind artists that we know of from the past 500 years. In fact, an interest in discovering something about the sense of touch, led him to assess all works according to visual standards—the outcome being that all were said to be good craft, but not fine art.[52]

The work of the sighted art historian, Volkmar Mühleis' *Kunst in Sehverlust* [Art in Loss of Vision] dating from 2005 is the opposite. He defines blindness in connection with phenomenological considerations[53] as 'dependent on one's point of view' and means this literally when he states that 'the balance of a person born Blind [...] is different to that of a sighted person'.[54] For a suitable method for analysing art by Blind artists,[55] he proposes taking the [blind] perception of the artist as the frame of reference. That means, for instance, 'illuminating sight as far as it reaches into Not-Seeing'. This should not lead to 'the metaphorical realm of the invisible' but 'to the tangibility of touch'.[56] With these considerations (comparable with the Blind Perception Style), Mühleis proposes that the art of Blind people should be understood historically as a haptic discourse.[57] This could be used to bring together a group of Blind artists, who had worked independently from one another with the Blind Perception Style. For Mühleis, the sculptor José Grania Moreira,[58] who went blind later in life, served as an example.[59] Moreira's way of working places at the centre the hand that feels forms.[60] On the basis of Moreira's considerations, Mühleis deploys a description of touch which primarily involves the hand and derives from the language of geometry.[61] In this procedure we can find two traditions of touch. Firstly, the hand is singled out as the prime organ of the sense of touch, with no involvement of the tactile faculties of other areas of the body.[62] Secondly, form is prominent as the central and primary category of awareness, while surface and material properties are ignored.[63]

Alongside the representation of Blindness in art, interest is also growing in art produced by the Blind. With their art, in turn, part of their perception again becomes part of the artwork, and with it, also of reception-oriented scientific approaches. At this point, a method is needed that not only recognizes Blind perception, but can extend to further modes of perception and possibilities of the sense of touch. To start with, it relates to something that in medicine has long been part of textbook knowledge, namely to take surface sensitivity or thermal irritability as analysis criteria.[64] The fact that art perception can anticipate both physiological as well as art-historical knowledge by way of the Blind Perception Style is the subject of the following section. With this we conclude the representation of content and the content of representation, and proceed to the matter of practice.

The Taxonomy of Touch

Georgina Kleege, who was quoted in the Introduction, not only provides a description of the problems under discussion but also proposes a 'Taxonomy of Touch'. These considerations form the basis of what follows. Since she developed them as a Blind art mediator, I read her text as being reflections on a Blind Perception Style and proposals for methodological guidance in the verbalization of tactile knowledge. To them, I should like to add my own tactile studies of objects

58. As far as Moreira is concerned: this is a sculptor who went blind later on. Further biographical information can be found in Mühleis, *Kunst im Sehverlust*. It remains to be seen to what extent the strategy of those who are Blind from birth differs, and whether Moreira's work can nevertheless be assessed as visual.

59. Mühleis, *Kunst im Sehverlust*, 92.

60. Mühleis, *Kunst im Sehverlust*, 100.

61. Mühleis, *Kunst im Sehverlust*, 101–104.

62. C. Benthien, Hand und Haut: Zur historischen Anthropologie von Tasten und Berührung, *Zeitschrift für Germanistik*, 8(2), 1998, 335.

63. Mühleis, *Kunst im Sehverlust*, 69.

64. R.D. Treede & U. Baumgärtner, 'Das somatosensorische System', in *Physiologie des Menschen. Springer-Lehrbuch*, R. Brandes, F. Lang & R. F. Schmidt (eds.), 2019, 652–657.

65. G. Kleege, 'The Art
of Touch: Lending a
Hand to the Sighted
Majority', *Journal of
Visual Culture*, 20 (2),
2021, 450.

66. F. Korner, 'Der
Betrug: Unantastbar',
*Form, Magazin für
Haltung und Design*, 295,
2022a, 33.

67. Korner, 'Der Betrug:
Unantastbar', 33.

68. Révész, *Die
Formenwelt des
Tastsinnes*, 1938a.

69. Korner, 'Der Betrug:
Unantastbar', 34.

70. Korner, 'Der Betrug:
Unantastbar', 34.

71. Kleege, 'The art
of touch', 451.

in the Museum Angewandte Kunst in Frankfurt, which were published in the design magazine *Form*.

Kleege presents seven elements of the practice of touch: firstly, under the keyword 'embodied knowledge', she describes how touch is used in many everyday and professional activities, for example, when working in the garden or fixing a car.[65] This is illustrated by means of the tactile exploration of a plate made by Theodor Bogler (1897–1968) in 1925–1926 at the Velten Ceramics Factories.[66] In the description we read: 'My fingertips linger on a surface for just a few moments, and an image, a form can already be detected which is immediately matched with a type of item'.[67] Form and surface interact, as it were, they suggest a memory of a shape and recognize the plate even though it had not been handled thoroughly.[68] At the same time as the memory is activated, the surface texture joins in:

> A little deep, slightly flattened, smooth and round in the middle, almost soft, rough and ascending on the outer edge to a vertical rim forming a glassy-porcelain border. Rough and smooth alternate, a light porosity nevertheless betrays something inelastic.[69]

The hollowing in the material's surface becomes even clearer when the plate's underside is felt: 'the material becomes all the more adhesive, but not sticky'.[70] While the form can be imprinted on the material, the material in turn lends its physical structure as a tactile experience. The term 'elastic' summarizes the touch sensation which depends on further material properties. While terracotta clay feels different to a glazed surface, the hardness of the material can nonetheless be detected through this surface. In the second section, Kleege summarizes this as 'the tools of touch'. She recommends first using the hands: 'The fingertips are good for general observations about form, texture and temperature'. After which the arms or the backs of the hands can also be used.[71] Even when the main focus is on the hands, the third to the seventh criteria form the basis for using the entire body as a tactile tool: active and passive touch is the difference between active gestures, such as stroking or pressing, and motionless placement of the hand to obtain tactile information. Pace and rhythm, the variation in speed and repetition of touch gestures; balance and symmetry, the use of two hands for simultaneous exploration to identify symmetrical or asymmetrical features of an object; sonority, the perception of sounds produced by touch, such as knocking or stroking; and scale, taking into account one's own body posture and movement in relation to the size of the artwork.[72]

If an object is bigger than a hand, it is necessary to explore it by means of movement sequences. 'Scale' is the best indication of the extent to which not only the hands should be involved. This is expressed in the tactile description of Marcel Breuer's 1925 B3 club chair:

> As I follow the cold metal bar backward over the armrest, I only feel as much as the width of my hand. I can use my entire arm, but it is still not enough to sense the entire structure. My hand keeps reaching forward; I'm now half-lying on the chair with my upper body to grasp the curve of the backrest framework. Everything I don't touch, I must imagine.[73]

Subsequently, the same text attempts to describe the tactile experience while sitting:

> The buttocks signal comfortable repose—in detail: firm support in the lower back, lighter contact above. The lower shoulder blade area rests comfortably, while the body weight tilts slightly backward.[74]

Based on Kleege's considerations, it can be maintained that by practicing the sense of touch, an ensemble of actions is created both by the hand as well as the entire body. The tactile process becomes a tactile movement or tactile performance. Everyday actions are the point of departure which can be condensed into their own strategy:

> You may already have a repertoire of strategies to make environments and objects conform to your physical particularities. These strategies will prove useful as you develop your own techniques for touching art.[75]

72. Kleege, 'The art of touch', 450–452.

73. F. Korner, 'Der Stuhl', *Form, Magazin für Haltung und Design*, 298, 2022d, 33.

74. Korner, 'Der Stuhl', 34.

75. Kleege, 'The Art of Touch', 450.

Exhibiting for
Multiple Senses

76. F. Korner, 'Das Matte: Unantastbar', *Form, Magazin für Haltung und Design*, 297, 2022c, 33.

77. Korner, 'Das Matte', 33.

78. Korner, 'Das Matte', 33.

79. Korner, 'Das Matte', 34.

80. F. Böhme, 'Gefühle', in *Vom Menschen: Handbuch Historische Anthropologie*, C. Ulf (ed.), 1996, 525–548.

Moreover, the aforementioned documentation and reflection together form an answer to the problem of the (not yet) linguistic character of the sense of touch, which was mentioned at the beginning of this essay. Moreover, the proposed considerations concerning methodology harbour another problem, which will be discussed further down. Using a final example I would like to demonstrate that the difficult part when discussing the perception of touch is how to name surfaces.

Form and temperature have already been mentioned several times, but the example of surface perception was limited to Bogler's ceramic plate. It entailed Kleege's familiar juxtapositions of rough and soft which alone did not, nonetheless, allow any precise definitions. This problem is reflected in the tactile description of two teapots in the TAC (The Architects Collaborative, 1945–1995) series designed for Rosenthal by Walter Gropius, Louis Albert McMillen and Katherine De Sousa.[76] The surface of one of the two teapots is described as follows: 'I get stuck, but I don't know on what. It could be a build-up of dust, rough yet smooth, a little unpleasant'.[77] And later, when comparing the two teapots:

> One version [of the teapots] is glossy, the other is matt. Those are visual impressions! The smooth one is finished and familiar, the matt one its opposite. I don't have the vocabulary to describe this sensation. Matt must be interpreted and so we enter the world of touch.[78]

Based on visual vocabulary, the roughness or irregularity is the most discernible for the sense of touch. When one attempts to describe it, one resorts to a series of associative terms of an affective emotional origin. 'It feels unpleasant, slightly sharp, repulsive, possibly disgusting'. That is the opposite to the glossy pot, the surface of which generally scored positive associations: 'pleasant, familiar, yielding'.[79] Even though emotional reactions do not constitute a precise descriptive vocabulary, they do reflect the pursuit of a stronger cultural-historical approach with which touch as 'feeling' is linked with inner emotions.[80] Beauty can also be attributed to those emotional states, so it is not surprising that the smooth teapot can be experienced as 'subjectively beautiful'.[81] In the end, 'Smooth means danger of slipping' is the only independent descriptive phrase in this text. There are no attempts to combine emotionally coloured adjectives and surface qualities, as we know from impressions of colour (for instance, 'unpleasant yellow'). This is different in the tactile descriptions of the club chair:

> The material is smooth. Leathery would be a suitable adjective, since cowhide was indeed used. But then it describes the material more than its surface. So again: it is smooth, but resistant to the touch. You don't slip as you would with a glazed surface, but need force to stroke it. The smoothness of leather[82] is abiding, centred on body heat and elastic.[83]

This text utilizes compound words to overcome the limitations of existing vocabulary for tactile experiences. Unlike the approach used in describing the TAC tea set, which relied on emotional responses, this text employs physiological modes of tactile perception. It incorporates interactive qualities such as 'holding firm', material properties such as 'elasticity', and thermal characteristics described as 'centred on body heat'. Through the formal strategies of analogy, association, and compound formation, two approaches for developing a language of touch focused on surfaces emerge. By combining both physiologically-oriented tactile terminology and vocabulary from the realm of emotional experience, a rich linguistic resource becomes available for verbalizing tactile sensations. This approach also reopens historical research perspectives, as etymologically, the concept of 'feeling' as sensory perception is closely related to emotional feeling, with the psychological interpretation developing only later in linguistic history.[84]

A Science of Knowledge about Touch

The thesis proposed at the beginning—that our sensory cognition of touch maintains its formal expression through corresponding linguistic idioms—was elaborated in the

81. Korner, 'Das Matte', 34.

82. The German term *Lederglätte* demonstrates a fundamental difference between German and English word formation. German readily creates compound nouns by combining words (here *Leder* [leather] and *Glätte* [smoothness]) to express nuanced concepts in a single word. English typically requires phrases like 'smoothness of leather' instead. This distinction becomes particularly significant by exploring tactile perceptions, where language often struggles to capture sensory experiences. At this point, I must settle for an inadequate translation, which will hopefully stimulate thoughts about appropriate linguistic strategies in English.

83. Korner, 'Der Stuhl', 34.

84. Binczek, *Kontakt*, 10.

85. P. Bexte, *Wo immer vom Sehen die Rede ist... da ist ein Blinder nicht fern: An den Rändern der Wahrnehmung*, 2013, 15.

86. Prange, *Die Geburt der Kunstgeschichte*, 37.

87. Prange, *Die Geburt der Kunstgeschichte*, 99.

88. Saerberg, *"Geradeaus ist einfach immer Geradeaus"*, 11, note 2.

preceding section. In the process, the exploration of tactile sensations has revealed a powerful historical link with thinking on Blindness. The presentation of blindness as an epistemic position at the beginning of the second section aims to consider blindness as an independent form of cognition—not merely as a stand-in for the sense of touch or as a symbolic or metaphorical reference to perception in general.[85] The Blind Perception Style evolves from merely being a representation of blindness to becoming its own form of knowledge production. This outlines a new field of art-historical work, bringing with it all the familiar research-ethical and methodological challenges.

Philosophical aesthetics was historically a necessary condition for translating the visual form of knowledge about painting into the theoretical and linguistic framework we now call art history.[86] An aesthetics of touch acknowledges the need to give proper recognition to a particular form of sensory experience not yet fully incorporated into the canon of scientific disciplines. Visual knowledge as described by for example Prange can serve as an exemplary model here. A prerequisite for this was knowledge of classicist literature and mastery of rhetorical topoi, as Prange demonstrates in Schlegel's painting reports.[87]

If aesthetics is a discipline that makes sensory experience communicable, as established in the introduction, then the language used by the Blind Perception Style is the expression of its specific sensory experience. This must be stated with utmost clarity, since Saerberg, as the principal witness of the Blind Perception Style, already noted the poetic form in its expression.[88] This form may appear resistant to sociological or other scientific knowledge production specifically because of its poetic nature—and it is precisely this aesthetic quality that constitutes the distinctive character of the Blind Perception Style.

Repetition characterizes the essence of practice, allowing tactile experience to become conceptualized through reflection. While connections to theories of embodiment and the phenomenological school of thought seem obvious, these connections reveal an important ethical dimension of aesthetic action: how we represent and engage with sensory experiences matters. These theories must therefore be continuously examined to determine the extent to which they might misappropriate blindness or tactile sensations as mere representational structures whose content does not actually align with the lived experience of the Blind Perception Style. And this relates to issues of accessibility. Being able to touch original artworks is not an accepted practice in museum and art historical contexts. We can only speculate how much knowledge remains unexplored as a result.[89]

This unexplored knowledge may include insights about craftsmanship, production techniques, and the specific properties of materials used in artworks. This is not to suggest that engagement with materiality represents a gap in art historical practice—on the contrary, this topic is gaining increasing momentum. Rather, what needs to be challenged is the implicit historical judgement that the sense of that is somehow incompatible with both fine art and the disinterested aesthetic engagement with art. This prejudice, articulated by Diderot, is perhaps the most deeply rooted misconception that art historical research through the Blind Perception Style must refute.

89. S. Saerberg, 'Sensorische Räume und museale Regimes: Von visueller Dominanz zu sensorischer Diversität', in *Wege zur Kultur. Barrieren und Barrierefreiheit in Kultur- und Bildungseinrichtungen*, A. Tervooren & J. Weber (eds.), 2012, 173.

Exhibiting for
Multiple Senses

BLIND PERCEPTION Style

Lilian Korner

GROW, MOSS ON A CANVAS

Smelling Memories

In the background we see a close-up image of a large jasmine bush, one of the scents that constantly trigger memories and sensations during the summer months. A reminder of holidays in Greece or Italy. Quote from an article by Donald A. Laird titled, 'What can you do with your nose?' (1936): 'the sense of smell determines much more of our behavior than we like to admit, or that we consciously realize... It is now shown that these memories of the past that have a peculiar haunting, emotional grip over us are often aroused by some fleeting odor.' In the top left corner is an image of a cat trying to jump onto a table. Cats are great 'stims'. Do you ever have a sniff at your cat? Or something else to help you calm down? At the bottom of the page is an image of a 'Boomy' ice cream, together with a photo of me as a child with my eyes closed and a large suntanned smile, leaning over a large white freezer, embodying the highlight of any summer holiday: lots of ice creams.

Can you still smell your favourite ice cream from childhood? Can you recall all the smells of your ex-lovers? How many smell-induced déjà vu moments do you have when you bike?

MULTISENSORY TO WHAT END?
Lessons of 'Tate Sensorium' and Intended, Potential and Emergent Objectives of Multisensory Exhibitions

Renata Pękowska

1. 'Tate Sensorium' was an immersive exhibition at Tate Britain (26 August–4 October 2015) created by Flying Object with collaborators Nick Ryan, Lizzie Ostrom, Paul A. Young, Marianna Obrist & Damien Ablart, and Tate producer Tony Guillan.

2. D. Lomas, in T. Pursey & D. Lomas, 'Tate Sensorium: An Experiment in Multisensory Immersive Design', *The Senses and Society*, volume 13, 2018, 361.

'Tate Sensorium' Lessons and Reflections

'Tate Sensorium'[1], staged in 2015, was arguably and in many ways a landmark exhibition. It incorporated and utilized both emerging technologies and analogue solutions in tackling the challenges of the 'sensory turn' attempts at incorporating several types of sensorial input in the experience of traditional pieces of visual art. In the case of 'Tate Sensorium', the artworks were four twentieth-century British paintings from the Tate collections: Francis Bacon's *Figure in a Landscape*, David Bomberg's *In The Hold*, Jonathan Latham's *Full Stop*, and Richard Hamilton's *Interior II*. This short analysis aims to recap some of the writing published during the exhibition and in the years since it was staged, both by its designers and co-designers and those who visited or, in some cases, 'did not experience it at first hand'.[2] I should also at the outset admit that I did not visit 'Tate Sensorium' and must rely on descriptions provided by others: those who visited the show and those involved in its design, development, and staging.

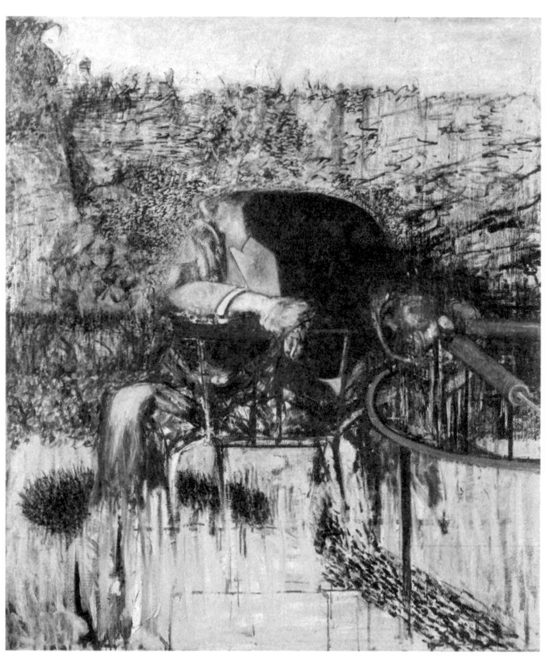

Francis Bacon, *Figure in a Landscape*, 1945.

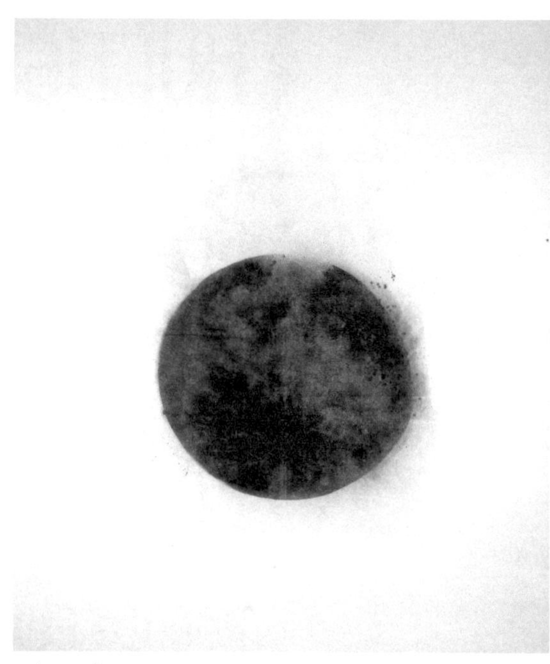

John Latham, *Full Stop*, 1961.

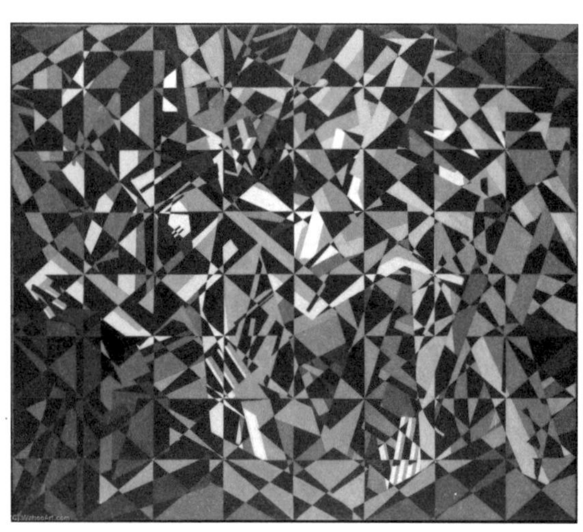

David Bomberg, *In the Hold*, ca. 1913–1914.

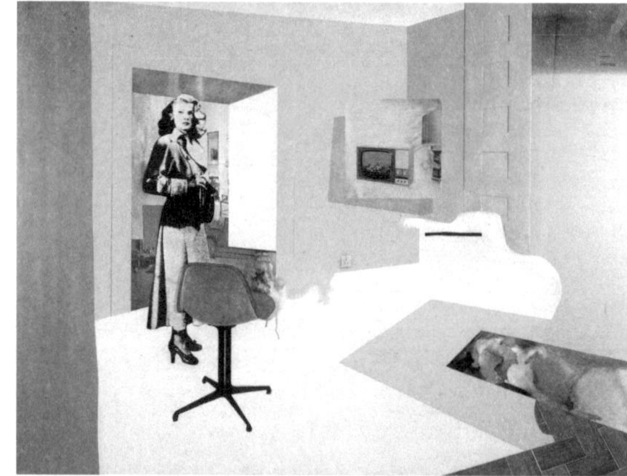

Richard Hamilton, *Interior II*, 1964.

Exhibiting for
Multiple Senses

3. T.Pursey, 'Does a Francis Bacon smell like bacon? Lessons from the Tate Sensorium', *The Guardian*, 2016.

I aim to expand on some of the themes revealed and present in the preceding body of written work dedicated to 'Tate Sensorium'. The time that has passed since the exhibition allows for a perspective that may provide new insights and points of reference. My focus is informed by questions related to my own research interests, including the challenges of linking the modalities of the visual and the olfactory. The scope of this analysis is also directly influenced by my background as an artist researcher who scrutinizes the potential of the multisensory exhibition experience in the context of digital attention economy and digital dependence. The digital context is also related to what I am going to refer to as 'flatness of experience'. I examine the intended objectives and reasons for staging the exhibition and their perceived levels of success. Based on the lessons of 'Tate Sensorium', the analysis examines strengths of its thoughtfully considered designs, its strategies of necessarily prescribed and highly mediated experience, and the risks of playing to the rhetoric of experience economy. It also looks into related issues of the potential threat of gimmickry or of diminishing the experience intended by the artists/creators of the original artworks.

The analysis also looks into possible potential and emergent functions and aims of multisensory exhibitions. I set out to reflect on the role of art in relation to limits of perception and awareness of perceptual habits, and the role of art experience in stimulating types of attention negatively affected by digital eye-to-screen interactions. I ask questions about what multisensory exhibitions might have to offer their audiences, intentionally or not, through their use of multimodal stimuli. I also examine the possibility of such shows to become sites where subjective, less recognized, or neurodiverse experiences and responses can manifest, be recognized and validated.

Connect the World with Art

'Tate Sensorium' was the result of the design studio Flying Object winning the IK Prize, a £70k commission which invites technology-related ideas to achieve what the brief and the objective described as a single sentence: 'Connect the world with art'.[3] The concept of the exhibition was to add one leading sensory clue to the visual experience of each of four chosen paintings, with other 'secondary' additional senses included. So, the objective of connection with art was to be achieved through sensory 'layering', described by multisensory expert Constance Classen as 'the multiple senses induced […] felt at the same time […] layered to produce embodied and immersive experiences that augment the 'visual' art experience'[4]. The word 'immersive' was also used by the director of Flying Object and one of the designers of the 'Tate Sensorium' exhibition, Tom Pursey. He described the experience that they wanted to create as 'immersive rather than detached […] more vivid and more memorable'[5], a deep involvement in 'that thing', a desire to make it 'more real'. The buzzword 'immersive' has possibly lost some of its sheen since then, but even at the time Pursey admitted his awareness of the 'threat of gimmickry'[6] underlying the attempts to create an immersive experience. Art historian David Lomas in the same jointly written article pointed to playing into the experience economy, and the ideas used by the exhibition team being borrowed from marketing-led tech strategies, whose goal is to create consumers, conditioned to believe they crave more sensations.[7]

It may be said that the idea of a deeper connection with art as a result of involving more sensory input is derived from the sensory turn concepts taking a stance against High-Modernist ocular-centrism. It may also lead to a point where 'only' a painting and its visual appeal becomes, as mischievously described by David Lomas, a 'perverse form of sensory deprivation'.[8] Trisha Austin, in her 2020 book on narrative environments and experience design cites Claire Bishop[9] who in her 2004 article criticized Bourriaud for assuming that 'optical contemplation' of an art object

4. C. Classen, *The Museum of the Senses*, 2017, 7.

5. T. Pursey & D. Lomas, 'Tate Sensorium: An Experiment in Multi-sensory Immersive Design', *The Senses and Society*, volume 13, 2018, 354.

6. Idem, 360.

7. Idem, 363.

8. Idem, 363.

9. T. Austin, *Narrative Environments and Experience Design: Space as a Medium of Communication*, 2020, 173.

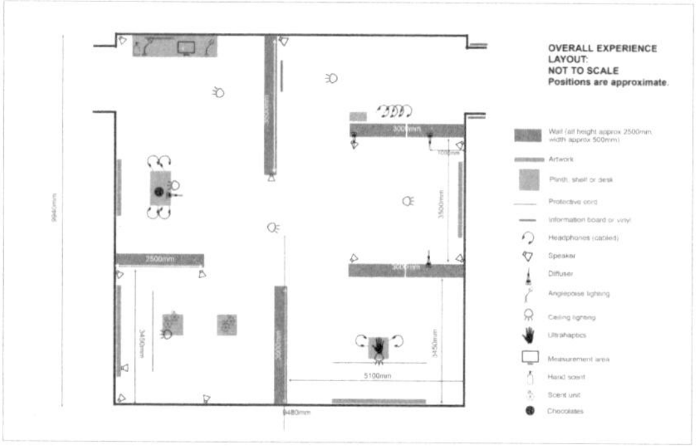

'Tate Sensorium' room plan design dated 4 August 2015. Image courtesy of Flying Object.

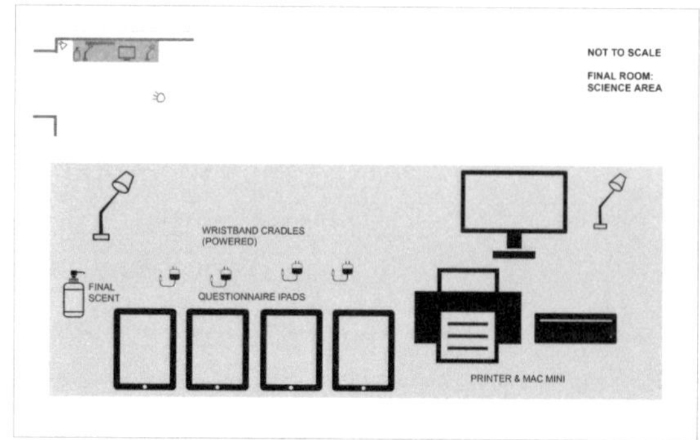

'Tate Sensorium' final room (science area) design dated 4 August 2015. Image courtesy of Flying Object.

10. C. Bishop, 'Antagonism and Relational Aesthetics', *Circa Art Magazine*, 2004, 62.

11. C.T. Vi, D. Ablart, E. Gatti, C. Velasco, & M. Obrist, 'Not Just Seeing, but also Feeling Art: Mid-air Haptic Experiences Integrated in a Multisensory Art Exhibition', *International Journal of Human-Computer Studies*, 2017, 10.

12. C. Classen, *The Museum of the Senses*, 2017, 7.

is 'passive and disengaged' (as opposed to intrinsically democratic relational aesthetics).[10] I would like to pause here and look more closely at the idea of contemplation. Contemplation might appear at odds with the necessarily highly mediated environments of some of the multisensory exhibitions, including 'Tate Sensorium'. As an intensely curated experience, it was strictly timed and prescribed. Visitors entered in groups of four, were divided into two groups of two for two of the paintings and had a specific amount of time for each exhibit (twenty minutes for the whole experience). This aspect was not enjoyed by everyone, as reflected in some of the critical comments that the exhibition designers received as feedback. The comments included words such as: 'prescribed', 'shepherded' or 'orchestrated', and descriptions of the feeling that they entered a space where all the choices had already been made by someone else, and stimuli such as smells and touch smoothly matched the visuals.[11] This might invite a question of whether such a controlled environment can be conducive to contemplation, which, it may be argued, can be seen as the condition for connection and for a special kind of private, mental immersion?

Against Flatness of Experience

Constance Classen stated that in an age of 'abundant visuality' a museum stands out 'not as an empire of sight' but as 'an extraordinary and sensuous landscape of things'.[12]

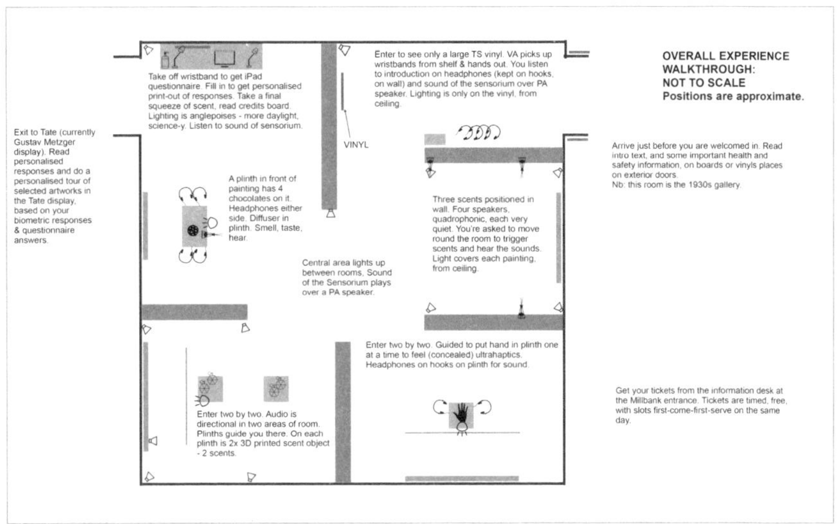

'Tate Sensorium' overall experience walkthrough design dated 4 August 2015. Image courtesy of Flying Object.

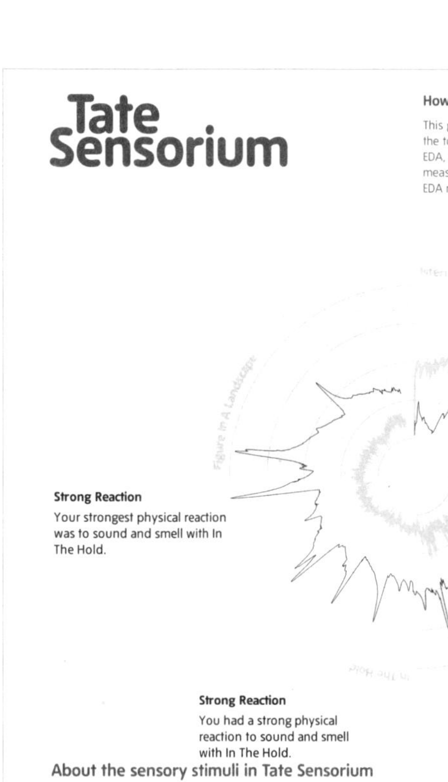

About the sensory stimuli in Tate Sensorium

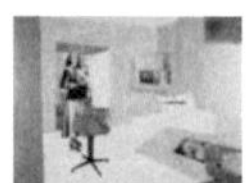 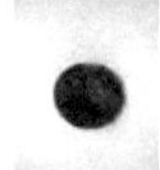 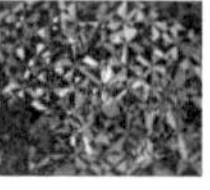 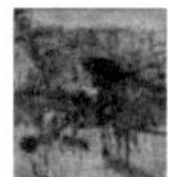

Interior II 1964
Richard Hamilton

Here, **smell** stimuli create a sense of a mid-century home and the impact of big brands by recreating the original scent of Pledge. The central character is brought to life with the scent of vintage hair-spray, and a glue/solvent smell hints at the collage process. The **audio** brings the viewer into the acoustic space of the central character. Some of the objects de-picted can also be heard, while sounds of paper and paint again suggest the creative process.

Full Stop 1961
John Latham

An Ultrahaptics device creates **touch** sensations on the hand in mid air, using ultrasound. These are sequenced with the **audio**. The artwork plays with positive and negative space, and the tactile-audio stimulus translates that as presence or absence. The sound especially emphasises the painting's black and white duality. The two senses work together to create a sense of scale, and of roundness, but also reference Latham's use of spray paint, and his iterative theory of mark making.

In The Hold 1964
David Bomberg

The **audio** brings the viewer into the painting, through two distinct planes of sound. The first reflects the geometry of the painting: acute angles, jagged sounds, reflecting Bomberg's quest for "pure form". The second evokes the subject matter - a ship's hold. The **smell** stimuli work in a similar way. The first scent is abstract: shrill, bringing out the blue colour. The second smells like the ship might: diesel and tobacco. Low concentrations of the second scent are present in the first.

Figure in a Landscape 1964
Francis Bacon

The **taste** of edible charcoal, sea salt, cacao nibs and smokey lapsang souchong tea bring out the painting's dark nature, and the wartime era in which it was painted - while a hint of burnt orange con-nects to flashes of colour and blue sky. **Smell** evokes the setting, Hyde Park: there's grass, soil, and an animalic, horse-like scent. **Audio** mirrors the smell and taste, while referencing the colour palette and the painting's visual texture; mechanised, industrial sounds are suggested in the subject matter.

'Tate Sensorium' personalized print-out of responses chart sample.
Image courtesy of Flying Object.

Museum objects and museum spaces, despite restrictions imposed on ways they can be interacted with, still offer a plethora of sensuous input. Tom Pursey commented on the Flying Object's decision not to add screens as part of the exhibition saying that an 'art museum contains sufficient

13. T. Pursey & D. Lomas, 'Tate Sensorium: An Experiment in Multisensory Immersive Design', *The Senses and Society*, volume 13, 2018, 356.

14. C. Classen, *The Museum of the Senses*, 2017, 18.

15. J.D. Porteous, 'Smellscape', in: J. Drobnick (ed.), *The Smell Culture Reader*, 2006, 101.

things to look at as it is' but also 'looking at something that *isn't a screen* may well be the reason a visitor enters the museum in the first place'[13] [emphasis mine]. Both parts of this sentence are of interest to this analysis, as the sufficient things to look at are presumably objects in the collections, but they are also things to look at which are *not screens*, which I argue provides a strong argument for seeing a museum visit and (an in-person) experience as an antidote to eye-to-screen interactions characteristic for an age of digital dependence. The museum objects are not flat—even if they are paintings or prints or drawings—they are three-dimensional objects, with their physical properties and their tangible materiality. The screens, so ubiquitous nowadays, are flat—not as objects, but as what they display, and what is looked at. Interactions with screens, even if they involve touch, are what I would like to refer to as 'flat experiences'. The touch of a screen is not what Classen refers to in her text quoted above as 'talismanic touching'[14] or a 'wondering touch' which she describes in relation to museum objects or to Rembrandt's painting techniques, which involved heavy layers of textured paint. Classen comments on the 'quality of enchantment' of the tangibility produced by painterly techniques creating an inducement to explore it, and while not encouraging anyone to touch the paintings, argues for the importance of investigating 'the appeal exerted by such works'. I argue that eye-to-screen experience, and its inherent flatness, is already vastly different from contemplating a physical object, even if only restricted to the visual manner. The object already has its myriad of material properties, which can be either sensed, suspected, or speculated upon, calling for the vast array of all previous personal sensory experience and data. So what happens if other sensory input is *added*? What about a sense as tricky to describe and to work with as smell?

Geographer J. Douglas Porteous described the smell-related memory as 'the vast structure of recollection, amid the ruins of all the rest', stating that 'time seems to play no role in odour memory'. In contrast with visual recognition accuracy, highly accurate within minutes but rapidly declining over time, smells can be recalled with the same degree of accuracy almost a year later.[15] Olfactory cultures writer Jim Drobnick claimed that synthetic scents as 'fashionable additions to the museum's repertoire of effects' where 'the use of smell as part of the "five senses experience" [...] gives the impression that an exhibition is a comprehensive, fully embodied encounter', but also stipulated that 'the rhetoric of total experience can be nothing but a gimmick'.[16] Experimental psychologist and crossmodal researcher Charles Spence in his 2020 article 'Scenting the Anosmic Cube' argued that augmenting visual displays with smell can result in widely varied levels of connection, or correspondence, between the visual input and added scents, 'not guaranteed to deliver a positive outcome *however that is defined*'[17] [emphasis mine]. Spence argued that the said outcome may depend on how the association between the artworks and scents is introduced or explained. According to experimental psychologist Richard J. Stevenson,[18] smell has some 'unique characteristics', as it can be a powerful retrieval force, but it may also induce strong negative emotions; it is also capable of inducing the sense of being part of the 'thing in question' and produce the sense of phenomenological proximity 'assuming that the odour is widely recognisable', which is a powerful potential but also warns of possible undesired effects. Cognitive scientist Jamie Ward stresses the importance of semantic congruency in multisensory memory formation; multisensory features, if meaningfully integrated, can lead to deeper encoded memories, which are generally considered to be remembered better.[19] Ward further states that the brain is quite capable of avoiding 'sensory overload' provided the sensory information is 'not conflicting', in another argument for congruency of the added multimodal input.[20]

How can this be applied to multisensory augmenting twentieth-century artworks? What kind of sound, scent, or taste would be considered congruent with an abstract or semi-abstract work? David Lomas defined the aim of 'Tate Sensorium' (therewith defining the expected 'positive outcome' in this particular case) as enhancing the encounter with the chosen artworks, making it more stimulating and thereby also more memorable. The work at the centre of his analysis was Francis Bacon's *Figure in a Landscape*, which, to him, in its purely visual form, already presents a brutal assault

16. J. Drobnick, 'Volatile Effects: Olfactory Dimensions of Art and Architecture', in: D. Howes (ed.), *Empire of the Senses: The Sensual Culture Reader*, 2005, 269.

17. C. Spence, 'Scenting the Anosmic Cube: On the Use of Ambient Scent in the Context of the Art Gallery or Museum', *i-Perception*, 2020, 4.

18. R.J. Stevenson, 'The Forgotten Sense', in N. Levent & A. Pascual-Leone (eds.), *The Multisensory Museum*, 2014, 161.

19. J. Ward, 'Multisensory Memories', in: N. Levent & A. Pascual-Leone (eds.), *The Multisensory Museum*, 2014, 278.

20. J. Ward, 'Multisensory Memories', in: N. Levent & A. Pascual-Leone (eds.), *The Multisensory Museum*, 2014, 281.

21. T. Pursey & D. Lomas, 'Tate Sensorium: An Experiment in Multisensory Immersive Design', *The Senses and Society*, volume 13, 2018, 362.

22. C. Spence, 'Scenting the Anosmic Cube: On the Use of Ambient Scent in the Context of the Art Gallery or Museum', *i-Perception*, 2020, 19.

23. D. Lomas, in T. Pursey & D. Lomas, 'Tate Sensorium: An Experiment in Multisensory Immersive Design', *The Senses and Society*, volume 13, 2018, 364.

24. R. Pękowska, 'Embodied Cognition and the Limits of Digital Museum Experience', *Museum International*, volume 74, 2022, 142.

on the senses. The questions asked is: what possibly could one hope to achieve through sensory augmentation of such an artwork? Lomas commented on the scent used for Bacon's painting. The painting started as a work based on a photograph of a seated figure identified as Eric Hall, Bacon's lover, in Hyde Park in London. The painting had other elements and layers added at a later stage, including images of African wilderness. Lomas comments on the smell being a direct reference only to the Hyde Park location, 'playing on the obvious', which overrides all of the other context: of the seater, or other possible sources used in the creation of the artwork. It leaves out the ambiguity and complexity, and sidesteps more controversial narrative threads related to the personal relations between Bacon and his subject.[21] It appears that in this case, congruency might come with a possibility of reduction rather than expansion, focusing on 'the obvious' at the expense of thorny entanglements. This possibility is what I refer to as 'flattening': erasing the nuance of multiple possible angles of the visual discovery of a complex artwork.

David Lomas also notes that offering a multisensory narrative might stand in stark contradistinction to what Bacon said about his own work, namely that his paintings meant and said nothing. The reflection is closely related to the concern expressed by Charles Spence, of 'whether it is actually appropriate to intervene between the artist and their audience'.[22] This question is even more relevant when considering artworks that 'withhold pleasure' and whose experience is that of absence, offering emotional depth and profundity.[23] Can my concept of 'flatness of experience', related to the digital realm, be again considered here, as a possible side effect, where augmenting becomes flattening instead? Can multisensory interpretations run the risk of simplifying or even obliterating the original, intended, and single-modally executed message—or lack thereof? And if so, are there any ways of negotiating this potential effect, by either working with living artists and developing multisensory exhibitions in dialogue with creators of original visual artworks, or by considering the ambient and embedded properties of objects and materials, thus achieving the 'not conflicting' memory-creating congruence which may lead to long-lasting cross-modal impressions.[24]

How Many Senses?

Considered in a wider context of ocularcentrism and the ubiquitous daily digital dependence, it can be argued that multisensory exhibitions have the capacity to create experiences for their audiences that can mitigate and respond to the flatness of eye-to-screen interactions. One way to achieve that is by adding other sensory input to visual artworks, as was the case with 'Tate Sensorium'. Exhibition designers can also employ certain strategies (as was also the case with 'Tate Sensorium') to prime their visitors for the focused, enhanced, multimodal experience of the collection items. In the case of 'Tate Sensorium', a team of experts who were hired to design the exhibition elements included interactive theatre designer Annette Mees and lighting designer Cis O'Boyle. They created an atmosphere for the exhibition, emphasizing the sensory presences and putting the visitors 'in the mood for a more sensory exploration of the artworks'.[25] This aim is reminiscent of a passage from Michael Fried's 1967 *Art and Objecthood* in which he discusses Minimal Art as a 'theatrical environment'. Fried quotes Robert Morris, who stressed the importance of having control over the entire *situation* [emphasis mine], the situation which includes and takes into account the beholder's body, where everything counts, not as part of an object, but as part of the situation, as the situation and its presence extort a 'special complicity' from the beholder.[26] The whole *situation* becomes in a way another sense, the sum of all sensory input, of the stimuli and of their awareness. It may be said that 'Tate Sensorium' team's efforts to create the whole environment of heightened awareness of the sensory presences can be described as one such constructed situation. Can a situation such as this evoke more sensory experiences than expected?

Caro Verbeek, an olfactory art historian, curator and researcher specializing in the cultural history of the senses, visited 'Tate Sensorium' in 2015.[27] I asked Caro about her memories and impressions, from the perspective of the nine years that have passed since her experience of the exhibition. She recalled that her strongest impression-memory was, surprisingly, not the smell, but how exciting it was to wait outside the door, in the line, and being led into a 'completely dark' space. She also remembered 'vividly' the last 'station'

25. Pursey, T., in T. Pursey & D. Lomas, 'Tate Sensorium: An Experiment in Multisensory Immersive Design', *The Senses and Society*, volume 13, 2018, 359.

26. M. Fried, Art and Objecthood, 1967, 155.

27. C. Verbeek, personal communication, 7 October 2024.

Exhibiting for
Multiple Senses

28. C. Verbeek personal communication, via Eva Fotiadi, 14 November 2024.

29. P. Law, personal communication, 7 November 2024.

with something to taste, as it was both exciting and scary to be ingesting something within an exhibition experience context, and the taste being 'very unexpected', and that it 'fit the painting' though she could not recall the painting. She remembered the chart of her skin response bracelet which she was given when entering, and the chart of her friend's response who visited the exhibition with her. Both of them showed a big response peak after the tasting experience. Caro also remembered a mid-air touch experience, with a tingling sensation that matched the shapes depicted in a painting (Jonathan Latham's *Full Stop*). She reflected on the reason for the smells 'not working' for her being the choice of particular smells to go with the artworks, which can work differently for everyone. She summed up the experience as: the darkness, the unexpectedness, and the guidance, particularly for the 'very challenging' sense of taste. Caro also described (in a separate message) the experience of her friend who accompanied her to 'Tate Sensorium', Piet Devos, who was a scholar specializing in perception and disability. Caro and Piet reminisced about their shared cherished memories when she visited him in a hospice, and Piet, who was blind, shared his memory of their trip to 'Tate Sensorium'. He said: 'I don't remember any of the other artworks but I clearly remember eating that piece of chocolate with salt inside, which was a surprising element. It was connected to a work by Francis Bacon' (source: conversation between Caro Verbeek and Piet Devos, 1 November 2024).[28]

Peter Law was one of the Flying Object team members who developed and designed 'Tate Sensorium'. He shared his comments and thoughts when asked whether the exhibition achieved its objectives and talked about his own experience and memories of the show.[29] Peter believed the exhibition had achieved its aims: the visitors were 'consulting' not only their vision but also the non-visual senses. They also took in the context in which the looking and sensing took place, and all of that seemed to have integrated into their experience of the paintings. In his opinion, the exhibition design left a lot of room for individual interpretations, while keeping the visitors focused on the artworks. When reminiscing about his own impressions of the exhibition, he described 'strong visual experiences', which he thinks were

OLFACTORY MEMORY

prompted by the non-visual stimuli, and which he could recall 'vividly'. He recalled the strong impression of the 'gritty visual texture' of one of the paintings, brought on by 'gritty chocolate material' in his mouth. This effect was memorable despite the fact that he chose and developed that chocolate material and had tested it several times; it did 'deepen' what he saw in the painting and the way in which it had been executed. Peter contrasted his own impression with that of a 'friendly art critic' who found that the multisensory stimuli were 'too directive', and 'got in the way'. He concluded with a reflection on a multitude of strategies that visitors might adopt when approaching a painting, and how what 'Tate Sensorium' did was to 'scaffold one strategy among many— a very sensory one'.

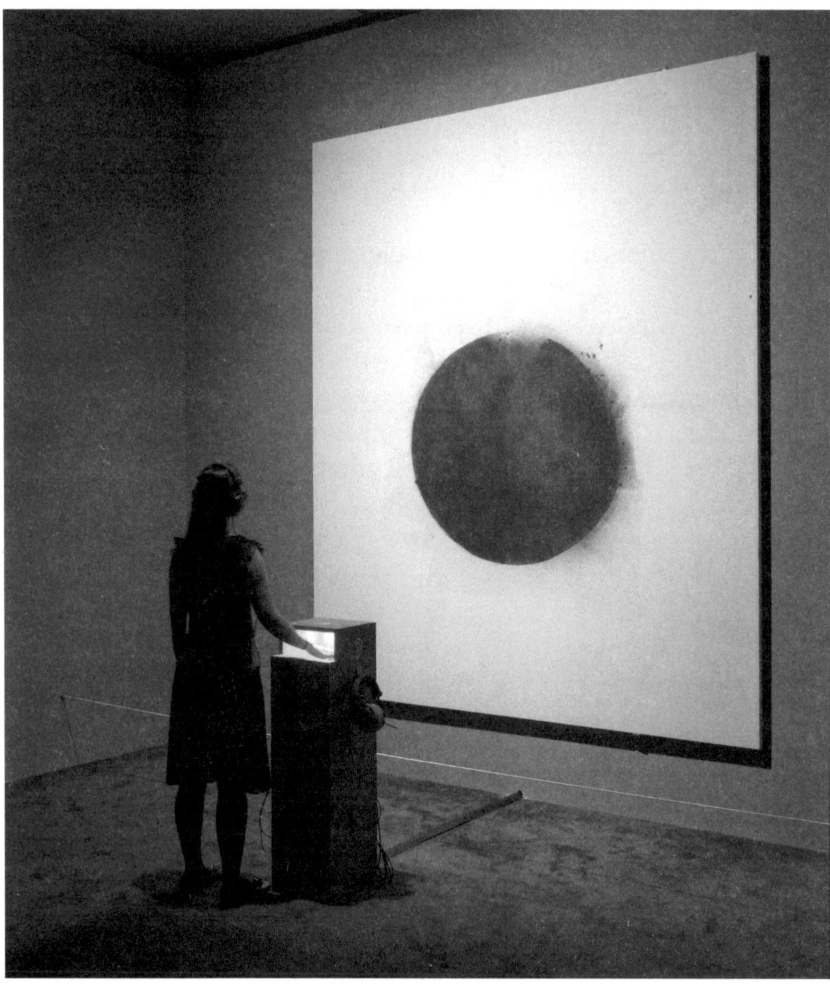

Installation photograph of IK Prize 2015: 'Tate Sensorium', Tate Britain. Showing the work *Full Stop* by John Latham (1961), 2015 © John Latham Estate, courtesy Lisson Gallery, London.

30. T. Pursey & D. Lomas, 'Tate Sensorium: An Experiment in Multisensory Immersive Design', *The Senses and Society*, volume 13, 2018, 354.

31. C.T. Vi et al., 'Not Just Seeing, but also Feeling Art: Mid-air Haptic Experiences Integrated in a Multisensory Art Exhibition', *International Journal of Human-Computer Studies*, 2017, 10.

32. D. Howes, Sensorium; *Contextualizing the Senses and Cognition in History and Across Cultures*, 2024, 5.

The recurring feature in the descriptions above is the edible element accompanying the Francis Bacon painting. For Caro, it had a surprising taste, which she thought 'fit the painting' (even though she could not recall the painting), it also felt unusual in being asked to ingest something as part of an exhibition. Piet Devos also remembered most vividly 'the chocolate with salt in it', and he recalled that it was connected to Bacon's painting. For Peter, one of the designers, it was the chocolate's gritty texture, deepening the visual experience of the gritty texture of the painting. It might be worth noting how the same experience was very different for the three people who described it. Peter's description does not mention the flavour, only the texture, which indicates that for him, the tasting experience was a haptic sensation, the sense of the inside of the mouth being touched by the 'chocolate material'. The descriptions reveal the subjectivity of responses, but the added sensory description also shows the complexity of the sensory exhibition element itself, in this case the tactile properties of the edible element, highlighting the interconnectedness and cross-containing of the different sensations.

So, what combinations and how many senses did the exhibition involve? And, furthermore, is there room in multi-sensory exhibitions for more than the widely recognized five senses? Tom Pursey described the hope that 'Tate Sensorium' would induce a more vivid and memorable experience 'by engaging *all the senses*' [30] [emphasis mine]. It also appears to have been the expectation of some of the visitors of 'Tate Sensorium', who reportedly indicated their disappointment that the experience was not as intense as they had anticipated. Their expectation had been something involving their 'whole body maybe', with one participant reportedly taking of their shoes 'expecting to be stimulated via their feet'.[31] David Howes, a theorist of the anthropology of the senses, reminds us that it was Aristotle in *De Anima* (On the Soul) who famously proclaimed that there are five senses, but this number has been contested since then at different times and in different cultures. During the nineteenth century 'numerous interoceptive senses came to be identified, such as proprioception or kinaesthesia'.[32] Howes also cites Walter J. Ong, who stated back in 1967 that

Renata Pękowska

by the sensorium we mean [...] the entire sensory apparatus as an operational complex [...] differences in culture [...] can be thought of as differences in the sensorium, the organisation of which is in part determined by culture while at the same time it makes culture.

Sensorium, according to Ong, includes communication technologies conceived as 'extensions of the senses'.[33] The dominant medium of communication has the strongest impact on the operations of the mind and of society, as the senses can be (and are) trained, socialized and technologized.[34] Howes concludes that the 'neurobiological model' of ten, twenty-one or thirty-three senses should be treated as contingent on the conditions of current beliefs and ultimately states that 'the senses are innumerable'.[35]

THE SITUATION BELONGS TO THE BEHOLDER
Multisensory Experience Manifesting Subjectivities

'The situation itself *belongs* to the beholder' is how Michael Fried[36] [emphasis in original] described Minimalist Art and its presence, adding that the works must somehow *confront* the beholder [emphasis in original]. I would like to expand on this comment and consider it in the context of the multisensory-augmented exhibition. How can the multisensory exhibition situation belong to the beholder? Tom Pursey[37] described the 'Tate Sensorium' experience as moving in and around the space, smelling, listening, while constantly looking at the paintings, letting the sounds and smells influence where to direct attention, noticing details or 'seeing prominent areas in new ways'. Seeing things in 'new ways' suggests developing your own, subjective response to the work seen. I would like to argue that the type of multisensory situation exemplified by 'Tate Sensorium' displays can serve not only to 'connect with art' but also to connect to one's own 'sensorium': a collection of memories, expectations, own levels of sensitivity to sensory stimuli, and finally to experiencing all of the above with a small group of other people in a room. Other people's

33. Idem, 9.

34. Idem, 10.

35. Idem, 12.

36. M. Fried, *Art and Objecthood*, 1967, 154.

37. T. Pursey & D. Lomas, 'Tate Sensorium: An Experiment in Multisensory Immersive Design', *The Senses and Society*, volume 13, 2018, 357.

38. Idem, 359.

39. J. Drobnick,
'Volatile Effects:
Olfactory Dimensions of
Art and Architecture',
in: D. Howes (ed.),
*Empire of the Senses:
The Sensual Culture
Reader*, 2005, 71.

presence is also a source of multisensory sensations, and it may affect someone's responses in a positive, but also in an inhibitive or discouraging manner. Other challenges may include sensory overload or lack of hedonic value, which might result in negative experiences; or an abstract approach to pairing sensory stimuli, which might result in disjointed sensations, preventing the connection rather than stimulating it. Using new technologies in multisensory exhibitions brings with it a novelty factor, which might quickly wear off; it also carries the risk of technology failings during the extended runs of shows.

Pursey described the wish to design a role for the visitor as a protagonist[38] who looks at paintings but also connects with their own senses and gains a 'better understanding of how their own perception works'. I argue that this awareness of own perception processes might be the biggest learning experience to take away from an exhibition like 'Tate Sensorium', where in a hyper-mediated situation, in the presence of a few precisely designed stimuli, we can more clearly perceive our own responses to separate slices and chunks of particular sensorial input. Those responses might include less recognized subjective reactions, such as a dislike of certain colours or sounds, sensitivity or lack thereof to smells, or disinclination towards certain textures. As vision is a dominant sense, it may be argued that bringing to the fore the embodied 'lower' senses, which require proximity, such as touch, smell or taste, are more likely to bring out these subjective responses, and make us aware of our own neurodiversity, and, by extension, of the neurodiversity and subjectivity of responses of others.

Already in 2005 Jim Drobnick[39] reflected on how the museums have been moving away from the need to be legitimized by 'master narratives and prescriptive interpretation', instead moving towards exhibitions that, by including other-than-visual sensory input, bring to prominence and highlight the 'subjective nature of knowledge production'. The visitors are thrown into an indeterminate situation in which they have to individually negotiate 'the tension between the museum's framing ideology and the immediacy of personal experience'. Tom Pursey in his closing remarks of the 2018 article considers what the visitors could take away from the exhibition, and asks whether, apart from it being something new to experience, there might be a greater goal to achieve, such as using multisensory strategies to 'challenge the kind of conventions that need challenging'.[40] I argue that the potential impact of manifesting invisible, diverse, and less recognized subjectivities could be the emergent and vital effect of multisensory exhibition experience. Considered in the context of the current homogeneity of ocularcentric, digital, eye-to-screen interactions and ubiquity of digital flatness of experience, this latent inherent aspect may turn out to be the multisensory exhibitions' greatest potential and prospective aspiration yet.

40. T. Pursey & D. Lomas, 'Tate Sensorium: An Experiment in Multisensory Immersive Design', *The Senses and Society*, volume 13, 2018, 360.

Exhibiting for
Multiple Senses

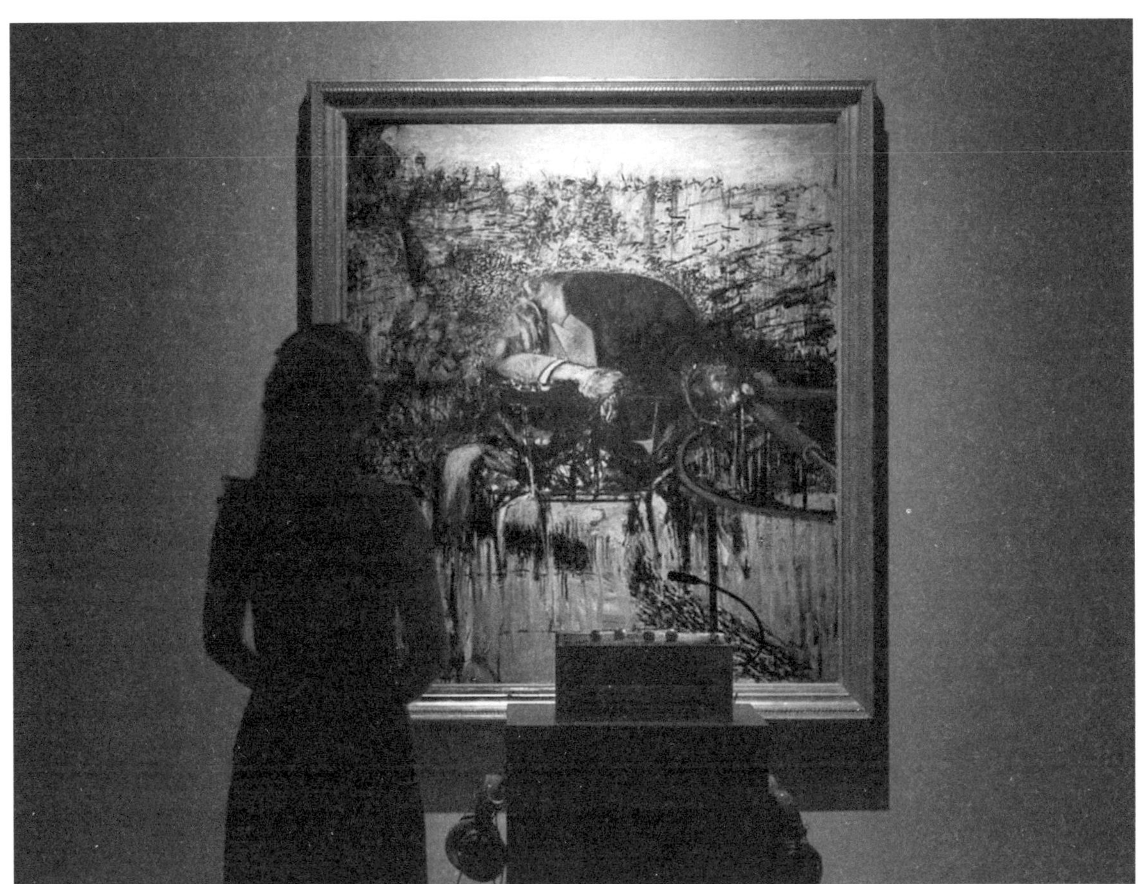

Installation photograph of IK Prize 2015: 'Tate Sensorium' at Tate Britain. Showing Francis Bacon's *Figure in a Landscape* (1945), 2015. The viewer is wearing headphones and eating chocolate. Photo courtesy of Tate Photography.

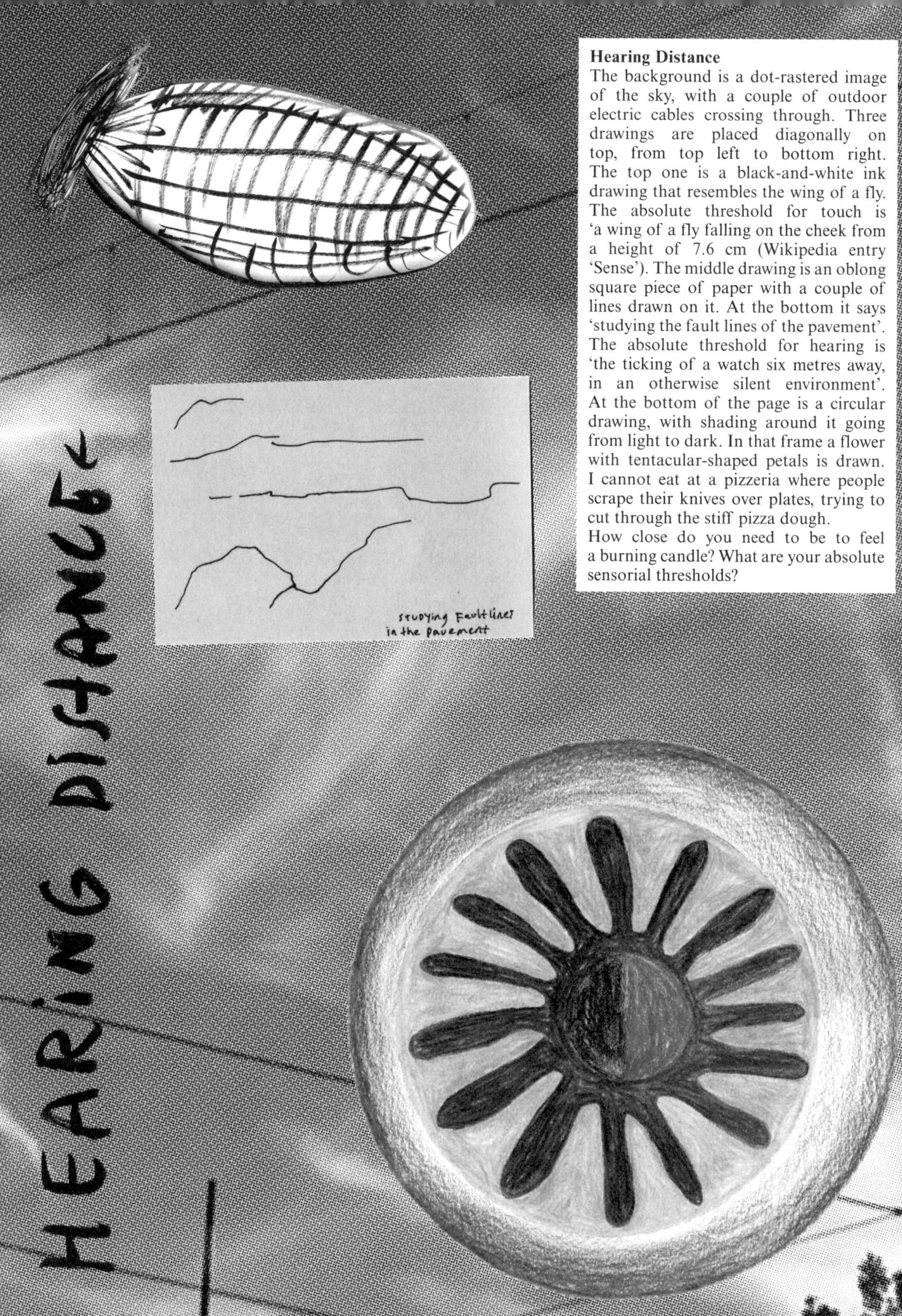

Hearing Distance
The background is a dot-rastered image of the sky, with a couple of outdoor electric cables crossing through. Three drawings are placed diagonally on top, from top left to bottom right. The top one is a black-and-white ink drawing that resembles the wing of a fly. The absolute threshold for touch is 'a wing of a fly falling on the cheek from a height of 7.6 cm (Wikipedia entry 'Sense'). The middle drawing is an oblong square piece of paper with a couple of lines drawn on it. At the bottom it says 'studying the fault lines of the pavement'. The absolute threshold for hearing is 'the ticking of a watch six metres away, in an otherwise silent environment'. At the bottom of the page is a circular drawing, with shading around it going from light to dark. In that frame a flower with tentacular-shaped petals is drawn. I cannot eat at a pizzeria where people scrape their knives over plates, trying to cut through the stiff pizza dough.
How close do you need to be to feel a burning candle? What are your absolute sensorial thresholds?

HEARING DISTANCE

BETWEEN CURATING AND CARE
Critical Inquiry and Feminist Speculations

Elke Krasny

What promise does the word curating hold in contexts that do not have anything to do with contemporary art or museum exhibitions? What are the meanings of care in recent exhibitions and art projects? Writing this essay is motivated by the interest in following words around as a form of critical inquiry to understand how words bestow meanings on new contexts and how the meanings of words and ideas are interpreted and shaped by non-verbal cultural articulations such as exhibitions. To me, following a word around is a critical research method, a form of cultural inquiry that invites critical analysis and feminist speculations. For some years now, I have very closely observed and studied two seemingly unrelated trends in the twenty-first century that have to do with the word curating and with the word care, and with the ideas, concepts, values, emotions and affects that are connected to these words curating and care. The word curating has been taken up in advertising and selling products and services in globalized capitalist economies. At the same time, the notion of care has become central to contemporary curating in the twenty-first century with very many different exhibitions, ranging from large-scale museum exhibitions to newly commissioned works for triennials and biennials as well as shows and public art organized by small-scale, self-organized, non-profit or activist art initiatives, having the word care in the title. As a research method, following around requires one to be open to noticing, to be persistent in this following, and to letting go of fast—too fast—acts of interpretation. Following around as a research method for critical inquiry develops an understanding of the meanings that the words that are followed around by way of reading these words in their new contexts and bringing a historical and etymological awareness to these current meanings. Following the word curating around led me to see that curating has travelled from the world of art and museums and entered into the experience and service economies.[1] Following the word care in the titles of exhibitions and curated programmes led me to understand that care, which has been relentlessly analysed as invisibilized, exploited, feminized, racialized and sexualized labour by generations of feminist Marxist activist theorists, militant researchers, and critical sociologists and which has been interpreted through ethics of care by feminist philosophers and environmental scholars, is at the centre of curatorial interest and thus very visible in the cultural field. Curators work on ideas and practices of care in relation to the conditions of our time, which are defined by structural carelessness, the afterlife of colonialism, the exploitation of labour, the extraction of resources, the global health crisis, pandemics, and the ongoing anthropogenic climate ruination, environmental destruction, and the ongoing mass extinction of species.

The first part of this essay titled 'Curated Consumer Capitalism' begins with sharing a few of the findings that show that curating appears in the context of contemporary capitalism. The second part is titled Curating Care and presents a ten-year overview on exhibitions that had the word care in their title. Starting with an exhibition that ran until January 2025, this overview, which is, of course, by no means complete, goes back to 2015 and shows how curating care was interpreted by curators in the contexts of art, architecture, design, activism, community-work as well as social, environmental, and reproductive justice. This recent history of curating care also shows that no two exhibitions interpreted the ideas and practices of care in the same way. On the contrary, each of the curatorial approaches in these exhibitions that have the word care in their title develops a distinct and specific understanding of care. I turn to the

1. In 2002, cultural theorist Mieke Bal published *Travelling Concepts in the Humanities: A Rough Guide*. In this book Bal examines how different disciplines make use of specific concepts in very different ways. Work between disciplines then makes it necessary to observe and study the ways in which concepts change, or take on different meanings, when they travel between disciplines or are shared by disciplines. My interest is in how words, and the associations and meanings they hold, travel to other contexts beyond their context of origin and how following words around can be practiced as a method useful for critical cultural inquiry. Mieke Bal, *Travelling Concepts in the Humanities: A Rough Guide*, Toronto, Toronto University Press, 2002.

Exhibiting for
Multiple Senses

curatorial statements and to the exhibition announcements on websites and social media platforms to present the aims and arguments that are being made in relation to care by the different exhibitions gathered here. Placing these two trends—the appropriation of curating by contemporary capitalism and the turn to care in contemporary curating—next to each other creates very interesting tensions. The third and concluding part of this essay takes up these tensions and provides feminist speculations on possible subterranean connections and contemporary currents that may have been the reasons for why the experience and service economies have eagerly embraced curating and why contemporary curating has developed an intense interest in care.

Curated Consumer Capitalism

Very curious to follow the word curating around and to understand how it travels in the economies of capitalist consumption, I have found myself standing in front of storefronts and taking photographs of the writings on shop windows that make use of the word curating to speak about vintage items or cosmetics. I have also found myself following the digital trail of airlines on social media platforms and the advertisements of the health and wellness industries. Over a longer period of time of following the word curating around and observing how it is used to advertise, and ultimately, sell products and services I could not help but noticing that curating is particularly used to advertise and sell products and services that intimately touch human bodies. Ranging from clothes to cosmetics, form travel to health and well-being, the word curating is used to describe curated clothing items, be they vintage or selected brands, curated cosmetics, in particular lipsticks, curated experiences in air travel and the travel industry at large, as well as customized services for health and well-being including mental health and all kinds of alternative medicines and healing practices. When the experience economy intimately touches the human body and the ways in which people are touched by how they feel about products or services they spend money on, the word curating comes into play. But it does not stop there. Also, money itself is being curated. We now have the word curated in relation to investing and financial services. Taken together, all this leads me to propose that we now have curated consumer capitalism.

One of my recent finds of the word curating on a shop window is on a nearby street in my Vienna neighbourhood, which is slowly, but relentlessly, gentrifying. In black letters on the glass window, the shop advertises 'Premium Vintage. Curated Cosmetics. Selected Books & Magazines. Rare Finds'. On 1 July 2023, I received an e-mail from Austrian Airlines Flight Service with the subject line 'Your curated travel information for Vienna–Copenhagen'. In a fifty-second-long promotional video shared on Facebook by Qatar Airways, the smiling faces of flight attendants are accompanied by the following message: 'Experience a journey where every detail is curated, because you really are the centre of our world'.[2] Offering 'branded lipsticks for women', a make-up brand operating out of Pakistan since 2007, states that 'our curated collection offers long-lasting, richly-pigmented shades, from runway-ready brights to everyday nudes, that glide on like a dream'.[3] The Curated Homes, according to their website a 'leader in the luxury property market', is a Malaga-based 'boutique Real Estate agency' that offers 'a collection of modern homes carefully handpicked to match your needs and expectations'.[4] Kechil Kitchen, a food consulting company in Singapore, 'curates menus with food storytelling'. On their website they state that 'at Kechil Kitchen, we embrace the richness of biodiverse, sustainable, food security and locally grown ingredients, each one carefully curated to transport you on a unique food story'.[5] Luminosity-Living, the practice of transformational psychiatrist Dr Shiv Dawson in Cape Town, which focuses on spiritual and personal development programmes, offers a '10-day curated 'in your own home' retreat to fast-track optimization'.[6] WealthBasket, an online investment and trading app, offers curated portfolios. On their website one can, for example, choose between 'smart momentum', a basket 'curated using factor-based investing strategy with a trifecta combination of Momentum, Value and Quality factors' or 'the sentiment opportunities', a basket 'curated using the forward looking view of analysts' insights'.[7]

2. See: Qatar Airways, promotional video, www.facebook.com/watch/?v=994326962065897, accessed 1 December 2024.

3. Luscious Cosmetics, Lips Worth the Limelight, www.iloveluscious.com/collections/lips?srslt id=AfmBOooewMHg3x6dJQ-a2euwcVwnokQ722FJej Xxzm1yM-e1f8FLaxHX, accessed 1 December 2024.

4. The Curated Homes, About Us, www.thecurated homes.es, accessed 1 December 2024.

5. Kechil Kitchen, www.kechilkitchen.com, accessed 1 December 2024.

6. Luminosity-Living, Offerings, www.luminosity-living.com/glow/, accessed 1 December 2024.

7. Share Market, 'Confused Where to Invest? Explore WealthBaskets', www.share.market/wealthbaskets, accessed 1 December 2024.

Exhibiting for
Multiple Senses

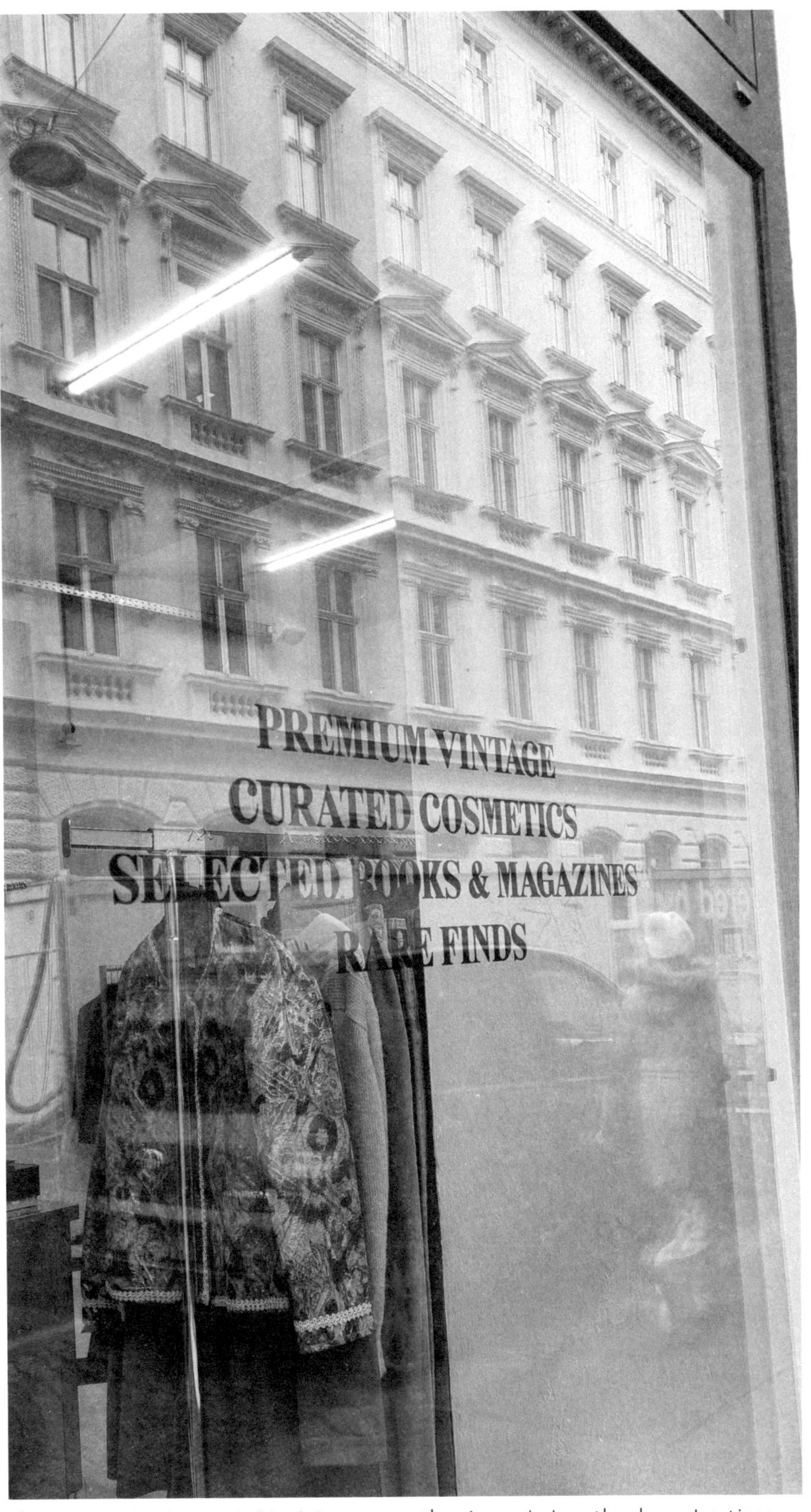

Shop window in Vienna. In black letters on the glass window, the shop advertises 'Premium Vintage. Curated Cosmetics. Selected Books & Magazines. Rare Finds'. Photo: Elke Krasny, 2025.

Having shared this very small selection from my findings on how the word curating is used in the contexts of the experience and service economies, I want to invite you, dear readers, to think of your own encounters with the word curating when you walk past storefronts, look at the offers of vintage clothing or the choices of lipsticks, when the airlines you book flights with communicates with you, or when you see advertisements for health and wellbeing treatments.

Curating Care

Very curious to find out how curators turn to the word care and use this word in titles of their exhibitions, I have found an abundance of recent curatorial work. One could even go so far as to say that care is taking centre stage in curating at this moment in time. Before sharing some of the exhibition titles with care in them and providing some contextual explanation how these exhibitions dealt with care as their subject matter, I should probably also add here that my own engagement with care in relation to curating with a specific interest in feminist perspectives on labour, architecture and spatial practices as forms of care, and in the etymology of the word curating, with its Latin root *curare* actually literally translating into care, spans close to fifteen years. My interest in how curating turns to care is therefore also deeply linked to my own journey as a feminist theorist, researcher and curator. In what follows I will establish a recent history of exhibitions on care. I will do so in reverse chronological order, starting with an exhibition that ran until January 2025 and going back to the year 2015. Even though this is, of course, not a comprehensive history including all the exhibitions which had care in their title, as this would go far beyond the scope of this article, the selection presented here serves to provide evidence that the word care was used in exhibition making in contexts of art, architecture, and design as well as health, well-being, and death, that the word care was used globally in many different parts of the world, and that the turn to care spanned across large-scale and well-funded projects to smallest-scale and grassroots exhibition making.

8. MFA Boston, 'Tender Loving Care', 22 July 2023–15 January 2025, www.mfa.org/exhibition/tender-loving-care, accessed 1 December 2024.

9. See: SaveArtSpace, 'Care Now, Care Forever', www.saveartspace.org/carenow, accessed 1 December 2024.

10. SaveArtSpace, About, www.saveartspace.org/home, accessed 1 December 2024.

11. art.feminist, We're reimagining reproductive freedom through art, www.instagram.com/art.feminist/p/C_5f9f6p3aK/?hl=en&img_index=1, accessed 1 December 2024.

Until 12 January 2025, the Museum of Fine Arts Boston, showed Contemporary Art from the Collection under the title 'Tender Loving Care'. Opened on 22 July 2023, this exhibition showing more than a hundred artworks from the museum's collection has been on show for the duration of eighteen months. The announcement on the museum's website explains how care is being understood by this exhibition. Starting with the argument that 'creating and looking at works of art are acts of care, from the artist's labour to the viewer's contemplation and appreciation', the exhibition announcement then goes on to describe museum care by stating that 'storage, conversation, and display are also ways of tending to art' to finally leave it open to the 'visitors to explore how contemporary artists trace and address concepts of care through their materials, subjects, ideas, and processes'.[8] Care here is very broadly described as characteristic to the making and the appreciation of art in general, as part of what museums do as they provide storage space, take care of the conservation of artworks and, finally, put artworks on public display, while the interpretation of how care is understood and made visible by the more than a hundred artworks on show is left open to the individual interpretation and understanding of visitors.

In November 2024, the non-profit organization SaveArtSpace in Brooklyn, New York, partnered with Autumn Breon, Aisha Becker-Burrowes & Ky Polanco, the co-founders of FEMINIST, and Martha Dimitratou of Plan C, who curated the public art exhibition 'Care Now, Care Forever', which was shown on ad space in Miami and Phoenix.[9] SaveArtSpace, who place 'culture over commercialism', uses billboards and advertisement spaces for public art and local communities.[10] In the open call to contribute to the project 'Care Now, Care Forever', which was published by the curators on Instagram and ended on 16 September 2024, the project was described as follows: 'Submit your vision for 'Care Now, Care Forever'—a nationwide billboard project transforming public spaces into powerful statements on reproductive rights! Your art could shape the future of care across America'.[11] The historical context of this public art exhibition is the post-Roe condition, that is the overturning

of Roe v. Wade, which since 1973 had guaranteed the right
to have an abortion across all the states of the United States
of America, in 2022, when abortion legislation was returned
to the individual states which was 'opening the door for states
to ban abortion outright' and creating a situation in which
'currently, abortion is illegal in 13 states'.[12] Care here refers
to the ongoing struggles for reproductive rights, which
centrally include abortion rights.

'Care Instructions' was the theme for the fifth edition of
the festival KLA ART, Kampala Contemporary Art, a
biennial project, which has been running since 2012. 'Care
Instructions' was chosen with the specific interest to invite
'artists and the general public to view cultural heritage
through the lens of care'.[13] KLA ART shows newly commissioned work, which is found through an open call. The call
asked artists to respond to questions like the following:

> What different ways of relating to each other,
> to the land and to other forms of life have been
> passed down to us through our clans, tribes, and
> communities, and can they be reformulated for now?
> Through the festival we will be questioning which
> care instructions are no longer being preserved,
> which care instructions would we hope to pass along
> to future generations and which ones we might want
> to invent anew.[14]

The festival's website shows that 'Care Instructions' perceives
of 'cultural heritage in Uganda as a series of instructions
that we have received on how we might live well'.[15] Creating
access to and reviving cultural heritage, which can provide
instructions how to care differently for the present, is necessary as 'oral tradition is breaking down due to globalisation
and rural-urban migration'.[16] The festival is understood as
'a space for artists and audiences to engage with indigenous/
local knowledge as care instructions and apply them to the
concerns of today'.[17]

From 16 January until 31 May 2024, the first edition of the
Guangzhou Design Triennial took place at the Guangdong

12. Center for
Reproductive Rights,
'After Roe Fell:
Abortion Laws by State',
www.reproductiverights.
org/maps/abortion-laws-
by-state/, accessed
1 December 2024.

13. KLA ART 2024, 'Care
Instructions', www.2024.
klaart.org/about/,
accessed 1 December
2024.

14. KLA ART 2024, 'Care
Instructions', www.2024.
klaart.org/about/,
accessed 1 December
2024.

15. KLA ART 2024, 'Care
Instructions', www.2024.
klaart.org/about/,
accessed 1 December
2024.

16. KLA ART 2024, 'Care
Instructions', www.2024.
klaart.org/about/,
accessed 1 December
2024.

17. KLA ART 2024, 'Care
Instructions', www.2024.
klaart.org/about/,
accessed 1 December
2024.

Exhibiting for
Multiple Senses

18. 'Matters of Care', Guangzhou Design Triennial 2024, www.wangnaiyi.com/Guangzhou-Design-Triennial-2024, accessed 1 December 2024.

19. Maria Puig de la Bellacasa, *Matters of Care: Speculative Ethics in More than Human Worlds*, Minneapolis, University of Minnesota Press, 2017.

20. 'Curating as an Act of Care', Guangzhou Design Triennial, 23 February 2024, www.e-flux.com/announcements/589715/curating-as-an-act-of-care/, accessed 1 December 2024.

21. Art exhibition 'The Circles of Care: Experience, Perception, Well-being and Peaceful Death', www.bacc.or.th/en/events/61526, accessed 1 December 2024.

22. Sharmila Wood, www.curatorsintl.org/about/collaborators/5772-sharmila-wood, accessed 1 December 2024.

23. 'Actions for the Earth: Art, Care & Ecology', curated by Sharmila Wood, www.curatorsintl.org/exhibitions/9836-actions-for-the-earth, accessed 1 December 2024.

Museum of Art. In the context of the Triennial's theme 'The Warm-beings', one of its exhibitions had the title 'Matters of Care'.[18] Curated by London-based Chinese curator Naiyi Wang, this exhibition used the title of theorist and scholar Maria Puig de la Bellacasa's book *Matters of Care. Speculative Ethics on More than Human Worlds*.[19] De la Bellacasa, who works at the intersections of feminist theory, care ethics, science and technology studies, and the environmental humanities, published *Matters of Care* in 2017, with the book immediately taken up not only in the contexts of reading lists assigned by university educators and theoretical inquiry across a number of different disciplines including, amongst others, sociology, philosophy, art and architecture history, and feminist studies, but also prominently in the contexts of cultural production and the visual as well as the performing arts. The aim of the exhibition 'Matters of Care', according to the exhibition announcement, which was published on e-flux, was to 'reimagine the politics and ethics of care'.[20]

In 2023, the Peaceful Death, Compassionate Communities Research and Development Foundation Thailand showed the art exhibition 'The Circles of Care. Experience, Perception, Well-Being and Peaceful Death' at Bacc–Bangkok Art and Culture Centre. The community-based exhibition focused on the 'ecosystems of care', aiming to articulate that 'intensive care, death, and bereavement is not just a medical experience'.[21]

In 2022 the travelling exhibition 'Actions for the Earth: Art, Care & Ecology' was launched by Independent Curators International and will be on tour until 2026. The exhibition was curated by Sharmila Wood, a Perth-based curator, who focuses on 'environmental, social and spatial justice'.[22] 'Actions for the Earth: Art, Care & Ecology' is comprised of eighteen artistic works that critically address coloniality and honour ancestral and Indigenous knowledge in order 'to grasp nature, health, and sustainability as intertwined'.[23] Care here is care for the earth as care for ancient beliefs, today's ruinous ecologies, and the precarious condition of human health.

From 23 September 2021 until 12 February 2022, Autograph ABP, the London-based non-profit photographic arts agency, showed the exhibition 'Care | Contagion | Community—Self & Other'. Curated by scholar of photography Renée Mussai, cultural historian Mark Sealy, and photographic artist Bindi Vora, the exhibition brought together newly commissioned works by ten UK-based artists who were invited to respond to the conditions of the Covid-19 pandemic and to 'look closely at their immediate environments'.[24] On Autograph's website we find the following paragraph that argues the meaning behind the title and the rationale of the exhibition as follows:

> Located as the symbolic bond between care and community, the word 'contagion'—its original meaning being 'together', and 'to touch'—evokes images of close contact, as well as ideas of potential exposure and transmission. […] How might we be better together as a community in the future? How to protect those who risk their lives in their commitment to care for others, working on multiple frontlines?[25]

From 1 November 2020 until 31 October 2021, State of Concept Athens, a non-profit contemporary art institution, which was founded by iLiana Fokianaki in 2013, curated an 'interdisciplinary research programme about the ethics and politics of care'.[26] Bringing together artists, cultural workers, activists, social workers, and writers, the programme included encounters, writings, and exhibitions and invited among others the Berlin-based Sickness Affinity Group, a support group by and for 'art workers and activists who are working on sickness/disability and/or are affected by sickness/disabil-ity',[27] the Melissa Network, an organization for migrant and refugee women in Greece, the Women to Women Collective/ Žene ženama, who use 'art to engage with women that were affected by war and displacement, and have found themselves living in Croatia',[28] and The Open School for Migrants in Piraeus, which 'has been active in the field of solidarity education since 2005'.[29] On their website, State of Concept explain the programme as follows:

24. Care | Contagion | Community—Self & Other, Autograph, 23 September 2021–12 February 2022, www.autograph.org.uk/exhibitions/care-contagion-community-self-and-other, accessed 1 December 2024.

25. Care | Contagion | Community—Self & Other, Autograph, 23 September 2021–12 February 2022, www.autograph.org.uk/exhibitions/care-contagion-community-self-and-other, accessed 1 December 2024.

26. State of Concept, 'The Bureau of Care', 1 November 2020–31 October 2021, www.thebureauofcare.org/about/, accessed 1 December 2024.

27. Sickness Affinity Group, www.sicknessaffinity.org, accessed 1 December 2024.

28. State of Concept, 'Encounter 3, Živi atelijer / Women to Women', www.thebureauofcare.org/2021/06/encounter-3-zivi-atelijer-women-to-women/, accessed 1 December 2024.

29. State of Concept, 'The Open School for Migrants in Piraeus', www.thebureauofcare.org/2021/03/encounter-2-the-open-school-for-migrants-in-piraeus/, accessed 1 December 2024.

Exhibiting for
Multiple Senses

30. State of Concept, 'The Bureau of Care', www.thebureauofcare. org/about/, accessed 1 December 2024.

31. Architekturzentrum Wien, 'Critical Care. Architecture and Urbanism for a Broken Planet', 25 April 2019–9 September 2020, www. azw.at/en/event/ critical-care- architektur-und- urbanismus-fuer-einen- planeten-in-der-krise/, accessed 1 December 2024.

32. Architekturzentrum Wien, 'Critical Care. Architecture for a Broken Planet', 25 April 2019–9 September 2019, www.azw.at/en/event/ critical-care- architektur-und- urbanismus-fuer-einen- planeten-in-der-krise/, accessed 1 December 2024.

The diminishing of care in all facets of human life has been one of the major effects of neoliberal austerity policies, that was made even more visible during the global pandemic of Sars-Covid19. [...] By 'leaning-in' and taking care of oneself, contemporary subjectivities of the so-called 'developed' world are tasked with the care of their overworked bodies, but are less and less interested in the well-being of bodies that are outside of the immediate realm of their family, class, working environment, neighbourhood, city, country.[30]

From 25 April 2019 until 9 September 2019, the Architekturzentrum Wien (Architecture Centre Vienna) showed the exhibition 'Critical Care. Architecture for a Broken Planet', curated by the Angelika Fitz and myself.[31] Bringing together twenty-one examples from Asia, Africa, Europe, the Caribbean, the USA and Latin America, it was our aim as architectural researchers, feminist theorists and curators to demonstrate that caring architecture and urbanism are, in fact, possible and that architecture can provide critical care by resisting the dictatorship of capital. We argued for architecture as critical care against the backdrop of climate ruination and planetary environmental destruction. On the Architekturzentrum's website Angelika Fitz and I described the project as follows:

A planet in crisis. The earth in intensive care. Man-made environmental and social catastrophes are threatening to render the planet uninhabitable. The situation is critical and, dominated by the interests of capital, architecture and urbanism are caught up in the crisis. The exhibition Critical Care shows how architecture and urbanism can contribute to repairing the future and keeping the planet and its inhabitants alive.[32]

On 20 September 2019, 'Wienwoche', an annual festival for art and activism, included in its programme 'Bitches & Witches', the curatorial project 'I Know I Care' by artist Jelena Micić. Resulting from an open working group, to which I contributed with a lecture on social reproduction and its spatial organization in the housing blocks of Red Vienna, 'I Know I Care' realized a number of care stations in a *Waschsalon* [laundry facility] at Wienerberg, one of the Red Vienna super blocks. The care stations were on view for one day, as the laundry facility is still actively used. Visitors to the exhibition included inhabitants of the Wienerberg public housing and the installations provided occasions to have conversations with inhabitants on their experiences of the invisibilization of care work. The project's interest in care was focused on reproductive labour and on the question how public housing organizes and spatializes gendered and feminized dimensions of care work. On the Wienwoche website these questions are addressed by Jelena Micić as follows:

> The reform in communal living transformed the living and working environment, but in which way did it actually emancipate and support the female labour force to challenge their social role(s)? In this sense, the notion of care will be addressed in relation to Marxist feminist perspectives, leaving space for confrontations, but also for commoning.[33]

From 15 September until 30 December 2018, the Palo Alto Art Center in California showed the exhibition 'Care and Feeding. The Art of Parenthood', curated by arts administrator Selene Foster and practicing artist and educator Andrea Antonaccio. According to Selene Foster, 'the exhibition was first conceived of when three Art Center staff members, including her, went on maternity leave around the same time'.[34] Included in the Artist Parent Index, an online database launched by Sarah Irvin, the focus of the exhibition is on how artists, who are parents, understand their situation through care and feeding. In the database of the Artist Parent Index, one finds the exhibition's curatorial statement:

> This exhibition explores the unique questions artists face, from both internal and external forces, when they become parents. It is our challenge to the once pervasive conception that artists cannot be dedicated to their creative work while raising a family.[35]

33. Jelena Micić, 'I Know I Care', 20 September 2019, www.wienwoche.org/en/archive/2019/festival-programm/projects/i-know-i-care, accessed 1 December 2024.

34. Karla Kane, 'Mom-and-pop art. Palo Alto Art Center nurtures 'The Art of Parenthood', 19 September 2018, www.paloaltoonline.com/ae/2018/09/19/mom-and-pop-art/, accessed 1 December 2024.

35. 'Care and Feeding: The Art of Parenthood', www.artistparentindex.com/items/show/391, accessed 1 December 2024.

Exhibiting for
Multiple Senses

36. 'Care and Feeding: The Art of Parenthood', www.artistparentindex. com/items/show/391, accessed 1 December 2024.

The curatorial statement also describes the mechanisms through which the art world discriminates against artists who are parents and care providers for their children.

> There are subtle ways the art world remains difficult for artists who have children. Very few residencies allow artists to bring their partners and children along, and those that do are highly competitive. These artists are often overlooked for opportunities because it is assumed they will not have the time. And the reduction in creative output that often accompanies having children can be interpreted as a failure to thrive by peers.[36]

From 21 June 2017 until 31 July 2017 the Vienna Biennial showed the public workspace Care + Repair curated by Angelika Fitz and myself for the Architekturzentrum Wien. We located Care + Repair in Vienna's largest inner-city urban transformation site proposing that new urban development should start from understanding and acknowledging the given care needs and arguing that the future is in need of repair. Rather than opening with a finished exhibition, Angelika Fitz and I curated a workspace with the working process being documented in a slowly growing exhibition. We created six teams, with each team composed of an international architect and a local person, who lives and works in Vienna and has expertise ranging from environmental to social concerns. Working in the Nordbahnhof urban development site, the six teams proposed and realized prototypes concerned with care and repair. Using a former warehouse, renamed as Nordbahnhalle, for daily public programmes, we collaborated with local organizations, NGOs and neighbours including among others the action committee Livable Nordbahnhof and the Integrationshaus, which focuses on needs-based support, legal support and psychosocial care for refugees. Care here is understood at the scale of urban development and the curatorial proposition is that of putting into practice a caring urbanism rooted in ecological and social justice accountable to environmental and social needs.

In 2016, the non-profit Instituto MESA in Sao Paulo, who seek to weave together art, culture, and society, and turn to 'the Latin roots of curatorship, curare, meaning care' to bring together 'artists, publics, researchers and context with a particular interest in the relations between art and health' launched the Art_Care project. The project was curated by art historian, educator and director of the Institute MESA Jessica Gogan and by researcher, curator and former director of the Hélio Oiticica Municipal Art Center Izabela Pucu. Interested in *Cuidado como método # 1* [Care as Method # 1], the project brought together 'researchers, artists, cultural workers, therapists, and administrators who work at the interfaces between the fields of art, health, environment, citizenship, and other forms of institutionality'.[37] Focusing on care, understood as 'a force of micropolitical action', the Art_Care project further aimed to contribute to changing the role of the artist and bringing art in meaningful conversation and collaboration with other fields. This is described as follows: 'By examining the diverse meanings, contradictions and possibilities of care, the project hopes to harness its potency as a political, ethical and aesthetic process'.

In September 2015, the Royal Academy of Fine Arts Brussels started a new Master's programme in exhibition practices under the title CARE with the aim 'to reflect and renew practices of exhibition and mediation'. Care here refers to the ways of working seen as necessary for making exhibitions and for processes of mediation:

> It is also a matter of looking and listening, as in an echo of the title of the programme, which invites us to 'take care'. Paying attention to the works, the artists, the qualities of places, the audiences, the installation and all the stages which structure the exhibition and make it exist. Also inventing oneself through singular projects which will take care to displace definitions.[38]

Here, care is not addressed as a thematic concern in curatorial work or as the specific subject matter for future exhibitions, but rather as an ethical imperative and a modus operandi, a method for working when making and mediating

37. Instituto Mesa, Art_Care Project, www.institutomesa.org/projects/art_care-project/?lang=en, accessed 1 December 2024.

38. CARE Master's programme in exhibition practices, www.centrale.brussels/en/care/, accessed 1 December 2024.

39. See: Elke Krasny, Sophie Lingg et al: *Radicalizing Care. Feminist and Queer Activism in Curating*, London, Sternberg Press, Publication Series of the Academy of Fine Arts Vienna, 2019; Elke Krasny and Lara Perry, *Curating with Care*, London, Routledge, 2023.

Exhibiting for Multiple Senses

exhibitions. Care then defines how one should work with artists, with artworks, with spaces, with audiences, and, perhaps, above all, throughout the entire process of all the invisible labours that are actually required for making an exhibition.

It seems that we have come full circle, between the very general approach to care as needed for exhibition making as proposed by the CARE master programme exhibition practices that was launched in Brussels in 2015 and the 2025 exhibition 'Tender Loving Care' in Boston, which posits that all creation of and looking at works of art are acts of care. While such a general view that care is required in exhibition practices, and that making art and engaging with art can be viewed as acts of care is interesting, my own inquiry focuses much more at what happens in the space between curating and care, when contemporary curators take care as their subject matter and aim to make contributions to social and environmental change, to conditions of health and education through the lens of care in relation to the crisis-ridden present.

Why 'Curated' in Consumer Capitalism? Why 'Care' in Curating?

In conclusion, I will share some feminist speculations on the meanings of 'curated' in consumer capitalism and the turn to 'care' in contemporary curating. I call these reflections speculations as, like all forms of critical inquiry and theorization, the evidence laid out can, could, and should always be open to more than one interpretation, and, of course, to interpretations beyond one individual view. This does not mean that speculations lack evidence. Quite the contrary. Feminist speculations, at least in ways in which I understand and practice feminist speculating as contributing to socio-natural-cultural theory, start from gathering evidence. In the context of this essay, the evidence was gathered by following the word 'curated' in consumer capitalism and the word 'care' in curating, more specifically through the titles chosen by contemporary curators for their exhibitions and programmes. Contemporary consumer capitalism uses the word 'curated' to speak of the work that has gone into sourcing and selecting products, to address the care given and attention being paid to the individual needs of customers in the contexts of services. While critical theorists of exhibition and museum practices have, for decades now, analysed how curating is historically implicated in the production of the master's knowledge, culturalization of colonial imperial patriarchal capitalism and how hegemonic curating, until today, functions as a form of gatekeeping, contemporary consumer capitalism embraces 'curated' precisely because of the associations with mastery. Knowledge, selection, refinement, taste, style—all these values are connected to the term 'curated' when applied to vintage, cosmetics, or records. These values are then bestowed on those who buy such 'curated'—that is selected and thus highly selective and individualized—products. While mass consumption of the past spoke to the availability of products for everyone, 'curated' products speak to elitism that can be purchased and therefore becomes accessible to many, while at the same time remaining distinct, individualized, and not available to the masses. 'Curated' thus promises, and ultimately sells, distinction by choices with the labour of selecting and choosing performed by those who curate products they then sell. While the word 'curated' effortlessly connects the mastery of knowledge to selected products, that is one knows why one is made to want or desire, and ultimately buy and own, something, 'curated' also speaks to dimensions of care in relation to service capitalism. When airlines communicate to their customers that they provide them curated seats or curated travel experiences, when hotels speak of curated views, when wellness providers speak of curated offerings, they not only appeal to the informed choices their customers supposedly made when choosing their services, but also to the individualized care and attention that has gone into creating and making these services available. Ultimately, 'curated' sells knowledge, taste refinement, and care. When spending money on 'curated' products and services, customers buy the feeling that they have made the right choice and invested in optimal self-care. Such is the culturalization of consumer capitalism that is articulated in the word 'curated'.

     While consumer capitalism values the notions of 'curated' as knowledgeable and careful selection, contemporary

ETHICS OF CARE

Exhibiting for
Multiple Senses

curators, in particular also anti-colonial, feminist, queer feminist and environmentally conscious and critical curators, have turned to the original meaning of curating, which is to care and to heal.[39] With curators producing cultural content and contributing to public discourse through exhibitions and other formats and platforms, the turn to care was articulated over the last decade in a large number of exhibitions. Looking back at a decade of 'care' in exhibitions, as I have done in this text, brings to the fore that taken together these exhibitions make a very wide range of different understandings of care legible and thus contribute to making different meanings held by care public. I continue to be very interested in, and impressed by, the ways in which curating has contributed to understanding the complexities, contradictions, and conflicts around care over the last ten years. And I am most appreciative of projects that create conversations, exchanges, and sometimes lasting collaborations beyond the art world, including, amongst others, the contexts of care labour struggles, citizenship activism and work with refugees, climate activism, health, parenting, or reproductive justice. Nonetheless, I keep asking myself how—and sometimes I even dare to ask if—this newly-won visibility of care through curating, which can also be understood as a culturalization of care, can and will contribute in deeper and more profound ways to socio-environmental transformation. Sometimes I have the nagging feeling that this visibility of care through curating is a form of cultural containment: that concerns and conflicts around care are addressed culturally, but not economically, infrastructurally, and politically. Most of the time, though, I feel that the turn to care in curating is more than a cultural hype and that continued engagement with care in the broadest sense possible will make some meaningful contributions to changing the conditions of care.

Orientation Inwards

A wavy line pattern covers the entire background of this page. The handwritten title is placed upside down at the bottom, to emphasize a change of viewpoint. In the bottom-left corner there is a hurricane warning flag consisting of two separate squares attached to the flag pole, each square has a smaller black square on it. On the top right there is a historical image of the semaphore alphabet, a signalling system using hand-held flags to represent letters and numbers. Below that image is a beanbag, or a kind of fluffy chair with a grass pattern on it. Above the flag, left to the semaphore image, is a miniature spongy tree. Nature as a stimulus, but only in the controlled environment of your own bedroom.

How do you sense when you're in danger? What signals does your body give off? Can your sensory perception be misleading?

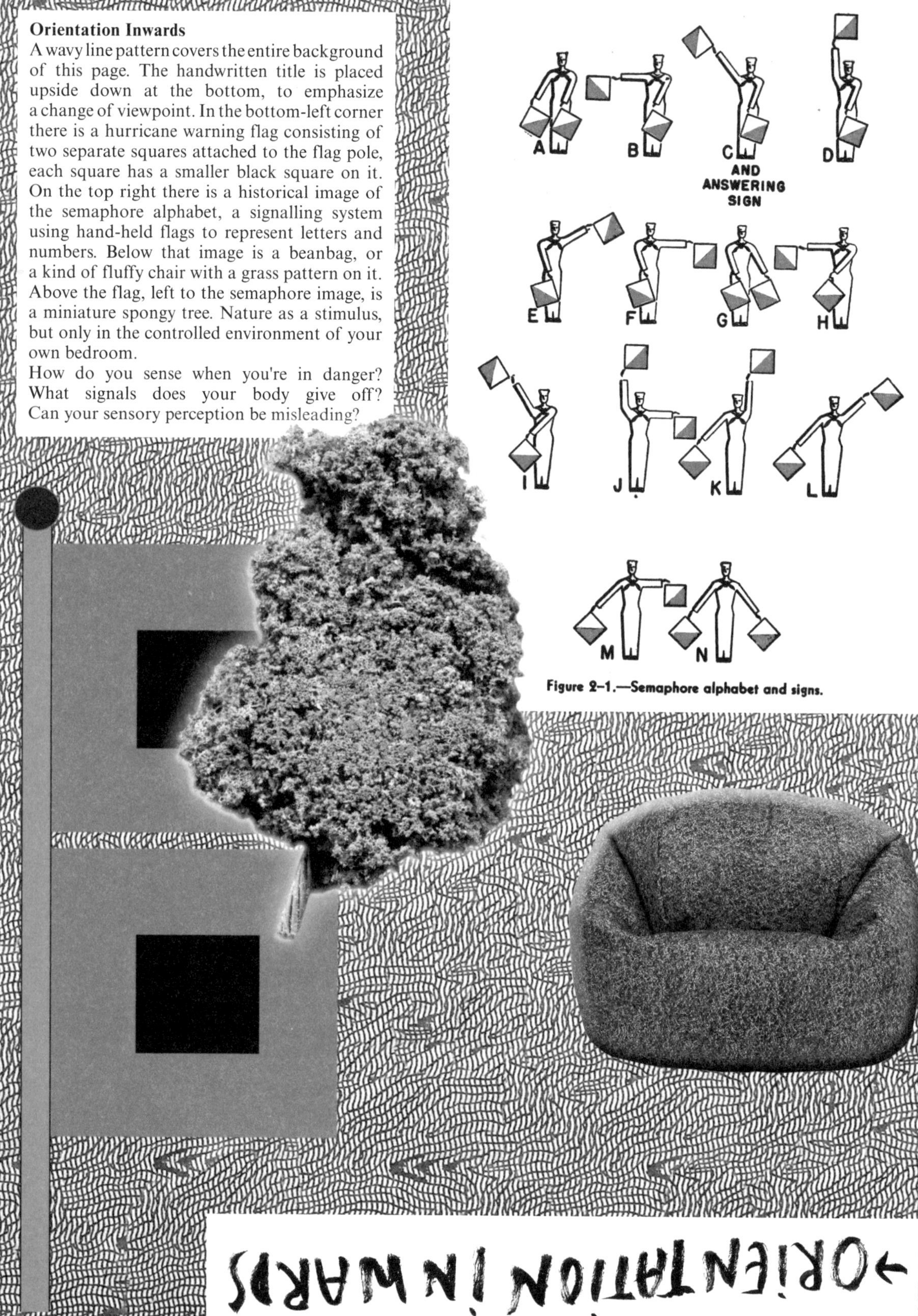

Figure 2-1.—Semaphore alphabet and signs.

VIBRAFUSIONLAB
A Centre for Reimagining Tactile Sensory Experiences

David Bobier

VibraFusionLab (VFL), founded in 2012, is an internationally renowned disabled-led creative research and development project that supports accessibility in art practices and art experiences. This has led us to working in the visual arts, music, sound art, theatre, dance, burlesque, circus arts, and performance with a particular focus on d/Deaf and disabled artists and audiences.

Our role is (as) facilitator and in service to those we collaborate with. We support the ideas, the expertise, and the individual capacities of our artists and arts organizations and facilitate a collaborative process that is supportive to our best capabilities.

VibraFusionLab specializes in inclusive technologies that furthers the desire of combining alternative language, communication, and emotional strategies and experiences into artistic practice and offers new and unique approaches for those with diverse abilities. Breaking down social, intellectual, emotional, and physical barriers is essential toward offering greater diversity and exchange of artistic experiences for both artist and audience. In exploring sensory transformation from one modality to another with particular emphasis on the tactile and sound visualization as forms of creative expression, it prompts consideration of multiple senses as channels of communication and exchange.

VibraFusionLab: the Backstory

On 5 May 2009, I heard of an event that was happening in a pub called Clintons Tavern on Bloor Street in Toronto, Ontario. It was promoted as the first ever concert for the deaf and was presented by the Centre for Learning Technology and the Science of Music, Auditory Research and Technology Lab through what was then Ryerson University. The university is now called Toronto Metropolitan University. The Centre for Learning Technology has also changed its name to Inclusive Media and Design Centre (IMDC).

This caught my interest as some years earlier, we had adopted two Deaf children. As our only children, we devoted much of our time to raising them in a culturally Deaf way by adapting to their cultural needs, such as learning American Sign Language, schools for the Deaf education and integrating them into the Deaf community by attending as many Deaf functions as possible.

With this in mind, I felt this concert was a must to attend. The promotional material advertised bands, in fact a 'cornucopia' of local bands, and a DJ. There was open captioning and sign language interpreters and music visualization. And there were three 'Emoti-Chair' prototype chairs.

Three years earlier the research team at Ryerson led by Dr Deborah Fels began experimenting with new ways of interpreting sound with the idea of placing chairs in the cinema for Deaf people to experience the sound as vibration. The research took on the name of the Emoti-Chair project. During the years leading up to the concert they researched the way nerves in the skin react to touch and uncovered how tactile vibrations are perceived by the brain, leading to understanding ways of communicating emotions inherent in musical notes and vibration.

Arriving at the Tavern, kids in tow, we experienced a mix of people, some signing and some talking. Interpreters were moving from one chair to another helping to facilitate communication. Taking the opportunity to impress, local bands were doing their best to attract attention while much of the audience, some impatiently and most with apprehensive excitement, were waiting in line to have their turn with the chairs.

Finally, it was my turn. It was a slumpy kind of

object covered in black canvas, something like a canvas deckchair but more slumpy. The person standing next to it explained that the chair was designed with two parallel systems of eight 'voice coils' running from the shoulder to the thighs using the human cochlea as a model for how to present vibrations to the skin. The voice coils, designed for both vibration and sound, moved up and down the parallel chain in response to the live music. Sitting in the chair and watching the band play, I was instantaneously hearing and feeling their voices and the music on my back and legs, or at least some of it. By that I mean there seemed to be gaps of sound and vibration if their voices went too high or their instruments reached a certain pitch. I learned later that the cells in our skin, unlike our cochlea, have a greater limitation for receiving and transmitting tactile frequencies to the brain. These cells embrace low frequencies, and they get very excited about giving us the capacity for feeling music in a frequency range that approximates 20Hz to 500Hz, remarkably less than what someone with excellent hearing can experience as sound, which can be up to 20,000Hz. While the chair was reasonably comfortable, it was low and difficult to get out of. It occurred to me at the time that while these chairs were fine for the non-disabled body they were limiting in access for some.

I left with a positive impression and within days I was contacting Dr Fels to see about visiting their research lab and getting another feel of the 'vibrating chair'. Dr Fels' response was quick and affirming.

And I could say the rest is history; for in fact, it was the beginning of something I had no way of imagining or thinking possible. Over the next couple of years, I made repeated trips to Toronto to explore their research more and to get to know who all these illustrious people were that were so committed to creating a chair that vibrates to music. As time went on, my own mind was working in future directions. I convinced the team that it would be interesting if we could trot some of these chairs out into the wilds of Toronto for a stint at the Toronto International Deaf Film and Arts Festival (TIDFAF) that was taking place at the time. For two days we hosted five Deaf filmmakers, oriented them to the chairs and invited them to create sound compositions

by feeling the vibrations through the chair. The filmmakers
were exuberant, and the chairs were happy. We followed this
refreshing outing of the chairs with a further-afield workshop
in London, a couple of hundred kilometres down the
road, and a dozen or so invited artists from the area. More
excitement and creativity ensued, and my future ideas were
becoming more crystallized. I was now ready to test them on
Dr Fels and the team back in the confines of academia. What
would happen if this technology and the chairs in tow could
be in a public space and available for practicing artists from
the community? What if we could invite d/Deaf and disabled
artists to experiment, to play, to share ideas, to create with
this technology? What if we could apply for arts grants to pay
these artists, so often marginalized by incapacity and poverty
through lived experiences to spend time in the Lab? What if
we could offer them a fully accessible way of creating with
sound/music, vibration, sound visualization, and motion
sensors?

      With these ideas in mind, I decided to bring them to
the attention of Dr Fels. To her insightful and astute credit,
she responded with enthusiasm and the suggestion that she
might apply for an inhouse Social Science and Humanities
Research Council grant to help establish such a place;
insightful and astute, but also daring. It seemed entirely
unlikely that we would be successful in receiving funds
to establish something outside of the university confines.
Universities love keeping control of such endeavours and
harbouring them within their hallowed grounds. To let three
years of funding slip out to the whims of artists seemed
highly improbable. But much to my surprise, word came
through that our proposal had been approved and the dream
of VibraFusionLab was being realized.

      In addition to Dr Fels and several other research
rock stars, one of the illustrious people on the Emoti-Chair
team was Maria Karam who was about to become Dr Maria
Karam through her own research working on this project.
I had earlier included her in my musings of establishing a
creative space for d/Deaf and disabled artists. With the soul
of a creative and the mind of an entrepreneur she could also
see the value in expanding the research into more practical
uses and letting the technology 'out of the barn' so to speak.

So, with three years of operational funding, a van
full of vibrotactile systems and a head full of magical notions
we filled the space and opened the doors of VFL in London,
Ontario. The rented space was large and on two levels. The
entrance level was wheelchair accessible, the second level
three steps up. The story was that it had been a brothel in a
previous life with smaller rooms upstairs. More recently it
had been a popular LP music shop called Dr. Disc.

VibraFusionLab had arrived at a time when the
beginnings of a somewhat consolidated emerging d/Deaf
and disabled arts movement were happening in Canada.
Additional funding from the Canada Council for the Arts
and Ontario Arts Council was soon acquired to run a
programme that mirrored my aspirations for the space. With
this money I could invite artists to come, and I could pay
them an honorarium and cover their travel, accommodation
and per diem costs. I could get Access funds to pay for interpreters. It was a dream realized!

In the early days Dr Karam came often to the Lab
to support artists in devising ways of using the technology,
regaling them with stories from her ongoing research days at
Ryerson and sharing wine in social gatherings in the evenings
with frequent visitors from the London arts community.
Musicians became the bulk of these visitors, mostly
apprehensive and unfamiliar with the notion of accessible
technology but with curious minds and requests for needing

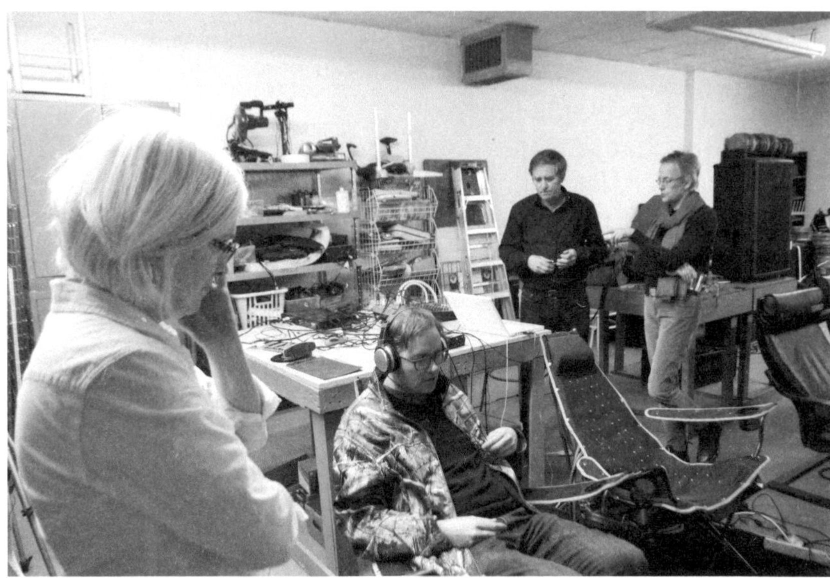
VibraFusionLab at Clarence Street, London, Ontario. Testing vibrotactile chairs.
Photo: David Bobier.

a place to play their music. The underground music scene in London at the time had a vital and creative pulse but with few places to exercise it. By the second year, the Clarence Street location had become a spark for alternative music with concerts happening one or two nights a week and occasionally three. In addition to the vibrations of the chairs there was another vibe happening.

Rarely did I charge rent for these events. For special occasions we would get a licence to sell wine and beer to make a small profit. I felt uncomfortable charging these youthful aspiring musicians when all they wanted to do was express themselves to their friends and peers through music. It was a venue for young adult angst and creative passion and outspoken desire, and I was fine with that. Mature bands came through and we had seasoned musicians and innovative composers, and new media sound artists as well. We had open-studio days when all varieties of people came in and we had guests who openly talked about their lives with synesthesia and cerebral palsy and autism and how vibration from the chairs affected them.

Over the three-year period our d/Deaf, disabled and able-bodied guests and experimental performers numbered in the hundreds. We partnered with a homeless support organization and Orchestra London, providing a number of vibrotactile chairs for a Christmas Concert fundraiser. We hosted live theatre productions for London Fringe. We opened the space for three nights of performances over two years for the Grickle Grass Music Festival. VibraFusionLab was establishing a name for itself as an alternative music venue and experimental space for accessible technology research and development.

But change is inevitable and the three-year funding through the SSHRC grant ran out. It was evident that the Lab had to shift to a different way of being while at the same time I wanted to understand what was happening in the UK around d/Deaf and disability arts. I knew that the rise of d/Deaf and disability arts in the UK in the 1980s came out of a broader political movement. Anti-discrimination legislation was finally achieved when the Disability Discrimination Act was passed in Parliament in 1995, but not before much campaigning by disabled people in the 1990s. I wanted to

Exhibiting for
Multiple Senses

meet these artists, see how d/Deaf and disabled arts organizations in the UK evolved out of this period and what it was like for them now.

I was successful in receiving grants from the Canada Council for the Arts to travel to the UK and Ireland. I connected with artists and arts organizations over a two-year period that I had researched prior to my travels. I also attended d/Deaf and disability festivals, such as the Bristol Festival, Edinburgh Festival's British Showcase, and the Unlimited Festival. The Unlimited Festival is held in the Southbank of London every two years and is the premier international multi-artform festival showcasing outstanding dance, performance, comedy, music, poetry, and visual art by d/Deaf and disabled artists. This was the most amazing opportunity for seeing a real cross-section of what was current in Deaf and disability arts and an inspiration for what is possible. It was a testament to the remarkable talents and capacity for innovation from a demographic population that is so often misunderstood and dismissed as incapable and unworthy.

In highlighting a few of the projects VibraFusionLab has initiated or partnered in, I will begin with 'Bodies In Translation: Activist Art, Technology, and Access to Life (BIT)', co-led by Dr Carla Rice (Canada Research Chair in Care, Gender, and Relationships, University of Guelph) and Dr Eliza Chandler (Director of the Office of Social Innovation, Toronto Metropolitan University), a leading-edge seven-year artistic creation research, technological innovation, and critical inquiry project. In 2018, VFL collaborated in an exchange project with Together 2012 (London, UK), sponsored by British Council Canada. In 2020 we began an ongoing national programme called Sync Canada led by UK-based disabled leaders Sarah Pickthall and Jo Verrent, combining leadership theory with one-to-one coaching techniques to develop d/Deaf, disabled and neurodivergent leadership in arts and culture. Other national partnerships in which we designed a range of accessible devices for both artists and audiences have included the National Access Arts Centre with disabled burlesque performers; continued collaboration with integrated dance organization Propeller Dance; double-leg amputee circus aerialist Erin Ball

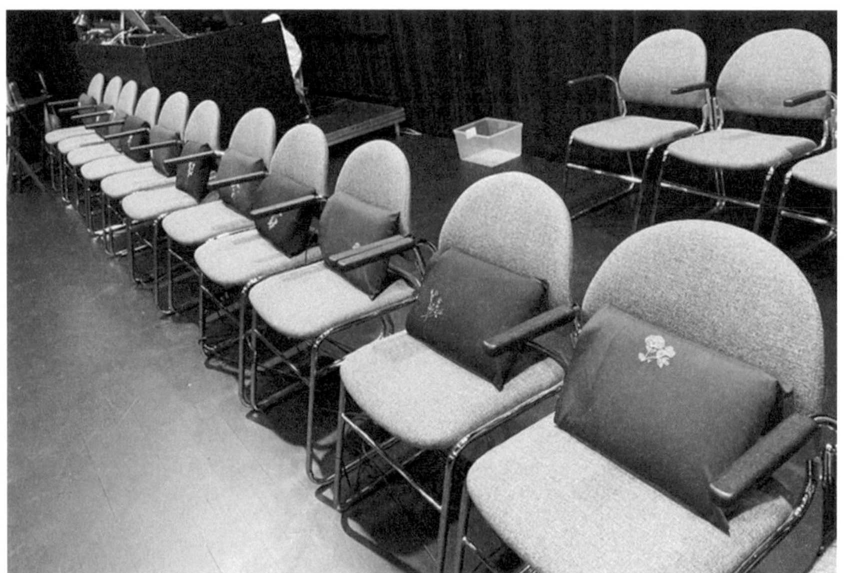

Installation with vibrotactile pillows for audience members, theatre performance
Je ne vais pas inonder la mer, by choreographer and dancer Sonia Bustos,
MAI (Montreal, arts interculturels), Montreal, Quebec, Canada, 2024.
Photo: David Bobier.

exploring motion sensors to control sound, vibration, and light; and partnering in a project called Carbon Movements in which five cm of black rice covering an entire stage was activated by motors in response to the movement of Deaf performer Connor Yuzwenko-Martin. VibraFusionLab has also worked with a number of theatres across Canada in providing specialized vibrotactile pillows for audience and performers to experience sound as vibration offering a more inclusive and accessible experience.

During this time in Canada there was renewed excitement with both the Canada Council and the Ontario Arts Council developing new streams of funding to support the d/Deaf and disability arts. Artists representing these communities were beginning to get support for their work and arts organizations were slowly forming, created and driven by members of these communities. At the same time VibraFusionLab was continuing to gain recognition and was functioning essentially as a mobile Lab, traveling to wherever we were invited to present or collaborate. With the new energy that was bubbling up in various parts of Canada we

Exhibiting for
Multiple Senses

were starting to receive more invitations at home as well.

However, this increasing interest in the work of the Lab led to new pressures on the technology resulting from the unique needs and ambitions of those we were working with. Adaptability of the technology for our collaborators was taking me outside of my capacities as I had lived my formative years in analogue production. I reached out to media artist and electronics engineer Jim Ruxton in the hopes that he would be interested in addressing these challenges. I met Jim a few years prior when we did a presentation on the early work of VibrafusionLab at the Subtle Technologies Festival in Toronto which he founded fifteen years previously. Jim graciously accepted my pleas for support and to this day, he continues to be my technical partner and the one who continues to innovate our specialized technology.

On 23 January 2020, Wuhan, China—a city of 11 million people—was placed under lockdown due to the 2019 Coronavirus outbreak. Two days later the first Covid-19 case in Canada was reported. On 30 January 2020, the World Health Organization (WHO) declared this novel coronavirus outbreak a public emergency of international concern. A few weeks later, on 11 March 2020, it declared Covid-19 a pandemic. The world was in lockdown!

Still without a permanent location to situate the Lab, Jim and I retreated into our respective studios, I to our converted school portable at home and he to his basement. The vibrotactile pillows that I had started creating from earlier Karam prototypes had been developing a bit of a popularity pre-Covid with the occasional sale order and temporary theatre placement. However, with new health regulations they no longer could be shared amongst people. They also required an additional mini-amp to operate them, adding to costs around rental and sales. We shifted our thinking to creating a vibrotactile device that was small, that would fit in a hand, and that was developed cheaply enough to be available for purchase by most people.

Of importance here is to explain an imperative of VibraFusionLab. Our artists, our audience, our 'family members', and those that we strive to connect with are of the d/Deaf and disabled demographic. As marginalized communities with often complex needs they tend to more typically

fall into a lower income stratum. This is always foremost
on our minds in determining any programming or ways of
considering support when working with these communities.
Is it within their income capacity? Can this device or system
be adjusted to fit all body types? Is it easily transportable? Is
it easy to hold or control? Are we embracing and facilitating
the needs and capabilities of as broad a demographic as
possible? Are we true to our initial guiding principles?

    With our new focus on developing a handheld
vibrotactile device, we enlisted a 3D design specialist Rod
Strickland to come up with a design that was comfortable
to hold in one hand and that would house the technology
required of a vibrotactile system—a transducer, a mini-amp
board with volume control, charging port, an outport pillow
connector and a rechargeable lithium battery. After several
3D printed tests, he came up with a design he called the
'potato' for reasons obvious from its shape. While it satisfied
our initial criteria, we were not happy with the printed material. We wanted a more environmentally sensitive material if
we were ever thinking of marketing it and we did not have the
finances nor access to a CNC machine if we wanted to test
a type of wood. The world was also slowly pulling itself out
from the depths of the pandemic and for the time being the
handheld prototype was put on the sideline and the popular
pillow became an option again.

    Before reviewing the period between 2022 and 2023,
I want to step back in time for a minute to recall a collaboration with Deaf UK-based dancer and choreographer Chisato
Minamimura. You will understand this momentarily as it is
a precursor to something we are finalizing as I write this. For
her production 'Scored In Silence' she invited us to design a
cabling system to supply individual vibrotactile devices for
theatre seating. For this we acquired a commercially available
device called the Woojer belt designed primarily for the
gaming industry. The new versatile cabling system allowed
us to install multitudes of these belts in a theatre, offering
additional access to the vibration of the sound production
to anyone, but targeted primarily to those with hearing loss.
We currently have the capacity to install 125 of these devices
for theatres anywhere in the world. For 'Scored In Silence',
Ruxton also designed a wireless vibrotactile system that

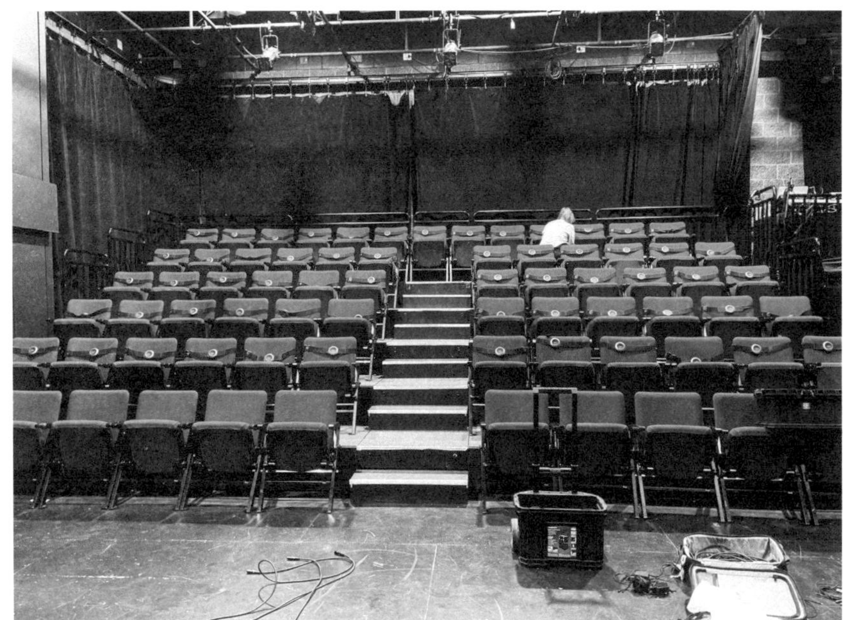

Installation with vibrotactile 'Woojer' belts for audience members, theatre performance Catfish by Alley Theatre, Cultch Theatre, Vancouver, British Columbia, Canada, 2023. Photo: David Bobier.

was placed in a small pocket on the back of Minamimura's costume so she could have added access to her own sound cues. This production was presented in Toronto and Hamilton, Ontario, in Canada, in Manchester, Brighton, Edinburgh in the United Kingdom, and elsewhere.

As restrictions lessened to occasional masking requirements, the belts again became a popular device. Smaller, more experimental theatres were awakened and responsive to the voices of those increasingly disenfranchised by the impacts of Covid and to artists gaining a breath of equity and hint of influence through the increased funding in Canada prioritizing the d/Deaf and disabled.

Was it the beginning of something more representative of equality? Was it possible that the canons of art were slowly dismantling; the doors opening ever so slightly to those forever discounted by the hierarchies of colonialism and capitalism? Could it be that worth, and important, and original might become terms that could be used to describe the emergence of artistic creativity from such a subverted place of existence?

With requests from theatres across the country I
travelled with suitcases full of Woojer belts, pillows, cables,
splitter boxes, tools, repair kits, and various other last-minute
thoughts from Halifax to Ottawa, Montreal to Toronto,
Hamilton to Edmonton, Kingston to Calgary to Vancouver,
with brief stints at home in between. It was now well into
2014, and other things were afoot that would change the fate
of VibraFusionLab once again.

Over several years we had collaborated on the odd
project with a not-for-profit organization in Hamilton,
Ontario called Centre [3] for Artistic and Social Practice. The
opportunity came up to partner with them on a renovated
factory space that would give us ample space to launch an
artist residency programme again and share our combined
studio resources. With much excitement we established
ourselves and dreamed of new possibilities only to have the
building sold out from under us within the year. The result
of this was to relocate to a smaller yet fully accessible space
in the downtown core of the city and in the proximity of
galleries and trendy restaurants.

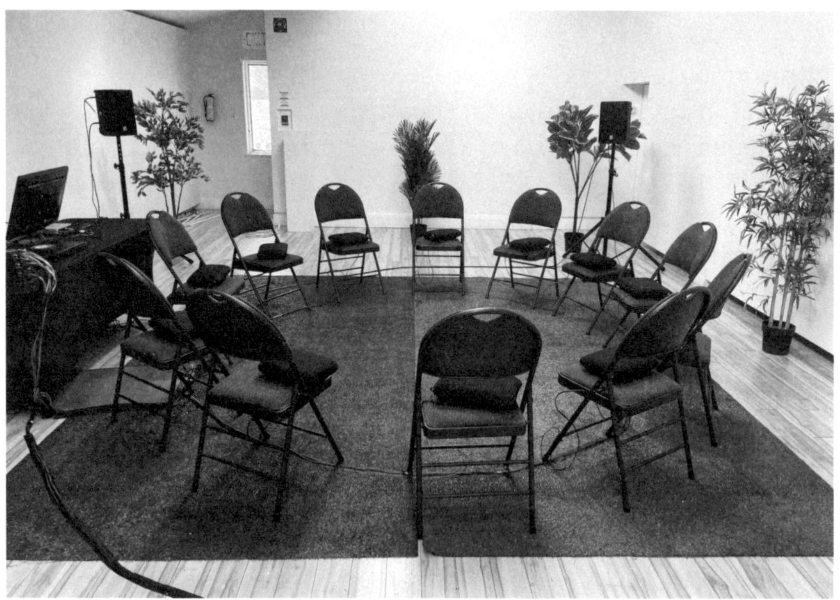

Leon Louder in partnership with VibraFusionLab, *Montreal Insectarium*, multi-day
installation including a sound composition from insect sounds channelled into
vibrotactile pillows offering an experience of hearing and feeling the insect
sounds, Music Gallery, Toronto, Canada, 2024. Photo: David Bobier.

VibraFusionLab: the Here and Now

We now have the capacity for continuing our research in further developing our specialized vibrotactile systems and accessible technologies with our ongoing emphasis on providing this research for the d/Deaf and disabled communities. It is home to our ongoing development of a wireless pillow and other wearable systems. It is also where our Haptic Voices project has happily found a place until it ventures off again in the new year.

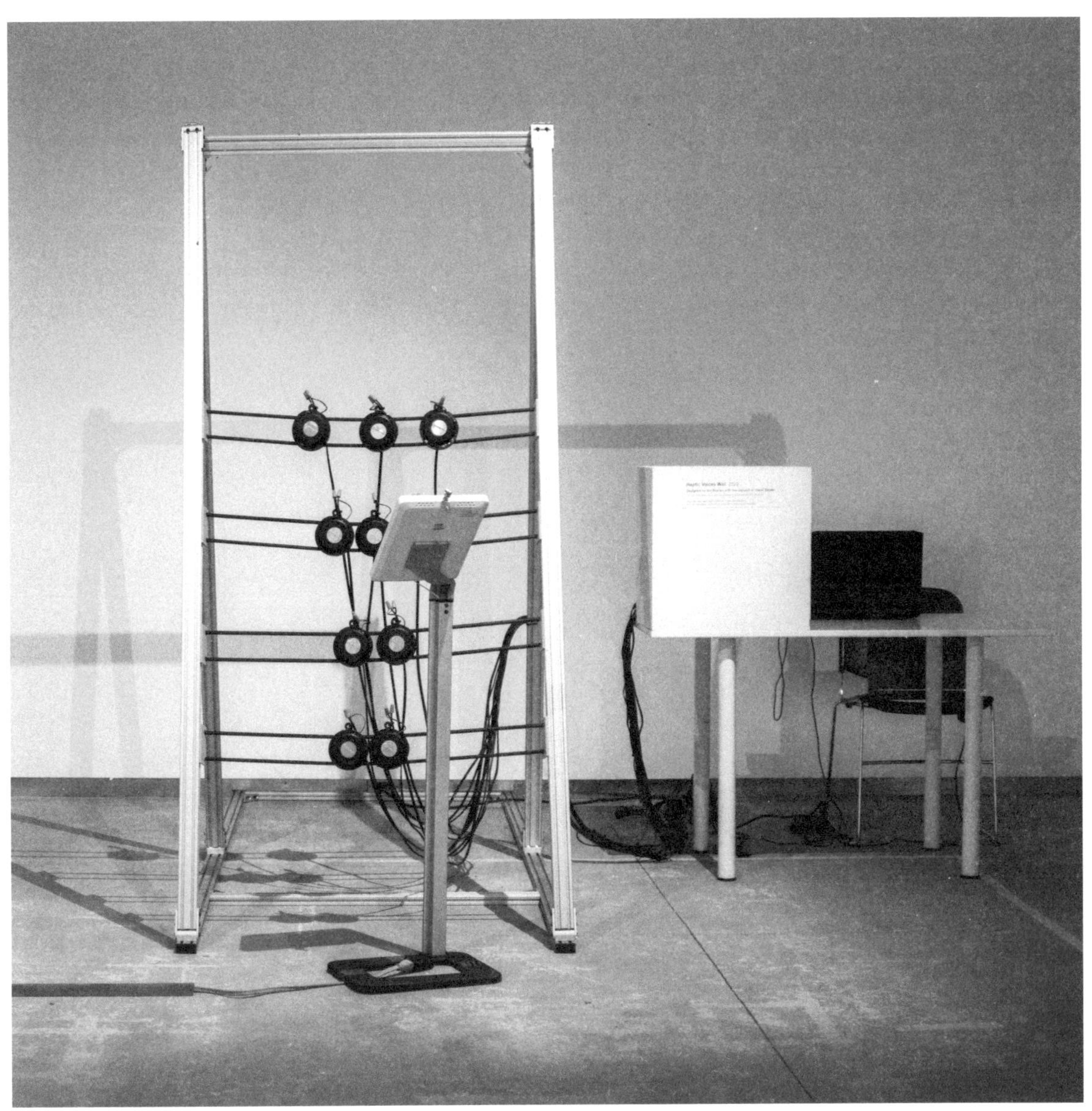

Jim Ruxton, *Haptic Voices*, installation, 2023, exhibition view, InterAccess, Toronto, Ontario, Canada, 2023.
Photo: David Bobier.

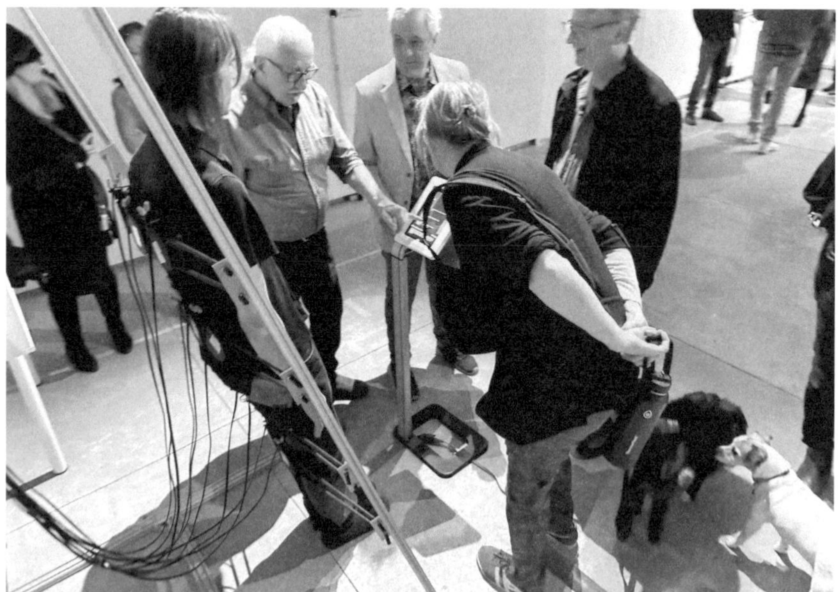

Jim Ruxton. *Haptic Voices*, installation, 2023, exhibition view, InterAccess, Toronto, Ontario, Canada, 2023. Photo: Leslie Putnam.

Haptic Voices is an interactive hybrid-online art installation. It works by having audio information, such as voice, music, or sound effects transformed into vibrations, allowing visitors to feel the music or sound through their haptic senses. They do this through a large-scale ten channel vibrotactile wall. A channel of sound refers to a specific path or route through which audio information (sound) is transmitted. In this case we have the potential for ten independent streams of sound signals.

Visitors are invited to stand against the wall to experience vibrations that are controlled by online participants who can chant, hum, and vocalize into the microphones on their computers as the sound is played through the vibrotactile transducers in the wall in real time. Online participants can control the position and location of the vibrations, manipulating through intensity and frequency components of the voice, or through the interface controlled by the participants' mouse. With a camera in the gallery facing the haptic wall, online participants can view how they are interacting with participants in the gallery. VibraFusionLab had not previously engaged with an online audience, marking this

Exhibiting for
Multiple Senses

major installation the first of its kind, transporting global 'voices' into an immersive tactile body experience. To date VFL has commissioned five sound compositions, designed explicitly for the vibrotactile experience.

Since inhabiting this new space, we recently hosted eight multidisciplinary artists from across Canada for three-week periods; three Deaf, three disabled, one indigenous, and one able-bodied, and there are lots more partnerships on the horizon.

VibraFusionLab: Future Forward

Imagining beyond the 'normal' in art making and art experiencing we question mainstream paradigms by asking 'who are missing as artists, who are missing as audience'. By emphasizing the importance of considering access as one of the starting points of creation we also emphasize the notion and relevance of 'access aesthetics' or simply 'integrated access'—the understanding that accessibility practices both remove barriers and contribute to the creative vocabulary of the work. Operating across disability culture and ethics of accessibility VibraFusionLab's work has been referred to as 'slow technology' by disabled Associate Professor Eliza Chandler. Lars Hallnäs, a researcher of slow technology, refers to it as a design philosophy that aims to create technologies that are good, clean, fair, and that support reflection and meaningful experiences with technology in everyday life.

VibraFusionLab's study of vibration as access to sound and music is still as much an idea as it is a space for research and development. The potential in considering vibration as a language of sharing experiences and as a means of communication feels limitless but worthy of our efforts. The quote 'Everything in life is vibration', attributed to Albert Einstein suggests that everything in the universe has a vibration, including thoughts, emotions, physical objects, and the energy that surrounds us. Who better to base one's motivations and creative endeavours on!

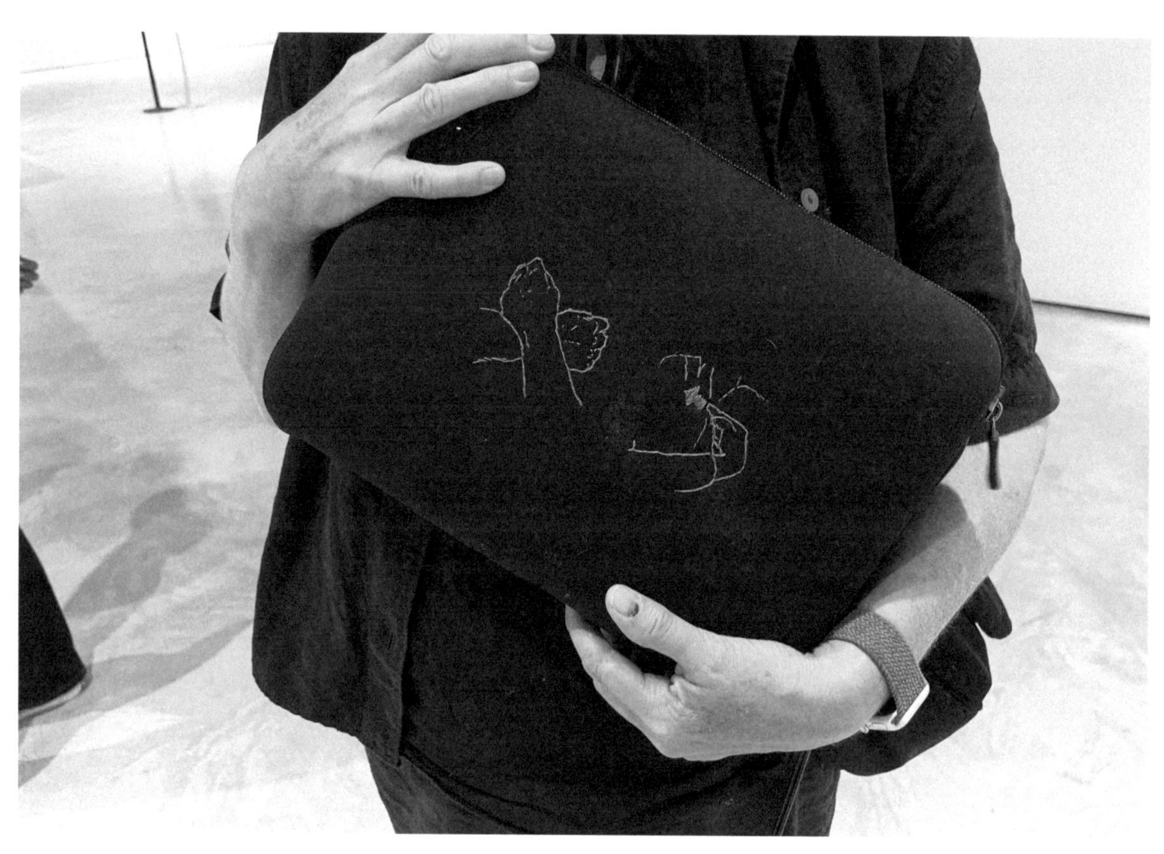

David Bobier, *Love Me*, 2024, detail view of installation 'Love Languages', Art Windsor-Essex, Windsor, Ontario, Canada. embroidery (American Sign Language for 'Love Me'): Leslie Putnam, curator: Julie Rae Tucker. Photo: David Bobier.

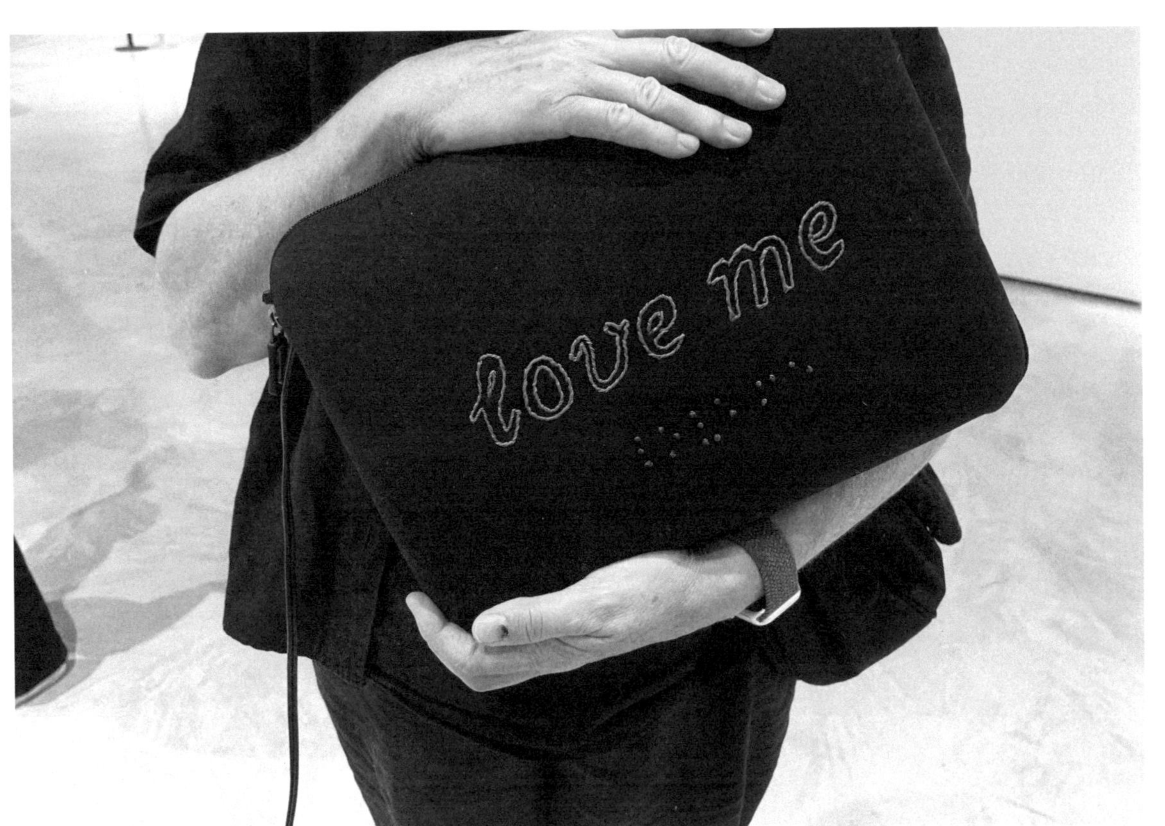

David Bobier

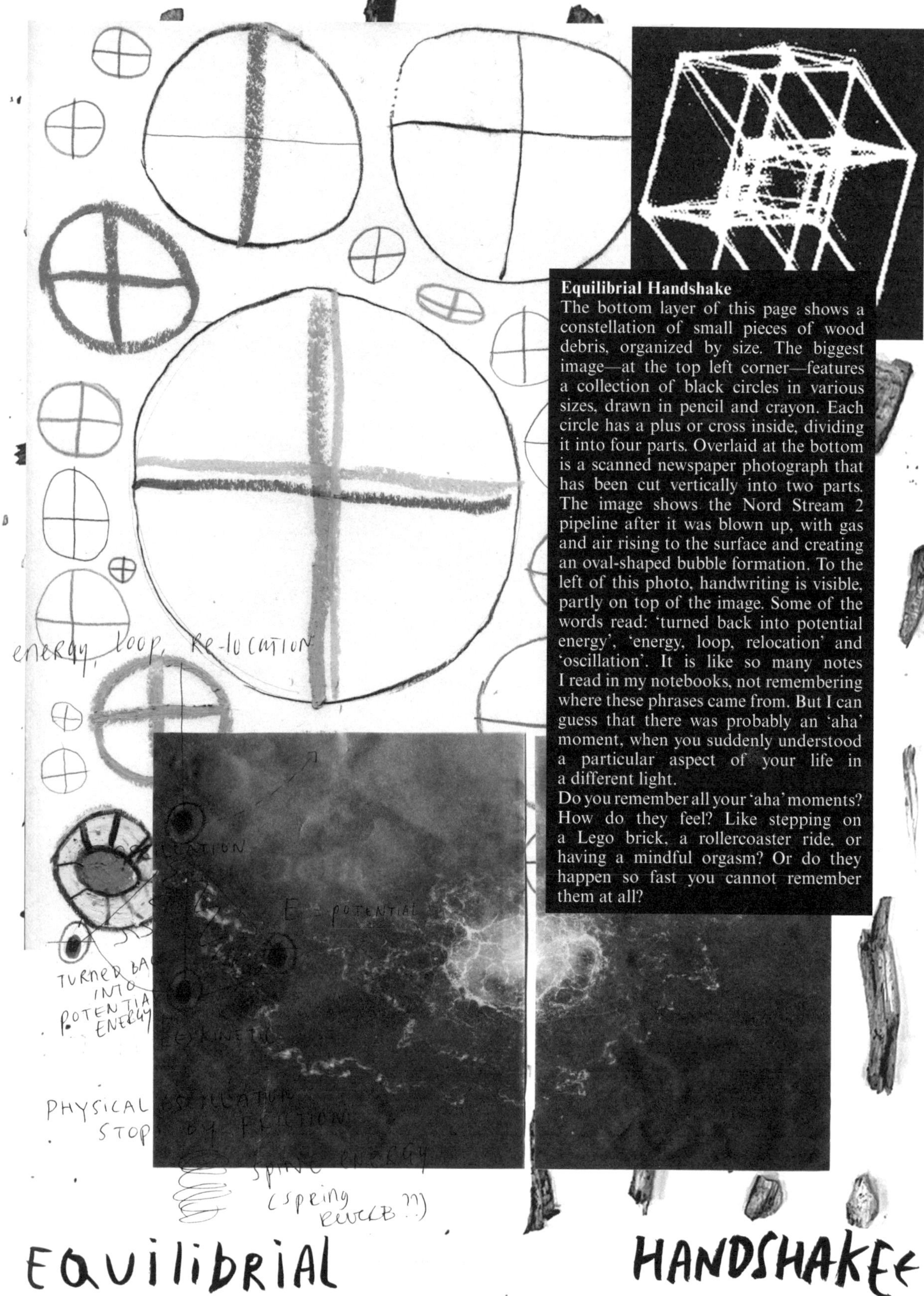

Equilibrial Handshake

The bottom layer of this page shows a constellation of small pieces of wood debris, organized by size. The biggest image—at the top left corner—features a collection of black circles in various sizes, drawn in pencil and crayon. Each circle has a plus or cross inside, dividing it into four parts. Overlaid at the bottom is a scanned newspaper photograph that has been cut vertically into two parts. The image shows the Nord Stream 2 pipeline after it was blown up, with gas and air rising to the surface and creating an oval-shaped bubble formation. To the left of this photo, handwriting is visible, partly on top of the image. Some of the words read: 'turned back into potential energy', 'energy, loop, relocation' and 'oscillation'. It is like so many notes I read in my notebooks, not remembering where these phrases came from. But I can guess that there was probably an 'aha' moment, when you suddenly understood a particular aspect of your life in a different light.

Do you remember all your 'aha' moments? How do they feel? Like stepping on a Lego brick, a rollercoaster ride, or having a mindful orgasm? Or do they happen so fast you cannot remember them at all?

ON TACTILE ARCHITECTURE, FROM VIBRORAISED RELIEFS TO THEATRE SPACES

A Conversation between Adi Hollander & Eva Fotiadi

There are two major projects that you have worked on over the last few years in which audible sound is translated into haptic experience: *The Body Imitates the Landscape* (2019–2020) and the series *Haptic Room Studies* (2022–2024/ongoing). Could you briefly describe the two projects and what led you from the former to the latter?

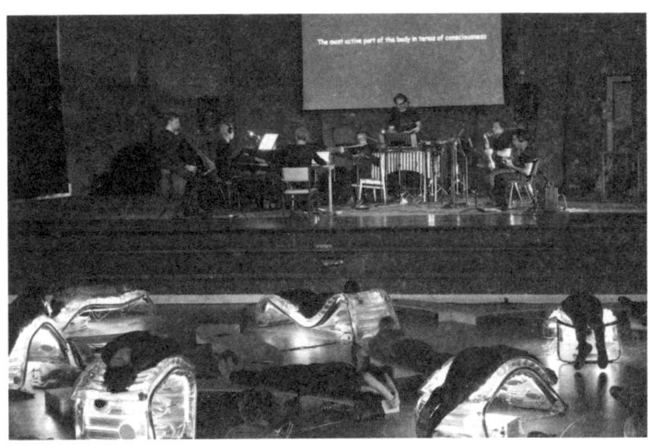

Adi Hollander and Claudio F. Baroni with MAZE Ensemble, *The Body Imitates the Landscape*, live concert presentation at The OtherAbilities Festival, Amsterdam, 2019. Photo: Ilya Rabinovitch.

The Body Imitates the Landscape (2019–2020) is a sound installation and live concert performance on which I collaborated with composer Claudio F. Baroni and the MAZE Ensemble. This interactive installation, which enables the human body to expand its listening possibilities beyond the ears to other parts of the body, was inspired by Michitarō Tada's book Karada about the 'school of the body'. The work uses sounds, text, gestures, movements, and space to address the 'body' as an archive of memory.

Based on excerpts from Tada's book, Baroni has composed an hour-long piece for MAZE Ensemble, where whispered voices reveal the hidden harmonies in ordinary speech.

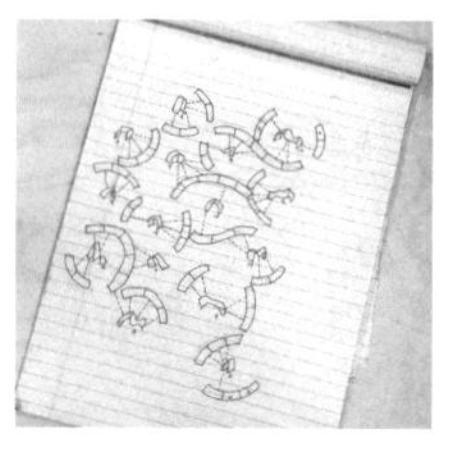
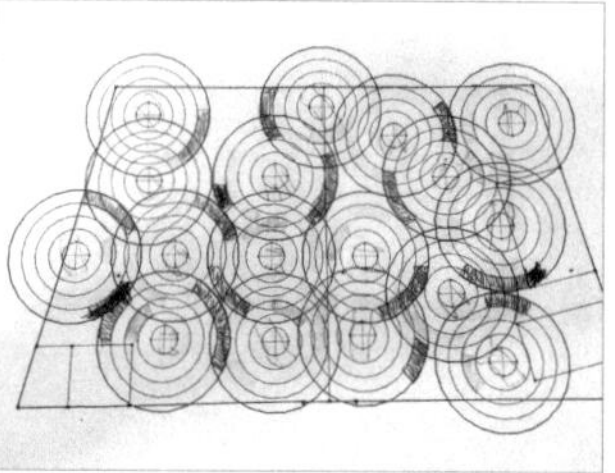

Planning the installation landscape *The Body Imitates the Landscape*, 2019. Photos: Adi Hollander.

1. The OtherAbilities (2018–ongoing) is an Amsterdam-based artists' initiative that explores the implications, potential, and attainability of intersensory translation through artistic research and technological experimentation. It serves as a hub for theoretical, academic, experimental, and practical projects, facilitating the creation of multisensory art and broadening art communication to wider audiences. The initiative was founded by Eva Fotiadi and Adi Hollander.

The process unfolds in three stages: selecting and recording the text with a narrator; conducting a spectral analysis of the voice; and finally, transforming the data into music.

The installation translates the textual experience of reading the book into a sensory one. Designed as a playground of sorts, it transforms music into vibrations felt through the body, fostering an intimate and private relationship between the audience and each object within the installation. The goal was to create a stage where the audience simultaneously consumes and participates in the work as performers.

Haptic Room Studies (2022–2024) (henceforth HRS) began as my collaboration with artists Andreas Tegnander, Ildikó Horváth, Sungeun Lee, and architect Yonatan Cohen. Our work focuses on 'haptic listening', a method for exploring the complex textures and layers of sound through somatic perception when the body is in contact with the room's interior surfaces, such as walls, floors, seats, or banisters.

This project represents the second phase of the OtherAbilities initiative, dedicated to sensory translation in art.[1] While in the first phase of this project,

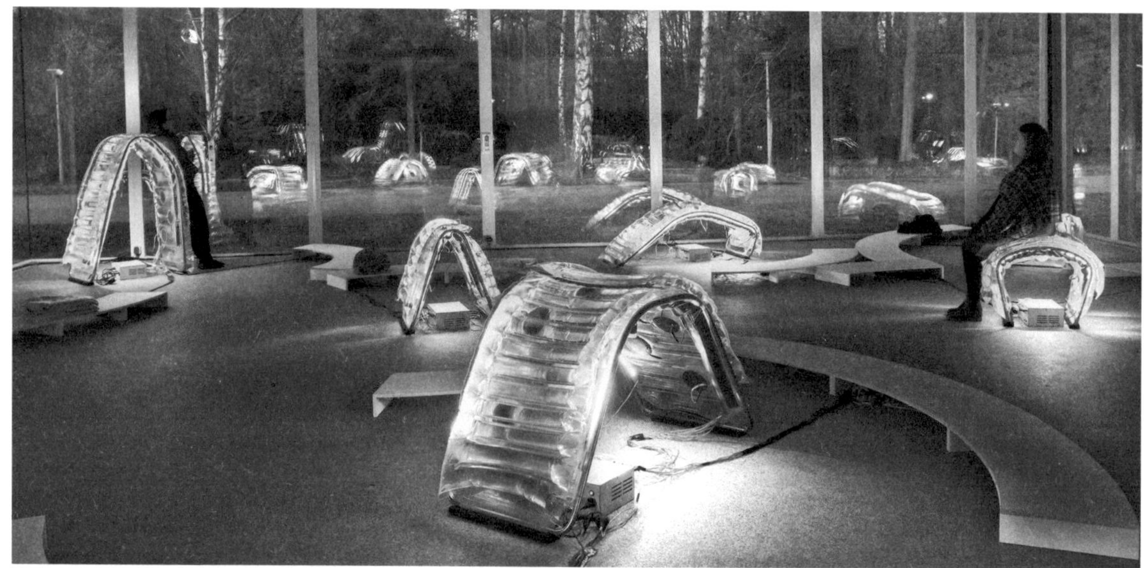

Adi Hollander and Claudio F. Baroni, *The Body Imitates the Landscape*, sound installation view, Zone2Source gallery Amsterdam, 2019. Photo: Ilya Rabinovitch.

 What do I Hear? (2021) explores prototyping technologies for sensory translation. The project aims to embed these technologies in the architecture of a gallery space, enabling the translation of sound- and movement-based artworks into vibration. Initiated by Adi Hollander and Eva Fotiadi. Participants: Andreas Tegnander, Mark IJzerman, Alina Ozerova, Ildikó Horváth, Claudio F Baroni, Maria Kandyla, Michele Abolaffio, VibraFusionLab-Collective, David Bobier, Jim Ruxton, Jenelle Rouse, Rebecca Kleinberger, Akito van Troyer, Mor Efrati, and Yonatan Cohen.

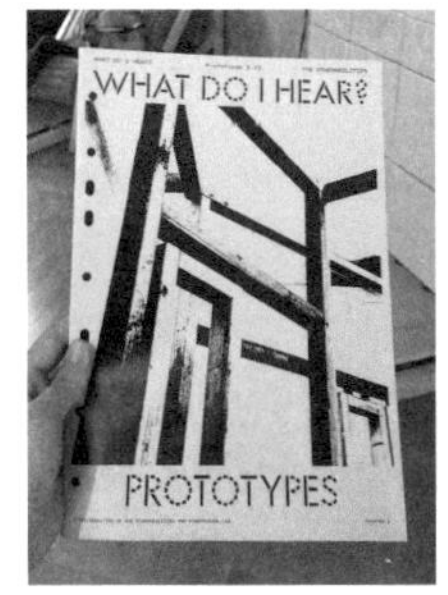

WDIH? Booklet (2021–2022). Photo: Alina Ozerova.

What Do I Hear? (2021) (henceforth *WDIH?*) we created prototypes that could become modules or tactile 'bricks' to create a haptic platform or an installation's architectural elements[2], in *HRS*, we refined our approach. We selected three tactile prototypes to use as building blocks—porcelain wall tiles, cushioned wall surfaces, and wooden floor tiles—chosen for their 'invisibility' and minimal distraction from the displayed artwork. These tools, when combined, allow us to create a multichannel system capable of simultaneously directing different sound parameters, such as density, harmony, direction, and spatialization. *HRS #1–#4* served as case studies, each exploring a distinct aspect of translating sound into tactility: concert, film, human voice, and nature. The presentations took place in institutions and spaces that allowed me to instigate a rethinking and redesign of architectural spaces for use by both hearing and non-hearing individuals.

What was the connection between the two projects?

Both *The Body Imitates the Landscape* and *HRS* are part of an ongoing exploration of tactility as both material and medium. With each work, I have discovered the boundaries of tactility and how to shape it, learning to create tactile spaces that offer two interesting directions. The first is creating spaces that serve as interfaces, translating complex, multi-channel sounds from existing artworks into a physical 'body experience' of listening. The second is developing tactile landscapes, where tactility generates a physical experience of sound—of an event, soundscape, et cetera. These haptic installations offer varied experiences: active listening for hearing audiences, an aid for people who are hard of hearing, or an alternative way to experience the many dimensions of sound.

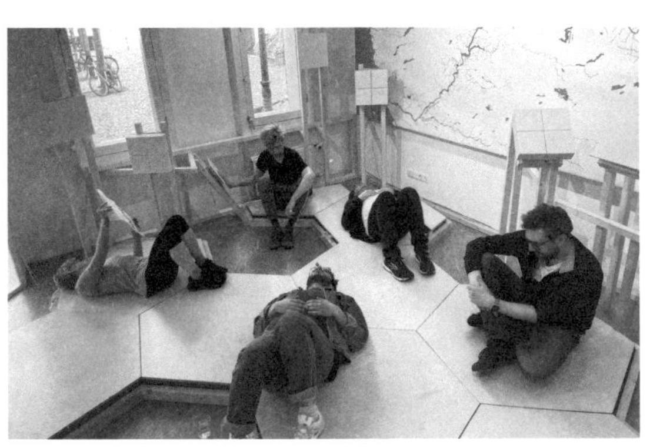

Adi Hollander in collaboration with Annea Lockwood, *Haptic Room Study #4: Questions about Tactile Spatialization: Between Hearing and Active Listening*, Movement Exposed Gallery, Utrecht, 2024. Photo: Adi Hollander.

Adi Hollander &
Eva Fotiadi

What were the technological advancements?

The Body Imitates the Landscape consists of seventeen modules— uniquely designed waterbeds resembling dancers' movements— augmented by sixty vibrating wooden benches. Arranged like a garden with many centres, the modules were spread around the musicians, each surrounded by cycles of low wooden benches, creating ripples of sound emanating audibly, physically, and visually from the modules.

The audience rested on water mattresses, which were placed over bass shakers, transducers, and bone conductors. Each device contains between eight and sixteen speaker outputs, with a total of 180 transducer speakers embedded through the installation. By using different transducers, I could cover a wide range of frequencies. The transducers, suspended in air pockets and in contact with the water mattresses, were pressed by the weight of the audience, amplifying the tactile experience.

In *HRS*, we created interior interventions within existing spaces, allowing people to watch a film or attend a concert by 'listening' to the sound through the vibrating architectural surfaces. These interventions were composed of three prototype units we designed during the *WDIH?* project: a Porcelain Membrane, a Sink-in Pillow, and VibroRaised-Relief. Each offered different sensations and possibilities for translating sound into tactile experiences. Crucially, the audience did not need to wear, hold, or look at anything in order to engage with and experience the installation.

The Porcelain Membrane is constructed from porcelain tiles, wooden frames, and rubber connectors.[3] It has outstanding sonic qualities, conducting a detailed tactile map that reflects the complexity of sound—frequency, rhythm, timbre, and dynamics.

The Sink-in Pillow comprises a round frame and a series of vibration-conductive pipes; all encased in a buckwheat-insulated cushion.[4] Each cylinder contains springs, metal tubes, and vibration motors, directing vibrations toward the user and away from the structure.

The VibroRaised-Relief are wooden floor tiles made of two layers of foam, rubber, and wooden plates.

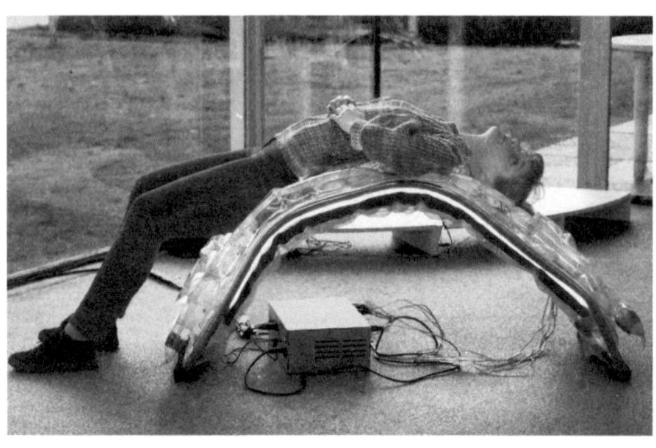

Different ways to interact with the module, Zone2Source Gallery, Amsterdam, 2019 Photo: Ilya Rabinovitch.

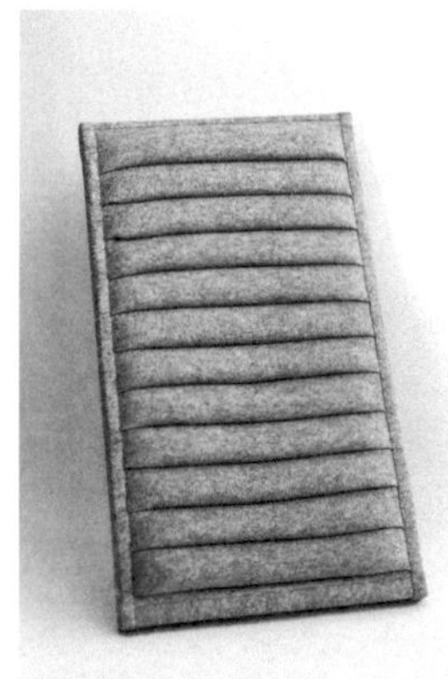

The Sink-in Pillow. Photo: Alina Ozerova.

They are designed for participants to experience sound spatialization. As a fundamental element of architectural space, the floor invites the audience to walk, sit, or lie down. Each tile includes four independently operated speakers, creating a dynamic soundscape as the body moves.

We developed a system that operates each speaker individually, controlling how sound travels between them. While *The Body Imitates the Landscape* uses stereo signals and different speakers to create complexity, in *HRS*, we treat sound spatially, sending thirty-two channels through the units. By combining surface sensations, varying heights, multi-channel setups, wide frequency ranges, and sound movement from speaker to speaker, we explored tactile spatialization. This approach highlighted different sound parameters, creating immersive tactile landscapes. Although each installation required unique considerations, our goal was to design a versatile sound system adaptable to any space. Artist Andreas Tegnander created a sound system that can operate up to thirty-two channels, with the potential to multiply to sixty-four or 128 channels, along with software to program sound movement between speakers.

Through our work on *HRS*, we gained significant insights into filtering sound for tactile experiences. For example, in *HRS #4*, the sensation of intense pressure when water crashes into a stone in a river felt so realistic, as if the water was striking the listener's body, as the sound conveyed the direction of the stream. A slower, thinner stream moving between stones was perceived as flowing between their toes, with many instinctively looking down to check if they had gotten wet.

What was the conceptual evolution?

The conceptual evolution of my work with tactility began with *The Body Imitates the Landscape*, where tactility shifted from a tool to both a material and a medium, influenced by my experience with haptic hearing as someone hard of hearing. After moving to Cambridge, MA, I missed my cats. A recording of their purring

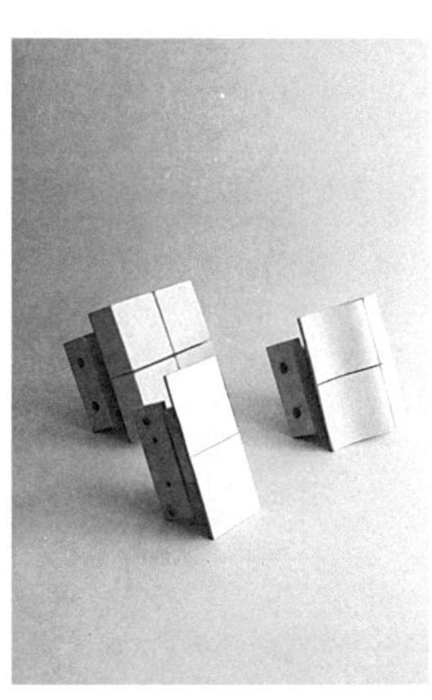

The Porcelain Membrane.
Photo: Alina Ozerova.

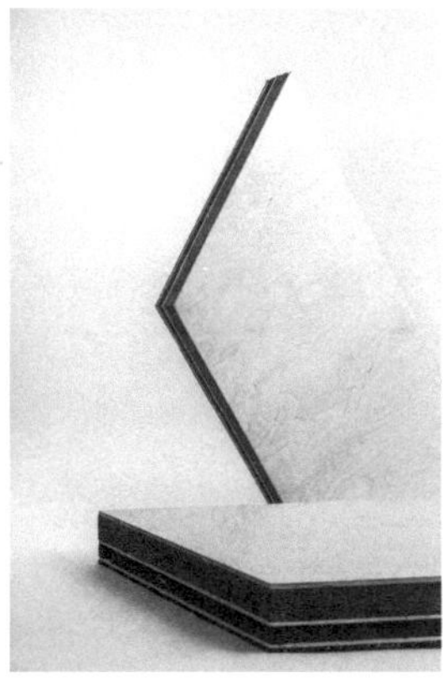

The VibroRaised-Relief.
Photo: Alina Ozerova.

played through a bass shaker attached to an air pillow, brought me comfort. The vibrations triggered memories and emotions, helping me 'hear' through touch. The experience made me curious about how tactile sensations could evoke sound and how tactile vocabulary could tell a story. I realized tactility could be treated like any material—wood or paper—to translate experiences into another sense.

In 2020, at the Eye Filmmuseum, I saw Chantal Akerman's *FROM THE EAST: Bordering on Fiction*. While walking between the TV screens, I felt the absence of sound, especially given how essential sound is to Akerman's work. I imagined a haptic floor that would allow navigation between soundscapes, helping to clarify the sound environment. This experience inspired the tactile floor tiles, developed as part of the OtherAbilities initiative. Our research questions included: What does it mean for a contemporary art space to become inclusive? How can we create spaces where no one is excluded from cultural participation? Who holds agency when art is mediated?

How was the idea of translating sound to touch adapted or expanded from a body-centric approach to an environment-centric one?

I am interested in investigating how spaces can host and enrich bodily experiences.

The OtherAbilities proposal aimed to make exhibition spaces more inclusive by integrating architectural elements—floors, walls, panels—with built-in sensory translation tools. Instead of offering assistive devices or guided tours, we want to redesign the

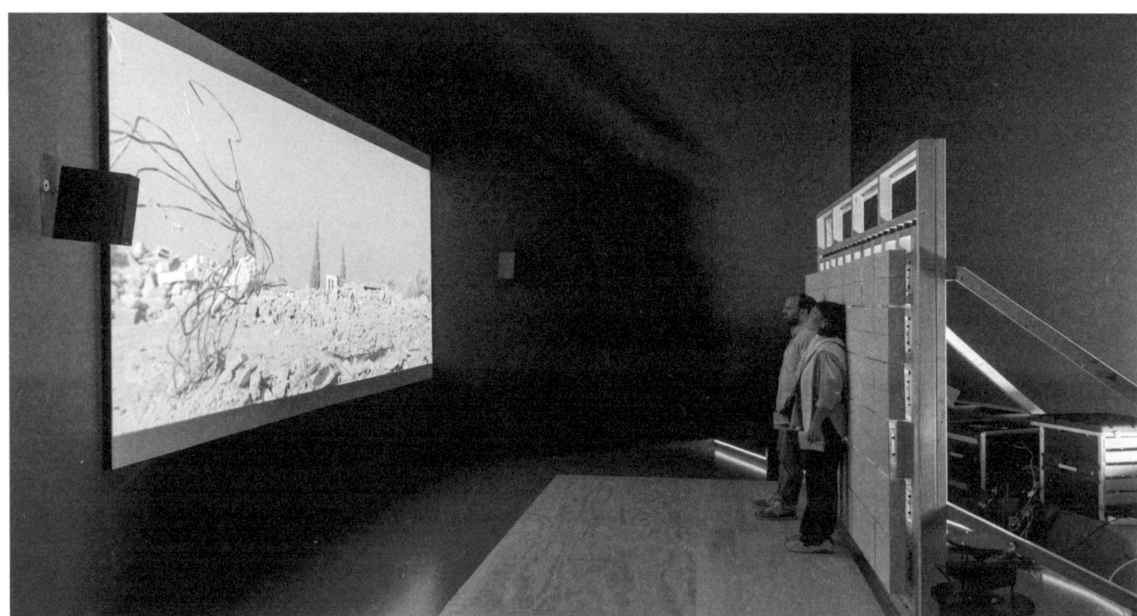

Haptic Room Study #1: Porcelain Membrane Wall, view from site-specific haptic room presentation at Van Abbemuseum, Eindhoven, as part of Dutch Design Week's Embassy of Inclusive Society exhibition, 2022. Photo: Konstantin Guz.

architecture itself to provide access to sensory engagement to both hearing and non-hearing audiences.

HRS #1: Membrane Wall was designed to translate the sound of a film from the Van Abbemuseum collection during the 2022 Dutch Design Week into a tactile experience.[5]

In film, sound and visual elements are woven together to create a complete universe. Sound is essential in storytelling: it conveys what happens off-screen, reveals characters' emotions, and offers non-visual and non-verbal insights into the protagonist's mind. Without sound, a film lacks a significant part of the creators' vision. To address this, we created a site-specific intervention in a room already set up as a black cube for a single film screening. In this haptic room, we built a three by two metres porcelain wall and a one-metre-wide floor along it, incorporating four types of transducers for a total of seventy-eight tactile speakers. This setup restored the film's audio cues through touch, creating a spatial haptic system where different sound channels are felt in different locations on the body, much like how the ear can differentiate between simultaneous frequencies (layers, sources, et cetera) without blurring them into one.

This work invites the public to 'listen' with their bodies without altering or distracting from the artwork on display.

It liberates the audience from relying on hearing or special devices, offering a more inclusive way to experience the film.

Since I first encountered your works back in 2004, you have always created space(s), literally and metaphorically. Working with the spatialization of sound is specific to projects of the last few years. Could you talk about space in your work and how it relates to sound, hearing, and haptic experiences?

In my practice, I create installations as 'places of exchange', composed of functional, site-specific sculptures experienced both as interior and exterior, formed through a dialogue with the venue. I am fascinated by how architecture and spatial design engage spectators through movement, touch, bodily experience, and sensory input.

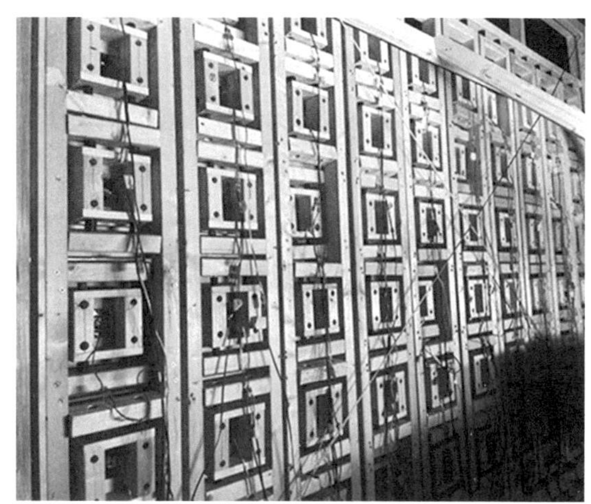

Backside view of *Porcelain Membrane Wall*.
Photo: Adi Hollander.

My projects aim to offer an alternative understanding of the senses and the way we interpret the world.

The concept of 'place of exchange' reflects public space as a way of thinking and experiencing public time. It raises questions such as: Who is my public? What exchange am I creating? How are the work's layers and the research behind it communicated? What social situations am I testing or offering? My works strive for a two-way exchange, transforming the spectator from passive observer to active participant, engaged through their senses.

I view installation art as a game with its own rules, where each work creates a unique world defined by space and time. Without written rules, the audience can choose to engage or remain passive. Play in art is not just intellectual or physical; it's a political and aesthetic tool that evokes doubt and questions: What does it mean to play? How do we play? Why do we engage in play? Like a language, play balances creation and destruction, offering freedom while also tempting us to break rules and experience pleasure.

6. *Public Space With a Roof* is an artists' initiative initiated by Tamuna Chabashvili, Adi Hollander, and Vesna Madzoski, who also run it.

You can see this approach in all Public Space With a Roof (henceforth PSWAR) projects as well as in my current haptic works, where I explore space through tactility as a medium, material, and tool.

With the PSWAR initiative (2003– ongoing), we have explored the role of the arts in society, the artist's responsibility, and the function of art institutions in the Netherlands.[6] We have translated theoretical ideas into concrete forms, creating exhibition formats that engage audiences both intellectually and physically.

This led to blurring the distinction between the artists' roles—artists as activists, producers, or curators. Each project resulted in an installation functioning as a rhetorical sculpture that provokes questions without predetermined answers. Our installations incorporated other artists' works as readymade, giving them new platforms to communicate with the public.

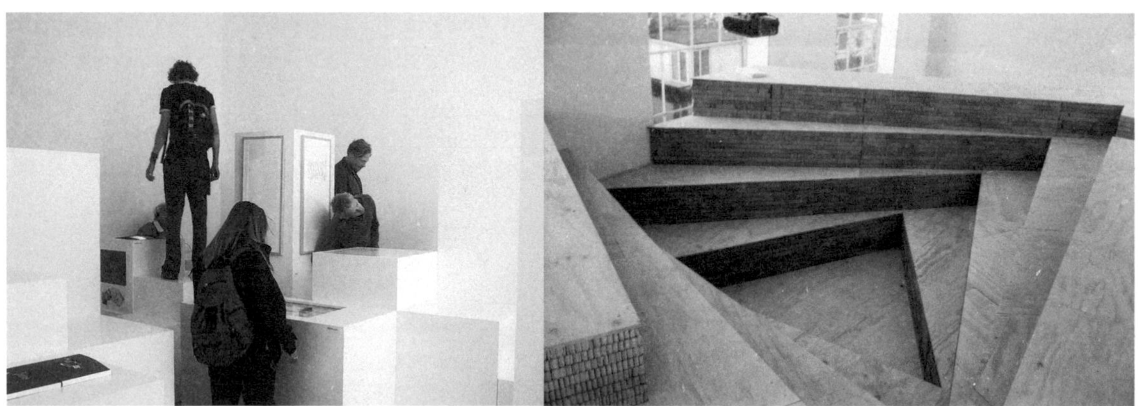

Public Space With a Roof artists' initiative, (left) *Pixel of Reality: What do you know? What do you see?*, Public Space With a Roof Project Space, Amsterdam, 2006, installation view; (right) *Endless Installation: A Ghost Story for Adults*, SMART Project Space, 2009, installation view. Both photos: Ilya Rabinovitch.

These spatial interventions go beyond aesthetics, challenging the positions of the artists and the function of exhibitions today. Each project required mastering new materials and techniques, much like my current work with tactility.

Creating haptic spaces is also personal, shaped by my experience with hearing loss. Born hard of hearing but only diagnosed at sixteen, I had already learned to listen with my eyes, unaware that my vision was defining and clarifying what I heard. This profoundly influenced how I create spaces that engage visually and sensorially. For hard of hearing or d/Deaf individuals, spatial organization is crucial—seeing the speakers, moving freely toward them when they speak, and managing the absence of background sounds are essential. Projects *WDIH?* and *HRS* were collaborative efforts but also personal discoveries for me, allowing me to experience space made of sound, which I often only grasp intellectually.

In *HRS*, we explored sculpting with tactile spatialization, using tactile objects to create physical spaces and evoke emotional responses. Tactility became a tool to transfer sound, translate works, and shape practical spaces that accommodate the audience—whether walking, sitting, leaning, or lying down.

Haptic Room Study #3: Conversation Piece comprises two units, each one linked to a microphone, which enables two people having a live conversation to sense both their own voice, as well as that of the other person, as vibrations across their bodies. We tend to connect a conversation primarily with the meaning of the words we utter. Strictly speaking, this meaning as such does not get 'translated' to a shared vibratory vocabulary. Or does it? What exactly is it that gets 'translated'? What does the haptic experience of somebody's voice in conversation consist of and what does it offer to the experience of a conversation?

A conversation is an exchange of ideas, thoughts, or information that involves speaking, listening, and responding. Beyond words, the

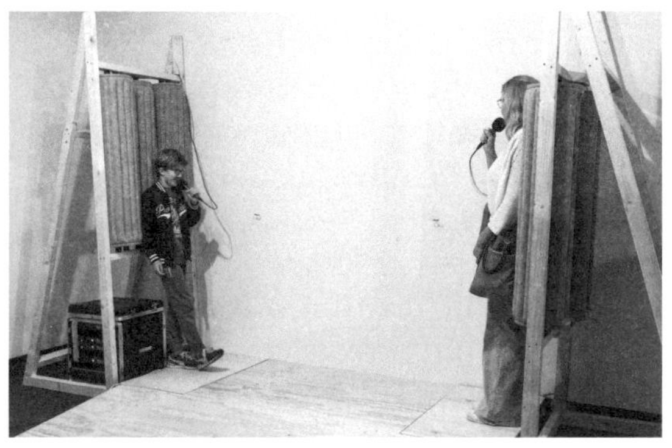

Haptic Room Study #3: Conversation Piece, site-specific haptic room presentation at Van Abbemuseum in Eindhoven as part of Dutch Design Week's Embassy of Inclusive Society exhibition, 2022. Photo: Konstantin Guz.

Adi Hollander & Eva Fotiadi

voice conveys additional layers of meaning—tone, pace and rhyme, volume, pitch, silence, accent, emotion, and more. These parameters are what gets translated—the voice itself. The meaning of words remains with the ears, lips (for lip-reading), or sign language.

In *HRS #3: Conversation Piece*, feeling your own voice allows you to feel your presence in the conversation. Are you speaking over the other person? Are you giving them space? And how does your voice physically feel when you are interacting with someone else?

We showed *HRS #3* at the 'Embassy of Inclusive Society' exhibition (Van Abbemuseum, Dutch Design Week, 2022) as an interactive installation for two people. Positioned near the entrance, it introduced visitors to haptic listening, preparing them for the tactile experience presented on the upper floor, where we presented *HRS #1: Membrane Wall* and Yael Bartana's film *Summer Camp* (2007).

I later presented another version of *HRS #3* at the Movement Explore Gallery in Utrecht, this time designed for four people. The focus remained on how we converse and on the personal impact of sensing both our own voice and the voice of others.

In *Haptic Room Study #4: Questions about Tactile Spatialization: Between Hearing and*

Active Listening, you have chosen to work with the composition *A Sound Map of the Housatonic River* by Annea Lockwood. While in the past a lot of attention was focused on trying to translate complex sound through the use of different channels, if I remember correctly, this fourth study has led to further questions of working with pure and bare sounds, probably even creating a vocabulary of sorts. Could you elaborate on these?

Complex sound involves multiple layers, such as overlapping channels or various sources of sound occurring simultaneously, like in a concert, theatre performance, or film. In essence, complex sound is a rich tapestry of different audio components that interact with each other, creating a more dynamic and textured listening experience. In contrast, pure sound refers to a signal without distortion or interference. With nature sounds, purity becomes crucial—while a hearing person can distinguish between wind and the sound of a singing bird, a hard of hearing or deaf audience might perceive the blended tactile sound as 'dirty' and 'noisy'.

In *HRS #4,* I focused on tactile spatialization, creating a sense of movement and direction within the space as visitors move around. This

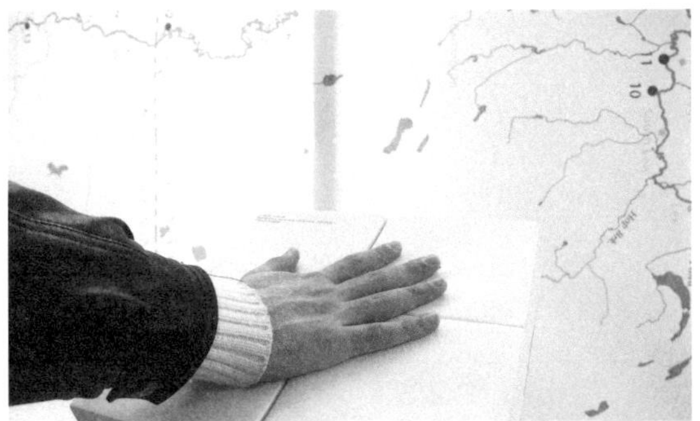

Interacting with the work, *Haptic Room Study #4*, 2024. Photo: Alina Ozerova.

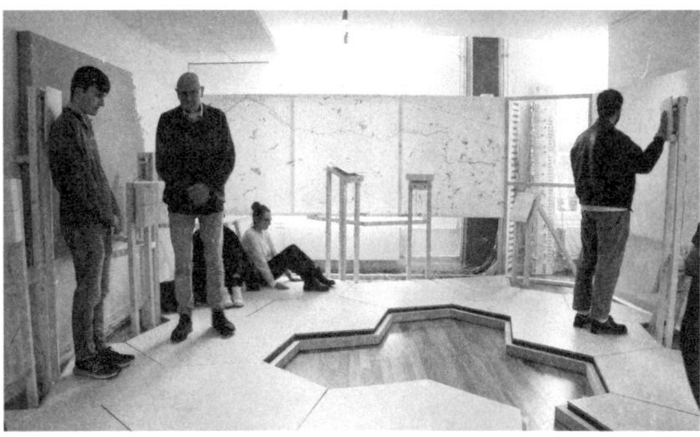

Different ways of interacting with the work, *Haptic Room Study #4*, 2024. Photo: Alina Ozerova.

study integrated all the components developed during the previous studies: the structure, sound system, software, and methods for filtering and translating sound into tactile experiences.

I was honoured to work with Annea Lockwood's composition *A Sound Map of the Housatonic River*, which traces the river from its sources in the Berkshire Mountains to its mouth at Milford, Long Island Sound. Using stereo microphones and underwater hydrophones, the piece captures eighteen unique soundscape portraits. My task was to create a tactile space that adhered to Lockwood's instructions, ensuring that the rich palette of water and the 3D soundscapes could be experienced through touch, just as they are through hearing.

This wasn't my first time working with nature and animal recordings. In 2016, at the REACH school for deaf children in Kolkata, where I worked with the pupils, we used haptic listening to engage with recordings of nature, animals, and urban environments. This process revealed sound colours and depths I had never imagined, but it also taught me the importance of clean recordings. Different sounds must

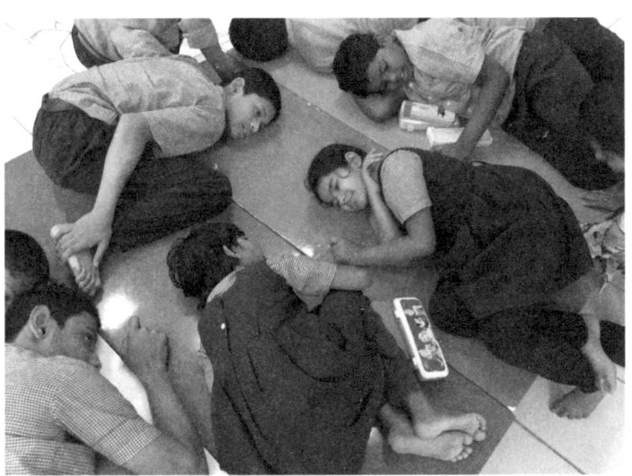

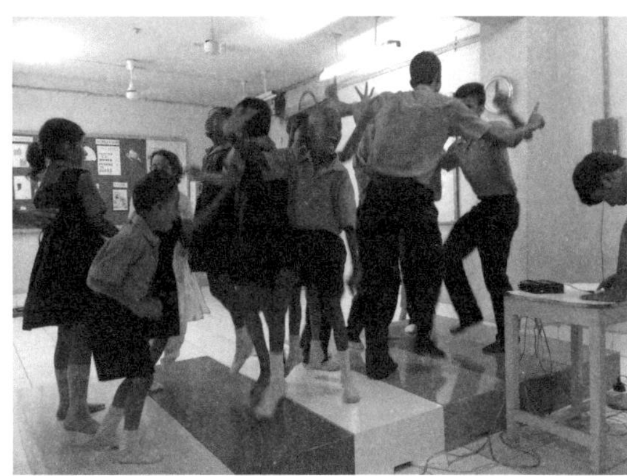

Adi Hollander in collaboration with sound engineer Sukanta Majumdar, *Tactile Platform: Or the manipulation of staging*. Workshop on tactile listening at the REACH school for the deaf, (left) Feeling-listening to soundtracks from nature, (right) First time dancing while feeling the music, Kolkata, India, 2016–2018. Photo: Adi Hollander.

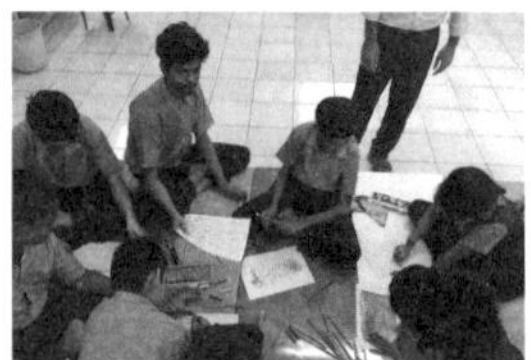
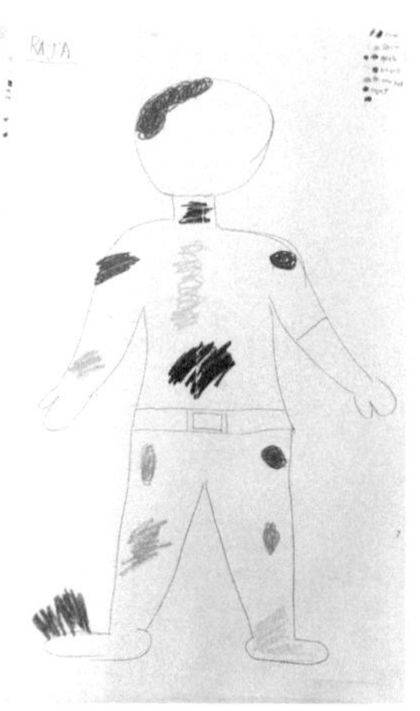

View from a workshop on tactile listening at the REACH school for the deaf, Kolkata, India, 2016–2018. Photos: Adi Hollander.

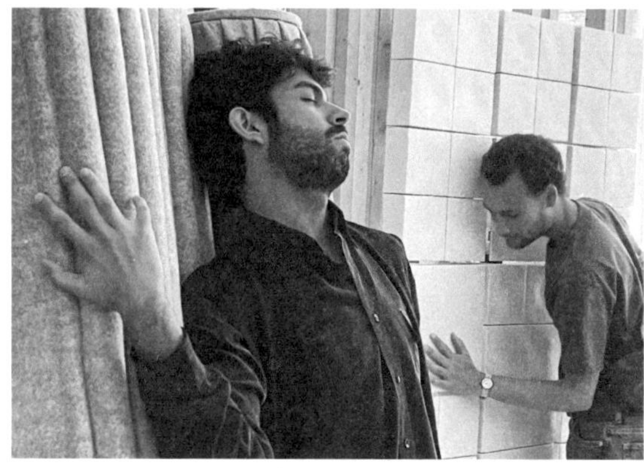

Haptic Room Study #2. Photo: Adi Hollander.

be separated through distinct tactile sources to avoid overwhelming the senses.

Playing and experimenting with the kids, I realized that high volumes or intense vibrations could mask finer tactile details and even become painful. Over time, we learned to recognize and memorize these vibrations, much like learning a new language—distinguishing the feel of a galloping horse, a Kolkata train, or heavy rain.

During the *WDIH?* process, we used nature samples as single 'words' in test workshops. I had always aimed to work with complex recordings of nature when we could use multiple independent channels, allowing visitors to experience change and the directional flow of sound as they moved.

    HRS #4, Lockwood's piece, with its rich palette of water and natural sounds, human voices, and city sounds, pushed me to further refine the tactile vocabulary. Focusing on purity and

clarity, I aimed to translate the energy and flow of the river into a tangible experience. This allowed participants to engage with the work through touch in a way that complements the auditory experience.

How does the translation of sensory experiences from one sense to another create a common ground between people with diverse hearing abilities? The experiences offered by such sensory translations cannot be considered as being the same for each individual with diverse hearing. Are they meant to be equivalents of some sort? What is shared exactly, and (how) does it comprise a proposal of inclusivity and equitability between hearing-diverse audiences?

Exhibiting for
Multiple Senses

In Alfred Hitchcock's famous forty-five-second shower scene in *Psycho*, composer Bernard Herrmann's score plays a pivotal role, slicing through the silence as sharply as the knife itself. Hitchcock's integration of sound and scoring into the film's visual world amplifies the suspense; without sound, much of the experience is lost. However, watching the scene without sound while relying only on subtitles was my only option. With *HRS*, on the other hand, I could feel each sound Herrmann used—the water, the moving curtain, the piercing violin—alongside the visual silence of Marion's scream and the knife's penetration. This gave me a 3D representation of the sound I could not hear, which the subtitle could not convey.

During the *WDIH?* research, we developed a sitting space for deaf audience members to attend concerts. One of our advisors, Jenelle Rouse, is an educator and artist with a PhD in applied linguistics and is also deaf, attended a concert by Claudio F. Baroni. Using two prototypes developed earlier, we placed her where she could see the performers.

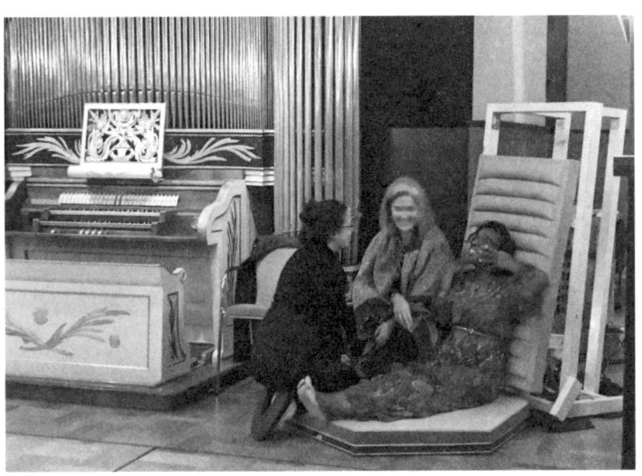

7. I. Claudio F. Baroni, *J'ai connu*, 2022; text by Géraldine Schwarz; a film by Sebastián Díaz Morales.
II. *Manual of Forgetting* (2019), by Yannis Kyriakides; text-graphic video based on forty-five aphorisms by Elias Canetti.
III. Phill Niblock, *Toegrooves*, 1991; slow-motion close-ups of flowers, without text or narration.
VI. Annea Lockwood, *Dusk*, 2012.

Afterward, she described how she felt the differences between instruments, as well as the density, direction, and force of the sounds. She beautifully expressed that, although she could see the musicians, her eyes were free—she could close them or look around—because she felt the music inside her body, like an acoustic box.

Rouse's experience helped us design the sound system, software, and speaker choices for *Haptic Room Study #2: Traveling Tactile Concert*. The installation, which accommodated four to six people, hosted four music pieces—three of which were accompanied by film.[7] Our goal was to transform silence, noise, or flat sound—typically requiring the eyes or other devices to perceive—into an experience where the body became the primary tool for listening, freeing the eyes for looking and reading.

After engaging with the three diverse pieces—through listening, watching films, and reading—participants' bodies gradually relaxed and learned to discern different vibrations, recognize tactile sources (multi-channels), and

Adi Hollander &
Eva Fotiadi

feel the subtle shifts of sound. By the final piece, many were able to enjoy feel-listening without visual input. We presented this work at the Echonance Music Festival in Amsterdam and the Milano Design Week, where it was well received. Visitors, even those with typical hearing, found the installation relaxing and deeply engaging. Tactility enhanced their concentration, allowing them to differentiate between overlapping tracks when felt on different parts of their bodies, feel the resonance of loud music even when inaudible, focus more intently on details even in noisy environments, and experience the surprise of feeling human voices and animal sounds through their bodies.

SOUND → TOUCH

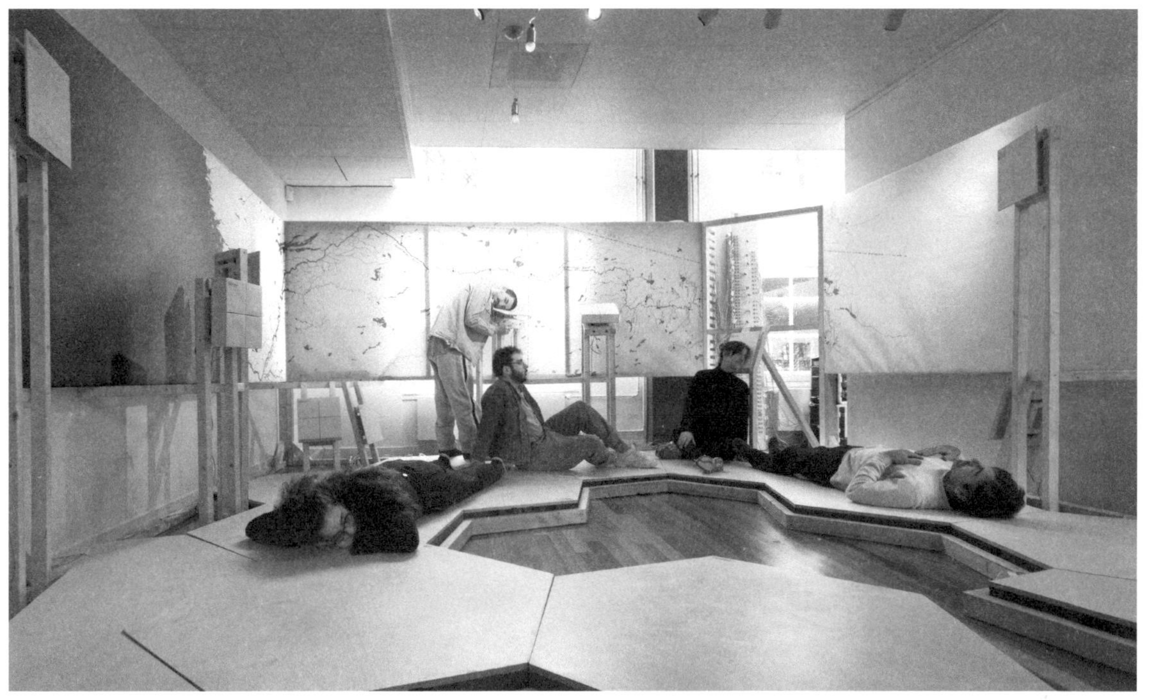

Adi Hollander in collaboration with Annea Lockwood, *Haptic Room Study #4: Questions about Tactile Spatialization: Between Hearing and Active Listening*, Movement Exposed Gallery, Utrecht, 2024. Photo: Ilya Rabinovitch.

(Un)Common Proximities

How are you connected to another person? What physical effects do these relationships have on your body? To what extent do the actions of others influence your body? In the film *Interstellar*, the Christopher Nolan sci-fi blockbuster from 2014, Dr. Amelia Brand discusses how love transcends time and space. Although this may seem like a clichéd Hollywood line at first, perhaps love is indeed a dimension that connects all human bodies. The closer the bodies are, the more connected they are in this dimension. We can interchange the word 'love' with 'time', as both are hard to measure in terms of experience. If time is a string that we walk on and all of these strings create a web that entangles everything, could it be that 'love' creates similar strings forming a web. This would mean that every action/force against a body that is inherently entangled in this web, has a direct impact on your own body.

On the background of this page is a pattern of diagonal thin lines. Overlaid are two landscape-oriented images of body imprints on a yoga mat. In the bottom right corner is an image of the basal ganglia, which are '…a group of subcortical nuclei, of various origins, located at the base of the telencephalon and in the upper part of the midbrain. They are strongly interconnected with the cerebral cortex, thalamus, and brainstem, as well as different other areas of the brain. They are associated with a variety of functions, including control of voluntary movements, procedural learning, habit learning, eye movements, cognition, and emotion.'

Do you feel the proximity of the people you love? How and where do you feel it? Is it located in a specific place and does it feel like a particular sensation?

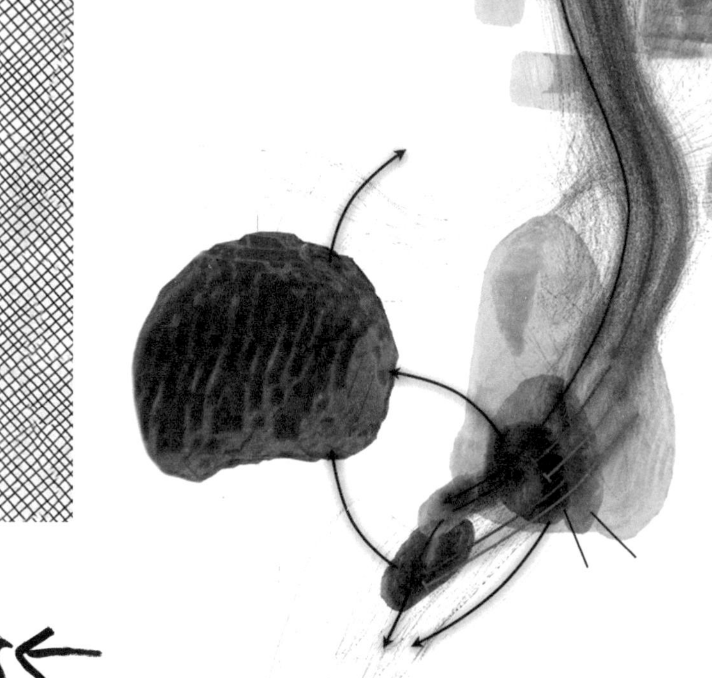

(un-) COMMON PROXIMITIES←

NEURO RECODING: KEYWORDS OF NOTHING MUCH
< Hacked Brain Processing in Dis:Ability >

Luca M Damiani

BRAIN-OVERLOAD

Neuro reCoding is a visually led and auto-ethnographic piece, to be considered also as a follow-up from some of my previous articles and research in neurodiversity and sensory conditions. Using writing, assistive-technology, and black-and-white images, here I experiment with the `abstraction` and `computing` of medical data from my neurological disability (impairment of my central nervous system function). This piece uses graphic techniques, visually reflecting everyday `sensory` processing of the surrounding environment and its difficulties, making the invisible `disability` visible. The aim is to show the 'disrupted' senses, which cannot usually be seen, as hacked aspects of brain overloads; here I create a composition or series of images whilst also using the fifty-five words method which is `performed` with and by patients with mental health and neuro-conditions, which allows us to write about intense hidden experiences `in moments` of extreme neurological pain. And so, here I will share some images as part of my experience of living with an invisible disability, trying to give you a 'window' into some of my diaries and processing. This piece aims to specifically create a contemporary and 're-coded' vision of disability, embracing various sensory experiences of neurological disorder in the processing of `sound, visual stimuli, seizures,` and `brain overloads.`

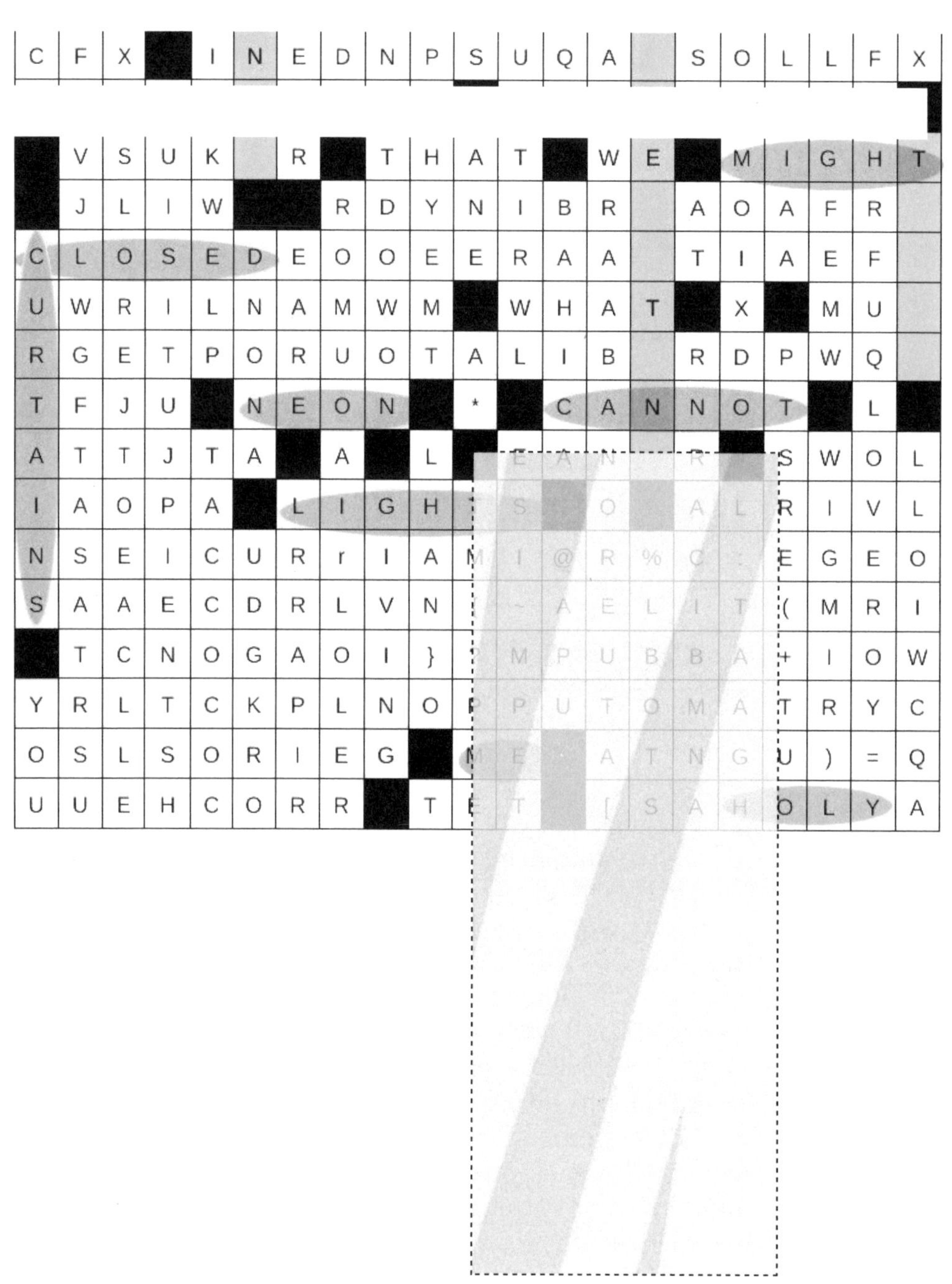

Exhibiting for
Multiple Senses

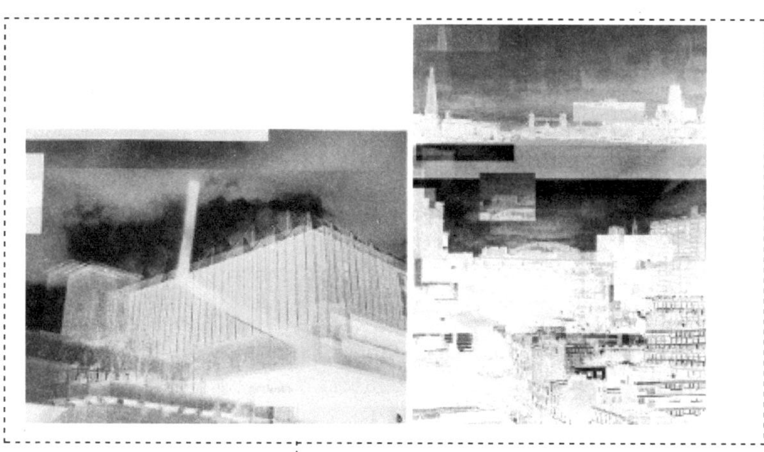

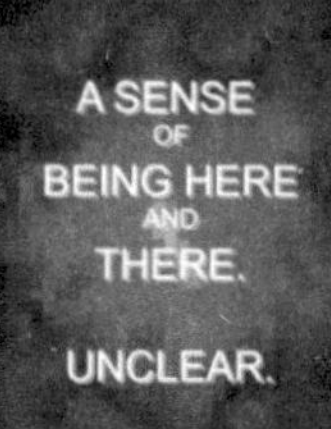
A SENSE
OF
BEING HERE
AND
THERE.

UNCLEAR.

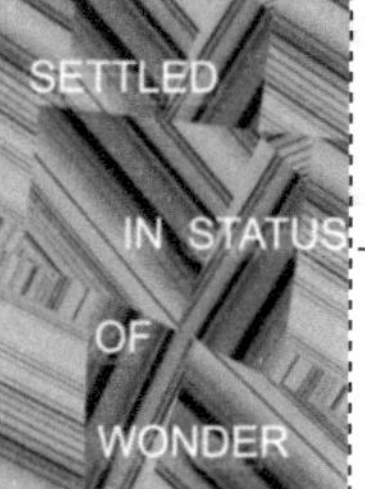
SETTLED

IN STATUS

OF

WONDER

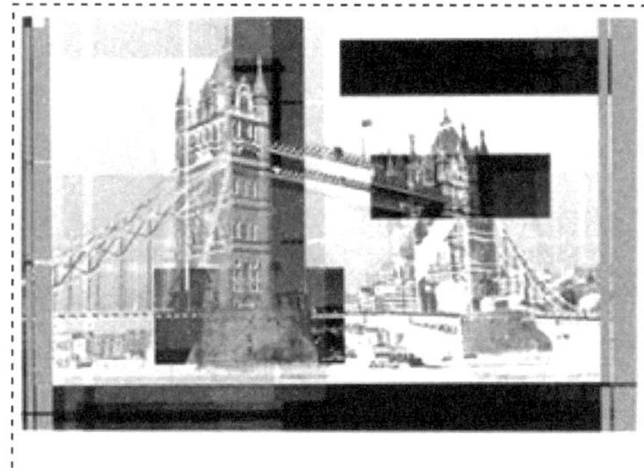

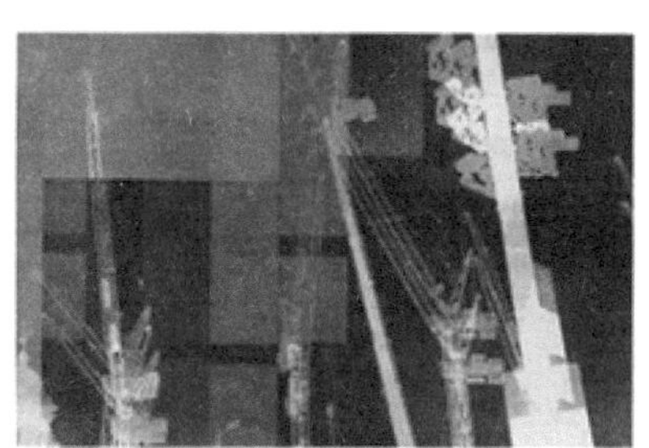

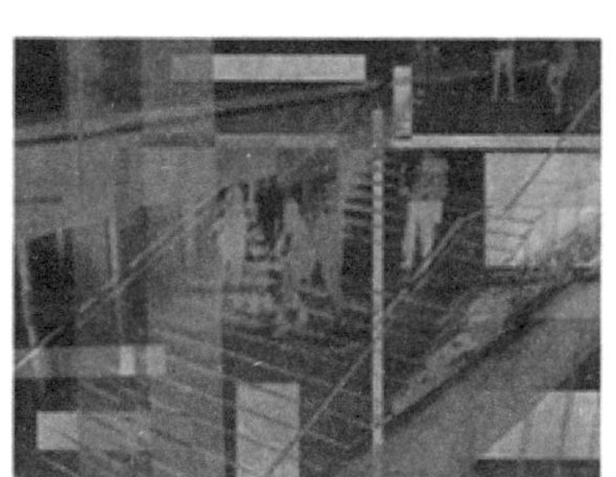

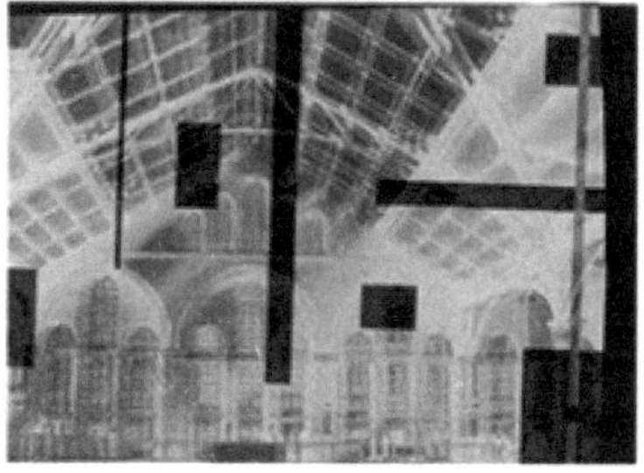

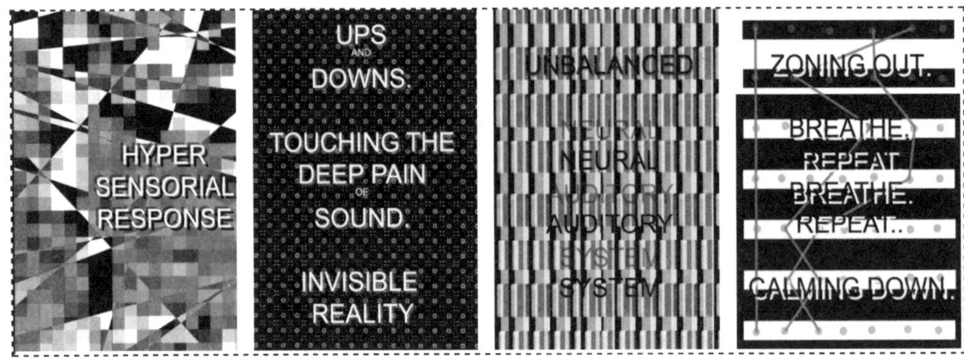

Fifty-five keywords that mean a lot
(whilst also mean nothing in the moment),
keep popping up in the journey:

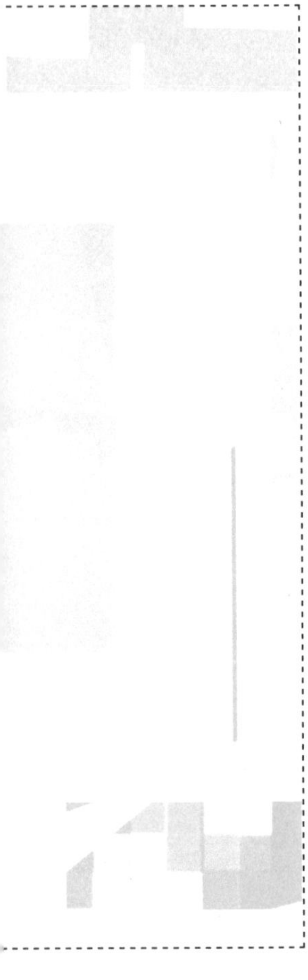

…Psychoactive Responses,   Compulsion,

Cognitive Behaviour Therapy,   Endorphins,
Eye Movement   Desensitization and
                    Reprocessing,
Manic,   Stabilizer,   Sectioning,
            Relapse, Resilience,

Disorder,   Condition,   High Functioning,   Insomnia,

Hyper Arousal, Memory,   Heightened, Triggers,

Bibliotherapy,   Post Traumatic Stress Disorder,
Neuroscience,   Neurodiversity,   Brain Trauma,

Impaired Central Nervous System,
Dissociations,   Seizures,   Black Out,   Hyperacusis,
Perceptual Postural Persistent Dizziness,
Vestibular Sensitivity, Emotional Dysregulation Disorder,
Clinical Depression…

As I look for conclusions, diagnoses, and ways forward,
sometimes it isn't straightforward to see the keywords and
find a way in. It is like a hybrid search-word building up in
a bleak present full of noise.

D		N	P	O	S	T	U	R	A	L	L	A	N	O	I	T	O	M	E
I	P	O								D	I	S	O	R	D	E	R		
S	E	I	Z	U	R	E	S				U		Y						
S	R	T									O			S					
O	S	A						V						T					
C	I	L			D	E	P	R	E	S	S	I	O	N				E	
I	S	U	Y	T	I	S	R	E	V	I	D	O	R	U	E	N		M	S
A	T	G	B	R	A	I	N			D	I	S	O	R	D	E	R		I
T	E	E	A													U			S
I	N	R		U		P	O	S	T	E		Y				R			U
O	T	S	L	M				R				T				O			C
N		Y	A	A		O	U	T	A			I			L	S			A
C		D	U				S		U			V		A		C			R
L			T						M			I	R			I			E
I			P						A			T				E			P
N			E						T		N	I				N			Y
I			C						I	E		S				C			H
C			R			B	L	A	C	K		N				E			
A	V	E	S	T	I	B	U	L	A	R	E								
L	I	M	P	A	I	R	E	D			S	S	E	N	I	Z	Z	I	D

	E	C	N	E	I	L	I	S	E	R			Y	R	O	M	E	M	I
		S	T	A	B	I	L	I	S	E	R					T			N
A			N									L:				R			S
R		H	I	G	H								A			I			O
O			H											P		G			M
U		R	P	F	U	N	C	T	I	O	N	I	N	G	S	G	S		N
S		U	R			H	Y	P	E	R						E	E		I
A		O	O			P							E			R	C		A
L		I	D		A					S			Y			S	T		
		V	N	R				M	O	V	E	M	E	N	T		I		
		A	E														O		M
		H	R	E	D	R	O	S	I	D	N						N		A
	T	E	V	I	T	I	N	G	O	C	O	M	P	U	L	S	I	O	N
		B															N		I
	D	E	N	E	T	H	G	I	E	H	S						G		C
P	S	Y	C	H	O	A	C	T	I	V	E								
						Y	P	A	R	E	H	T	O	I	L	B	I	B	
				C	O	N	D	I	T	I	O	N							
						G	N	I	S	S	E	S	O	R	P	E	R		
		D	E	S	E	N	S	A	T	I	Z	A	T	I	O	N			

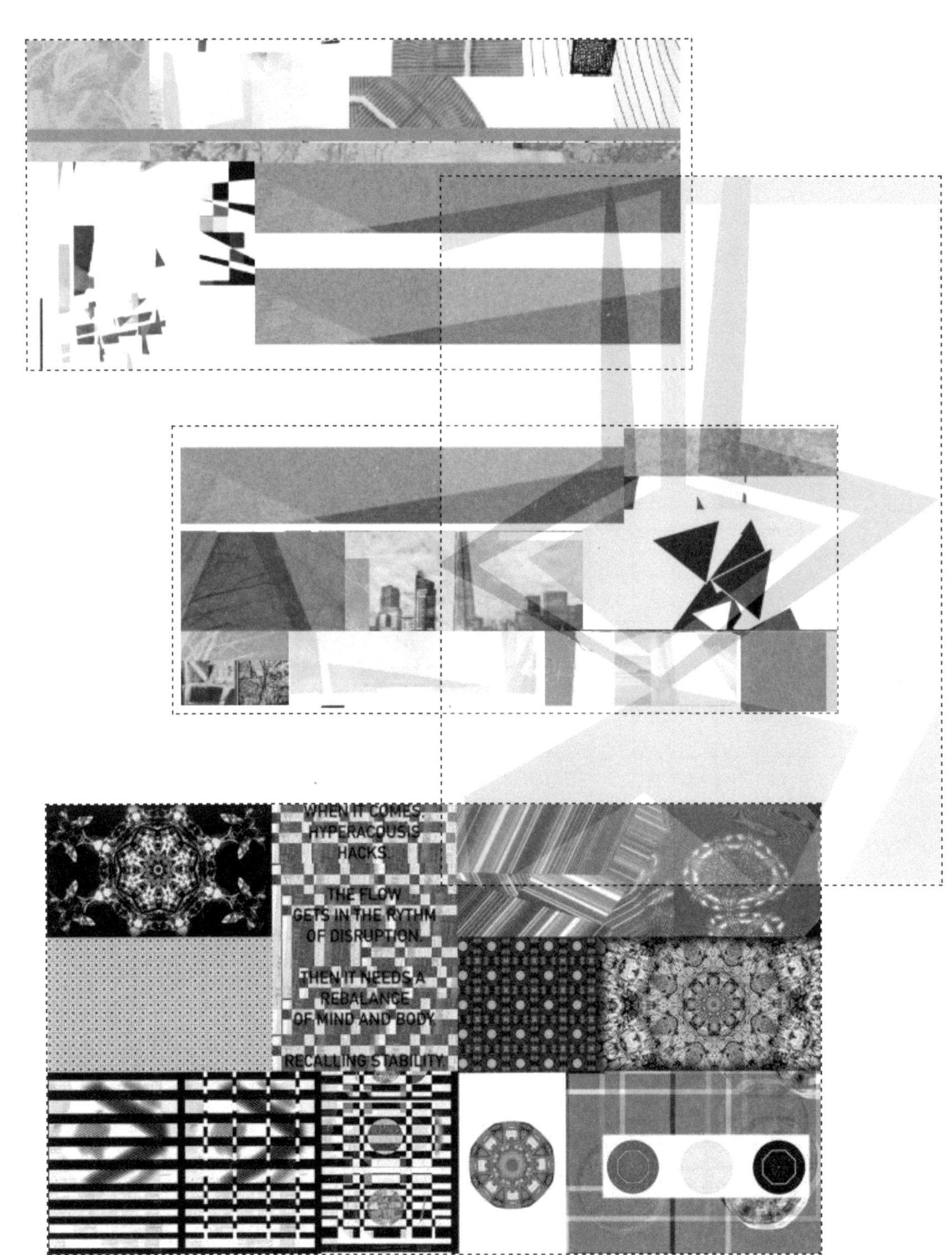

Exhibiting for
Multiple Senses

I

N

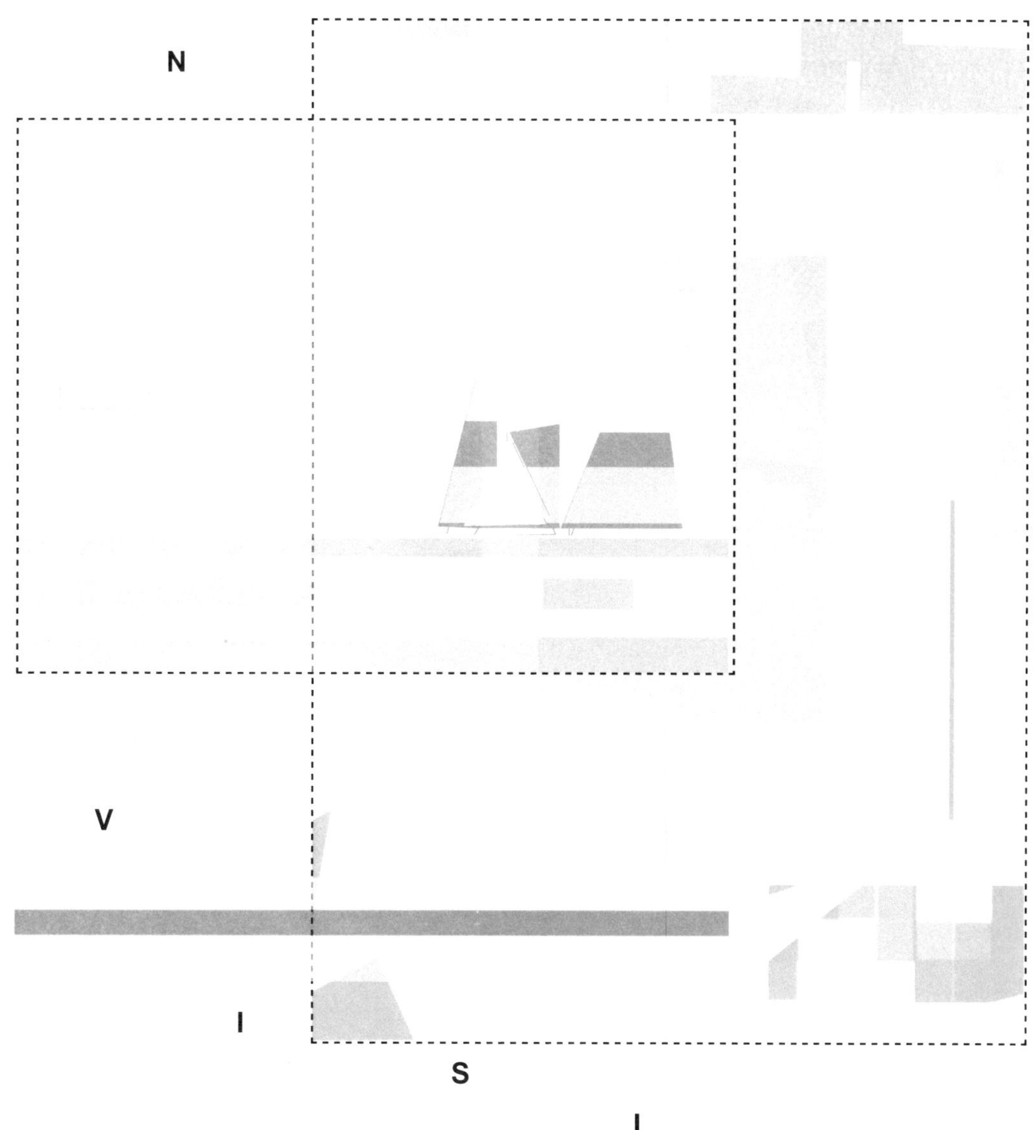

V

I

S

I

B

L

E

DISRUPTION

OF

TREMOR

MEMORY

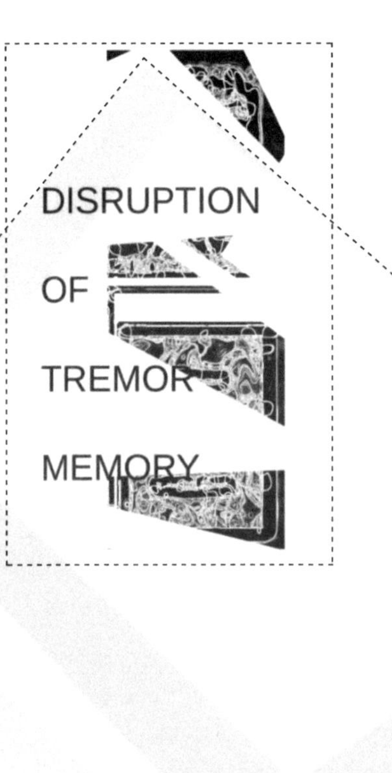

COMPUTED

IN

SPIN

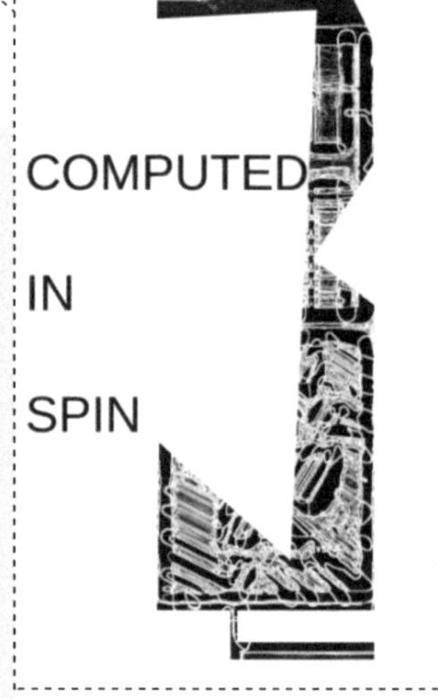

OF

BROKEN

FREQUENCI

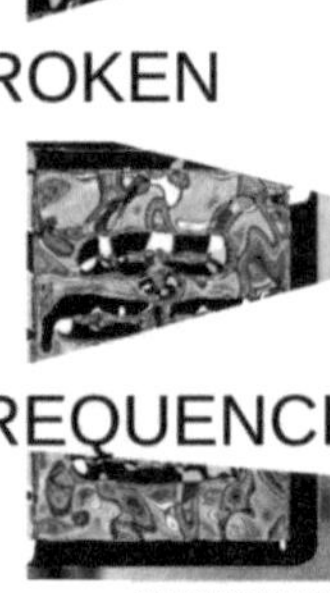

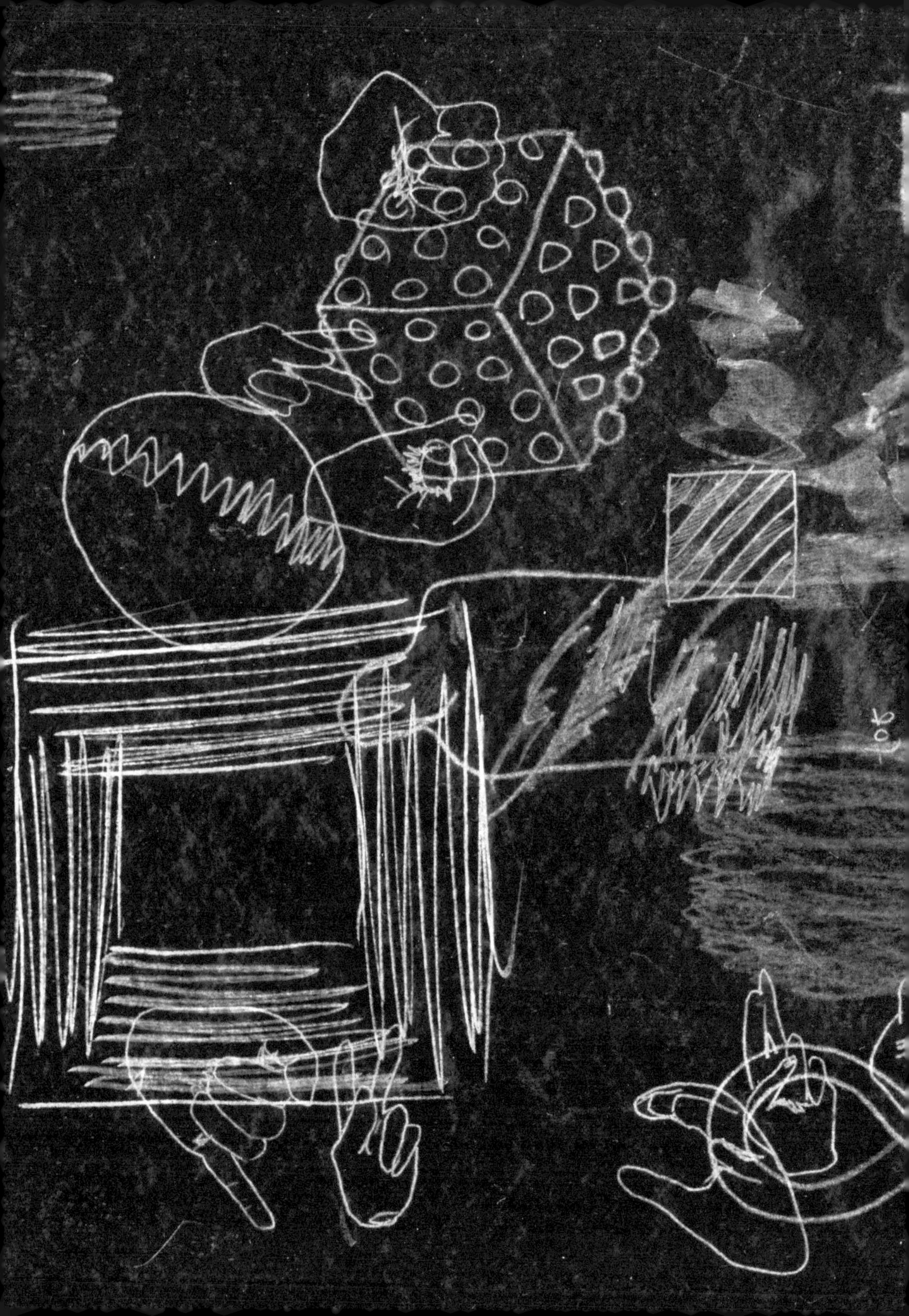

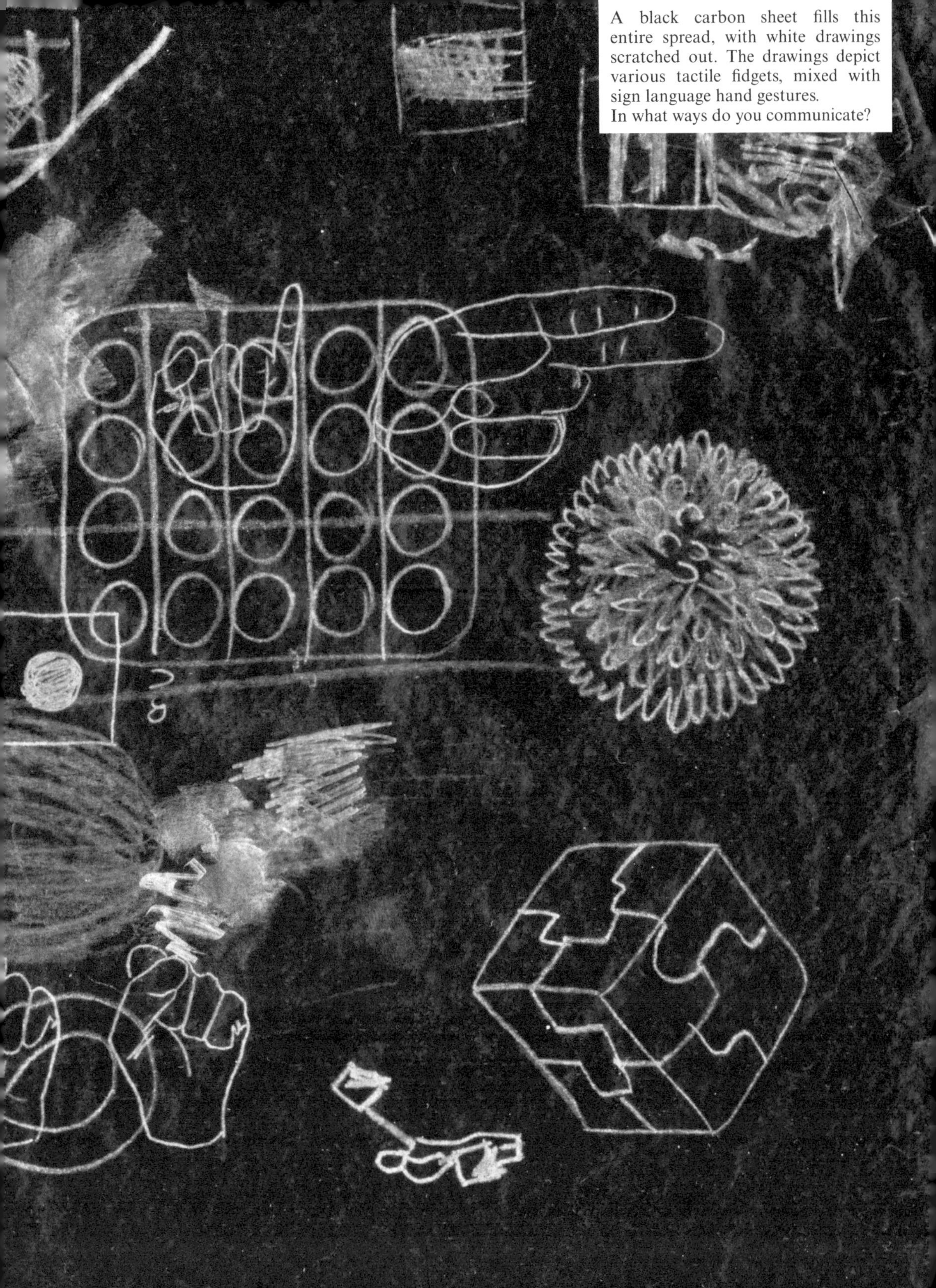

A black carbon sheet fills this entire spread, with white drawings scratched out. The drawings depict various tactile fidgets, mixed with sign language hand gestures.
In what ways do you communicate?

Biographies

David Bobier (1949) is a hard of hearing and disabled media artist whose creative practice is researching and developing vibrotactile technology as a creative medium and language of expression. This ongoing work led to his establishment in 2012 of VibraFusionLab in Ontario, Canada, a creative multi-media, multi-sensory centre that has gained a reputation as a leader in accessibility for the Deaf and disability arts movement in Canada and internationally. As a practicing artist his exhibition career includes eighteen solo and over thirty group exhibition projects across Canada and in the United States, France, Costa Rica, and the United Kingdom.

Bobier has served in advisory roles in developing Deaf and disability arts Equity programmes for both Canada Council for the Arts and the Ontario Arts Council and was an invited participant in the Canada Council for the Arts—The Arts in a Digital World Summit, and a panel presenter at the Global Disability Summit in London. He has recently been nominated by the Canada Council for the Arts for a Governor Generals Innovation Award.
bobierdavid.com
vflvibrafusionlab.com

Luca M Damiani is an artist, author and university fellow, focusing his ongoing creative practice and research on neuroscience/health, technology, and nature. Luca has a neurological disability and has had various visual art books and academic articles published, as well as being exhibited internationally. He has worked and collaborated with institutions such as BMJ Medical Humanities, BBC, Science Gallery, Computer Arts Society, Disney, Yale University, Jewish Book Council, The Times of Israel, TATE, and V&A.
lucadamiani-art.com

Eva Fotiadi is a historian of contemporary art based in the Netherlands. She is a researcher at the Center for Applied Research in Art, Design and Technology and lecturer at St Joost School of Art & Design. Previously she was a researcher at Free University Berlin, Princeton University and a lecturer at the University of Amsterdam. She is interested in public art, participatory art, exhibition histories, diversity with focus on disability. She is the author of *The Game of Participation in Art and the Public Sphere* (2011). Her articles have appeared in English, German, Greek, Dutch, Russian, and Arabic.

David Gissen is an author, designer and educator based in New York. His work challenges the manner in which architecture and urbanization instantiates concepts of physiological and biological normality, naturalness, and functionality. David has published the books *The Architecture of Disability* (Minnesota, 2023); *Subnature: Architecture's Other Environments* (Princeton, 2009); and *Manhattan Atmospheres* (Minnesota, 2013). His essays have appeared in *Artforum, Art in America, Grey Room, E-flux, Domus, Abitare, The Harvard Design Magazine, AA Files, Log*, et cetera. His architectural and urban design work has been exhibited at the Venice Biennale (2016 and 2021), the Canadian Centre for Architecture, and the Centre for Architecture in New York, among other venues.

davidgissen.org

Adi Hollander (1976) is an artist based in Amsterdam, the Netherlands. She studied at the Rietveld Academy, Amsterdam, and earned an MS from MIT, Massachusetts. Her installations, conceived as 'places of exchange', feature functional, site-specific sculptures exploring architecture's influence on perception through sensory engagement. She cofounded Public Space With A Roof (2003) and The OtherAbilities (2019). Recent projects include 'Haptic Room Studies' (2022–2024); 'What Do I Hear' (2022); and 'Body Imitates The Landscape' (2019–2020). Recent publications include *What Do I Hear?* (2022).

Hettie James (1994) and Stephanie Farmer (1986) are a freelance artist curator/curator duo. James studied at Kingston University and Farmer at The Ruskin School of Art and The Courtauld Institute. They focus on audience experience, perception and communication in written, spoken and heard formats, exploring interpretation, language and the role of the curator, artist, and audience. Together they have curated 'Ensemble', an Arts Council funded exhibition at APT Gallery, London, 2024 and 'A Garden with Animals', 7B Agar Grove, London, 2022.

instagram.com/hettiejames
instagram.com/stephuaf

Georgina Kleege (1956) is Professor Emerita of English at the University of California, Berkeley, where she taught courses in creative writing and disability studies. Her recent books include *More than Meets the Eye: What Blindness Brings to Art* (2018); *Blind Rage: Letters to Helen Keller* (2006); and *Sight Unseen* (1999). Kleege lives in New York City.

Lilian Korner, born in 1996 in northern Germany, is a Blind art scientist, inclusion activist, art educator, and access dramaturg. They study Aesthetics at Goethe University in Frankfurt. At the intersection of the disability movement and cultural studies, Lilian Korner is interested in marginalized forms of (sensory) knowledge and their expression. They develop art education inspired by the perceptual approaches of Blind people, as seen in projects like 'With All Senses' at the Museum of Modern Art Frankfurt and the Museum of Applied Arts Frankfurt.

Elke Krasny PhD, is Professor at the Academy of Fine Arts Vienna. Krasny's research is concerned with histories and practices of transnational feminisms, politics of memory and dimensions of care and social and ecological justice in architecture, urbanism and contemporary art. Publications include *Critical Care: Architecture and Urbanism for a Broken Planet*, edited with Angelika Fitz (MIT Press, 2019); *Curating as Feminist Organizing*, edited with Lara Perry (Routledge, 2023); *Living with an Infected Planet: Covid-19, Feminism and the Global Frontline of Care* (transcript, 2023) and *Feminist Infrastructural Critique* (2024), edited with Sophie Lingg and Claudia Lomoschitz. (fkw-journal.de/index.php/fkw/issue/view/89)
    elkekrasny.at

Renata Pękowska is a visual artist and researcher based in Dublin, Ireland. Her current research project examines exhibition-related creative practices as sites of attention care, in the context of attention economies of online platforms. Most recent publications include 'Seeking Attention' (*Mimesis Journal* Vol. 13 No. 2, 2024) doi.org/10.13135/2389-6086/9937, 'Can drawing workshops take on a role of attention care?' (B. Widdis, ed., Museum Ireland, 2023) irishmuseums.org/museum-ireland-2023.pdf, 'Embodied cognition and the limits of digital museum experience' (*Museum International* Vol 74, 2022, Routledge) doi.org/10.1080/13500775.2022.2157571.

Caro Verbeek (1980) is an art historian, educator and author. Her PhD research was focused on the role of the senses (specifically smell) in art history and museology. She currently works as a curator at Kunstmuseum Den Haag and as an assistant professor at Vrije Universiteit Amsterdam. Her aim is to (re)narrate and curate art history as a multisensory phenomenon. She recently wrote the book *On the Nose: A Brief Cultural History* (translations in 2021, 2024, 2025, 2026). A recent museum project includes: 'Clapping to the Beat of Piet (Mondrian)' (Kunstmuseum Den Haag, 2022–2024).
    futuristscents.com

On the Design and Chapter Opening Images of this Book

Lotte Lara Schröder (b. 1988, Amsterdam) is an artist and graphic designer, interested in ecological and natural phenomena. Her free work consists of drawings, paintings, and collages, often combined with sound or objects. Lotte created the overall book and cover design, as well as the opening collages of each chapter.

For these opening pages Lotte was inspired by the faculties of smell, touch, taste, sight and hearing and how these are being influenced by others, by our surroundings, by nature, and by our own subjectivities. With her collages she wants to invite the reader to open up to certain ambiguities, to take the opportunity to use our nose, ears, eyes, skin and mouth to explore the unexpected around us.

The descriptions of these images give additional clues on how one can concentrate on the use of the senses, and how these may spark other sensations.

termsofcircumstance.org

Publisher

Valiz is an independent international publisher, addressing contemporary developments in art, design, architecture, and urban affairs. Our books provide critical reflection and interdisciplinary inspiration, often establishing a connection between cultural disciplines and socio-economic questions.

valiz.nl

INDEX OF TERMS

Index of Names

Index of Organizations

Exhibiting for
Multiple Senses

Index of
Exhibitions and
Projects

Exhibiting for
Multiple Senses

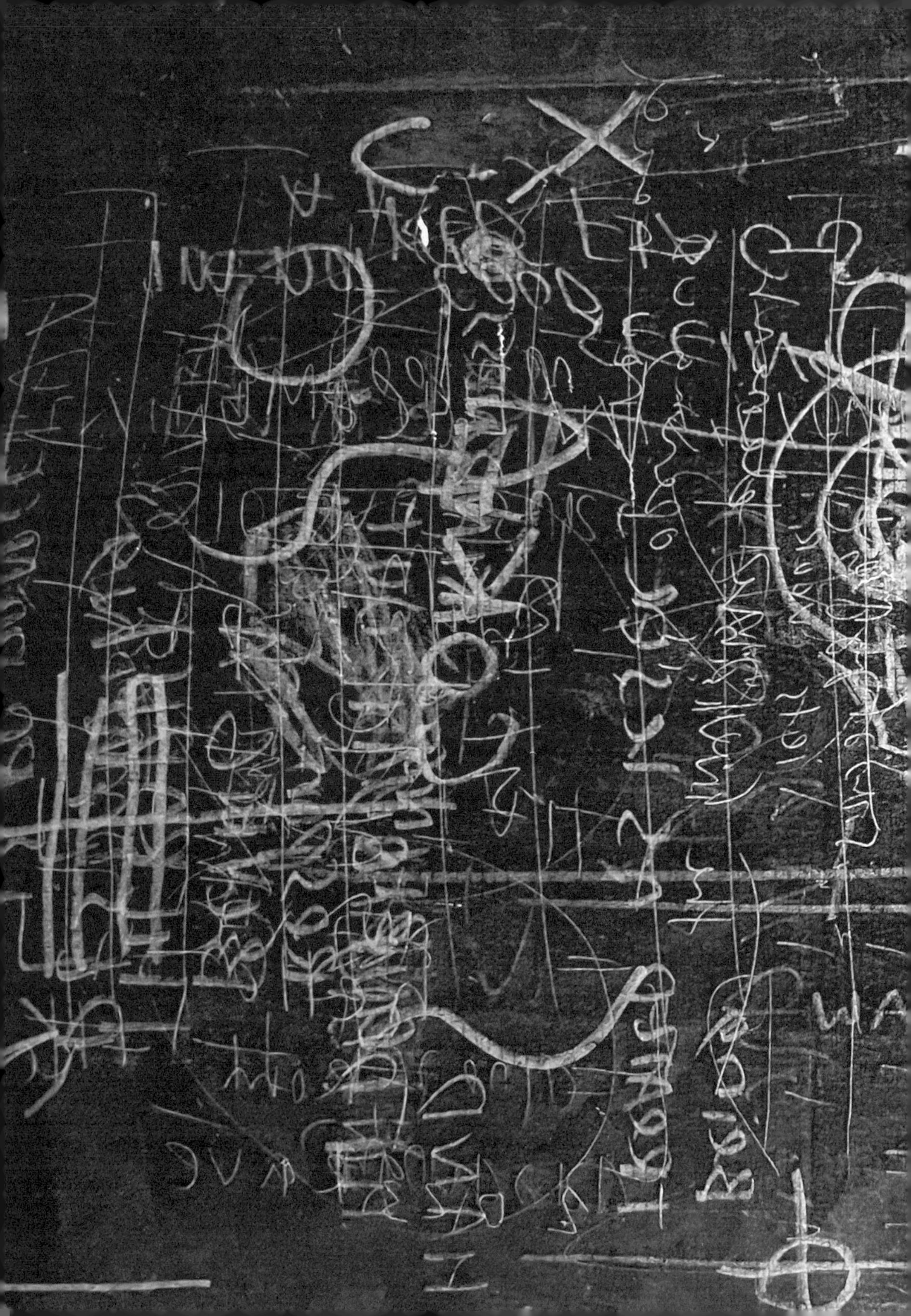

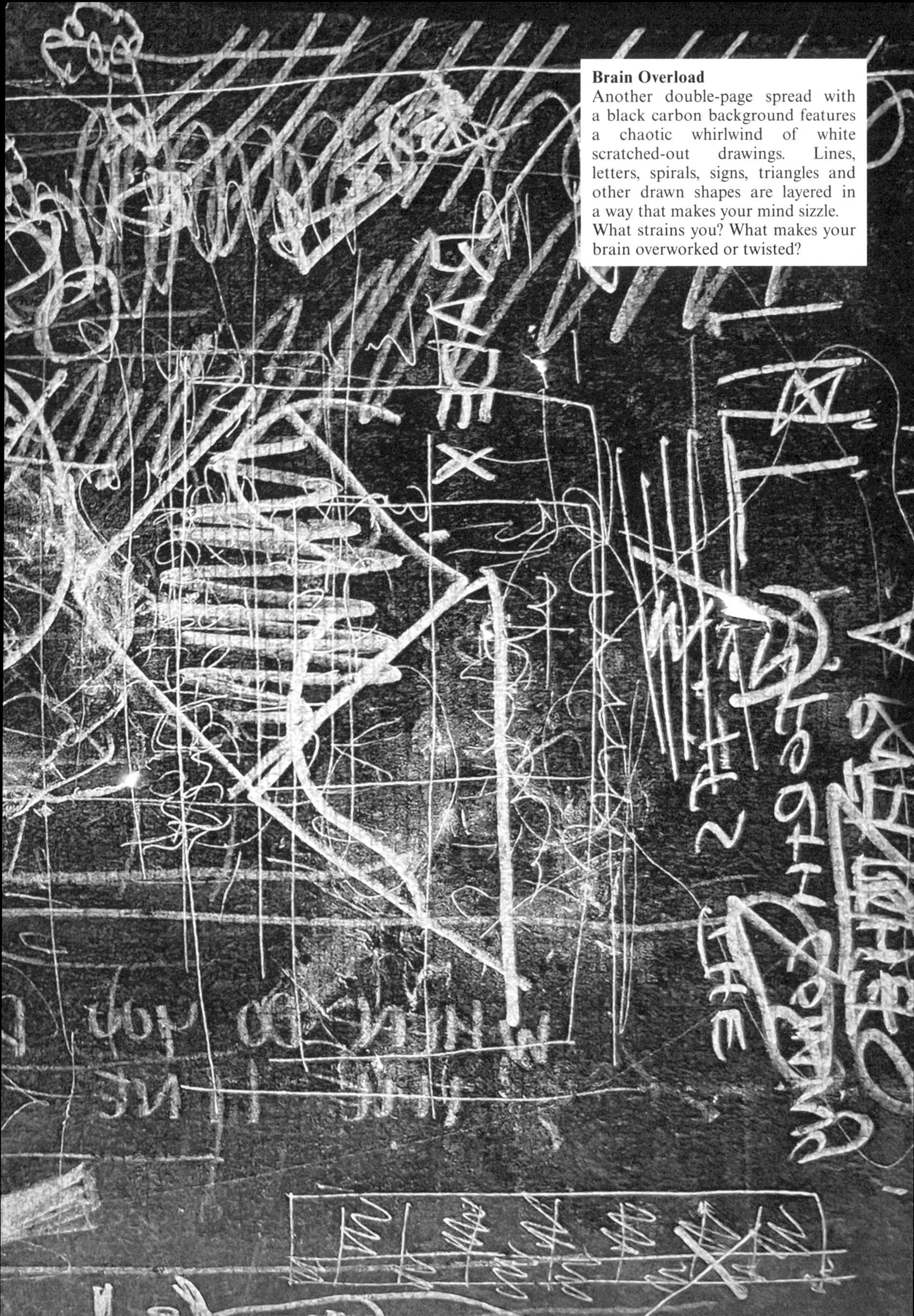

Brain Overload
Another double-page spread with a black carbon background features a chaotic whirlwind of white scratched-out drawings. Lines, letters, spirals, signs, triangles and other drawn shapes are layered in a way that makes your mind sizzle. What strains you? What makes your brain overworked or twisted?

COLOPHON

Editor
Eva Fotiadi

Contributions by
David Bobier, Luca M Damiani, Stephanie Farmer & Hettie James, Eva Fotiadi, David Gissen & Georgina Kleege, Adi Hollander, Lilian Korner, Elke Krasny, Renata Pękowska, Lotte Lara Schröder, Caro Verbeek

Project Editor
Simone Wegman/Valiz

Copy-editing
Eugenie Tee

Proofreading
Robin Straaijer

Index
Jesse Muller

Translation
Wendy van Os-Thompson, German-English
(Lilian Korner, 'Aesthetics of Blind Tactile Sensations, Attempts at Describing the Tangible')

Graphic Design
(incl. visual chapter openings, theme images, cover) Lotte Lara Schröder, termsofcircumstance.org

Typefaces
Times New Roman MT Std
Slight Change by David Jonathan Ross
Open Dyslexia Mono by opendyslexic.org

Paper
Munken Print White 100 g/m2, 1.5
Arena Natural Rough, 200 g/m2

Lithography
Wilco Art Books, Amersfoort

Printing and Binding
Wilco Art Books, Amersfoort

Publisher
Valiz, Amsterdam, 2025
Astrid Vorstermans
www.valiz.nl

This book has been generously supported by the:
• Mondriaan Fund
• Cultuurfonds
• De Gijselaar-Hintzen Fonds
• Avans Centre of Applied Research for Art, Design and Technology (CARADT), Breda, NL, caradt.nl

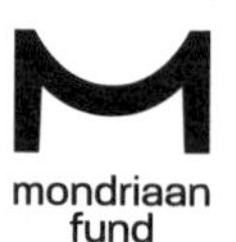

mondriaan fund

De Gijselaar-Hintzenfonds

het Cultuurfonds

caradt.nl
avans

International
Distribution
NL/LU: Centraal Boekhuis,
www.centraal.boekhuis.nl
BE: Epo, www.epo.be
GB/IE: Central Books,
www.centralbooks.com
Europe (excl GB/IE)/Asia:
Idea Books, www.ideabooks.nl
Australia: Perimeter,
www.perimeterdistribution.com
USA, Canada, Latin-America:
D.A.P., www.artbook.com
Individual orders: www.valiz.nl;
info@valiz.nl

ISBN 978-94-93246-48-5
Printed and bound in the EU, 2025

Notes & Reflections

The PLURAL series focuses on the intersections between identity, power, representation and emancipation and how these evolve in the arts and in cultural practices. The volumes in this series aim to do justice to the plurality of voices, experiences and perspectives in society and in the arts, and to address the history, present and future meaning of these positions and their interrelations. PLURAL brings together new and critical insights from artists, arts professionals, activists, cultural and social researchers, journalists and theorists.

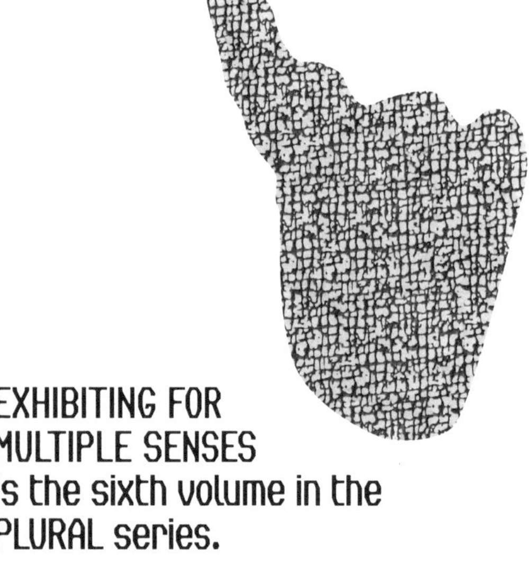

EXHIBITING FOR MULTIPLE SENSES is the sixth volume in the PLURAL series.

ISBN 978-94-93246-48-5
Printed and bound in the EU, 2025

The other PLURAL volumes are:

Feminist Art Activisms and Artivisms
Katy Deepwell (ed.)
ISBN 978-94-92095-72-5

SHAME! and Masculinity
Ernst van Alphen (ed.)
ISBN 978-94-92095-92-3

Design Struggles:
Intersecting Histories, Pedagogies,
and Perspectives
Claudia Mareis & Nina Paim (eds.)
ISBN 978-94-92095-88-6

Mix & Stir:
New Outlooks on Contemporary Art
from Global Perspectives
Helen Westgeest & Kitty Zijlmans (eds.)
ISBN 978-94-93246-05-8

Queer Exhibition Histories
Bas Hendrikx (ed.)
ISBN 978-94-93246-13-3

Love and Lightning:
A Collection of Queer and
Feminist Manifestos
Sarah van Binsbergen, Liz Allan,
Jessica Gysel, Sara Kaaman (eds.)
ISBN 978-94-93246-47-8
(forthcoming 2025)